PUBLICATIONS
OF THE
ARMY RECORDS SOCIETY
VOL. 24

ROMAINE'S CRIMEAN WAR

The Army Records Society was founded in 1984 in order to publish original records describing the development, organisation, administration and activities of the British Army from early times.

Any person wishing to become a member of the Society is requested to apply to the Hon. Secretary, c/o the National Army Museum, Royal Hospital Road, London, SW3 4HT. The annual subscription entitles the member to receive a copy of each volume issued by the Society in that year, and to purchase back volumes at reduced prices. Current subscription details, whether for individuals living within the British Isles, for individuals living overseas, or for institutions, will be furnished on request.

The Council of the Army Records Society wish it to be clearly understood that they are not answerable for opinions or observations that may appear in the Society's publications. For these the responsibility rests entirely with the Editors of the several works.

The Society's website can be found at
www.armyrecordssociety.org.uk

1600–1939

A carte-de-visite of Romaine of about 1860. (Reproduced by kind permission of the Victoria and Albert Museum, London.)

ROMAINE'S CRIMEAN WAR

The Letters and Journal of
William Govett Romaine
Deputy Judge-Advocate to the Army of the East
1854–6

Transcribed, edited and annotated by
MAJOR COLIN ROBINS
and members of the
CRIMEAN WAR RESEARCH SOCIETY

Published by
SUTTON PUBLISHING LIMITED
for the
ARMY RECORDS SOCIETY
2005

First published in the United Kingdom in 2005 by
Sutton Publishing Limited · Phoenix Mill · Thrupp · Stroud
Gloucestershire · GL5 2BU

British Library Cataloguing in Publication Data
A catalogue record for this book is available from the British Library.

ISBN 0-7509-4287-8

Typeset in Ehrhardt.
Typesetting and origination by
Sutton Publishing Limited.
Printed in Great Britain by
J.H. Haynes & Co. Ltd, Sparkford.

Contents

Illustrations

Figures

Maps

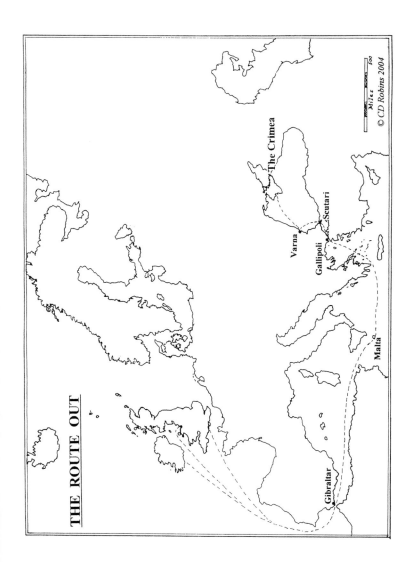

THE ROUTE OUT

The Crimea

Varna

Scutari

Gallipoli

Malta

Gibraltar

Miles 500

© CD Robins 2004

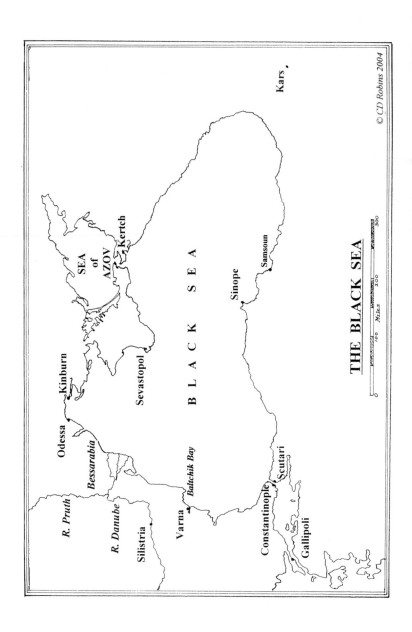

THE BLACK SEA

© CD Robins 2004

Kars

SEA of AZOV

Kertch

B L A C K   S E A

Samsoun

Sinope

Odessa

Kinburn

Sevastopol

Bessarabia

R. Pruth

R. Danube

Silistria

Varna

Baltchik Bay

Constantinople

Scutari

Gallipoli

Miles
0   100   200   300

xiv

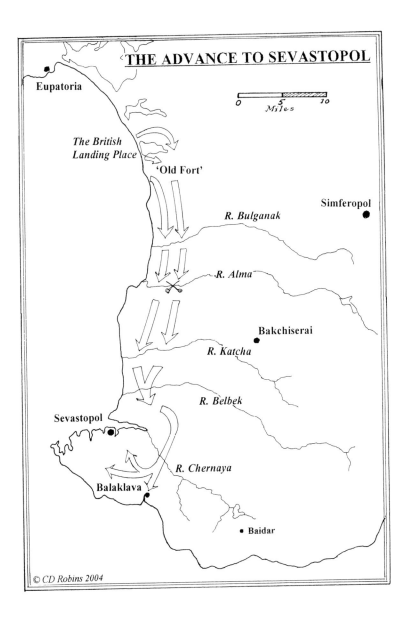

THE ADVANCE TO SEVASTOPOL

Eupatoria

0   5   10
Miles

The British
Landing Place

'Old Fort'

Simferopol

R. Bulganak

R. Alma

Bakchiserai

R. Katcha

R. Belbek

Sevastopol

R. Chernaya

Balaklava

Baidar

© CD Robins 2004

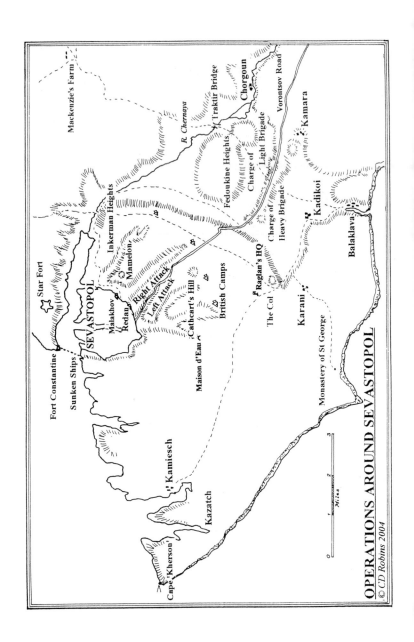

Mackenzie's Farm

Star Fort

SEVASTOPOL

Fort Constantine

Sunken Ships

Malakhov
Redan
Mamelon
Inkerman Heights
Right Attack
Left Attack
Maison d'Eau
Cathcart's Hill
British Camps

R. Chernaya
Traktir Bridge
Chorgoun
Fedoukine Heights
Charge of Light Brigade
Vorontsov Road
Kamara

Raglan's HQ
The Col
Charge of Heavy Brigade
Kadikoi
Balaklava

Karani

Monastery of St George

Kamiesch

Kazatch

Cape Kherson

Miles
0   1   2   3

OPERATIONS AROUND SEVASTOPOL

© CD Robins 2004

xvi

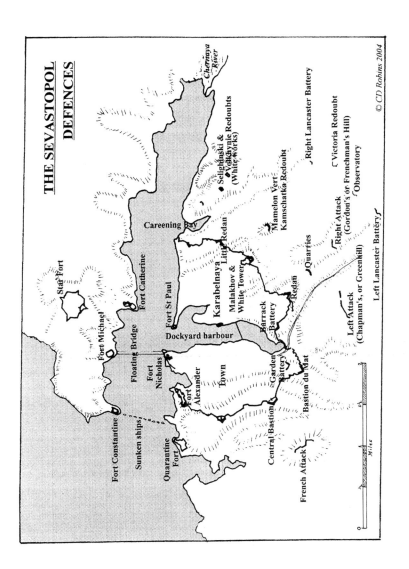

THE SEVASTOPOL DEFENCES

© CD Robins 2004

Cherriaya River

Selighinski & Volhynie Redoubts (White Works)

Right Lancaster Battery

Mamelon Vert
Kamschatka Redoubt

Victoria Redoubt

Careening Bay

Little Redan

Right Attack
(Gordon's or Frenchman's Hill)
Observatory

Star Fort

Quarries

Fort Catherine

Karabelnaya

Malakhov &
White Tower

Redan

Left Lancaster Battery

Fort St Paul

Fort Michael

Barrack
Battery

Floating Bridge

Left Attack
(Chapman's, or Greenhill)

Dockyard harbour

Fort
Nicholas

Garden
Battery

Town

Fort
Alexander

Fort Constantine

Bastion du Mat

Sunken ships

Central Bastion

Quarantine
Fort

French Attack

Miles

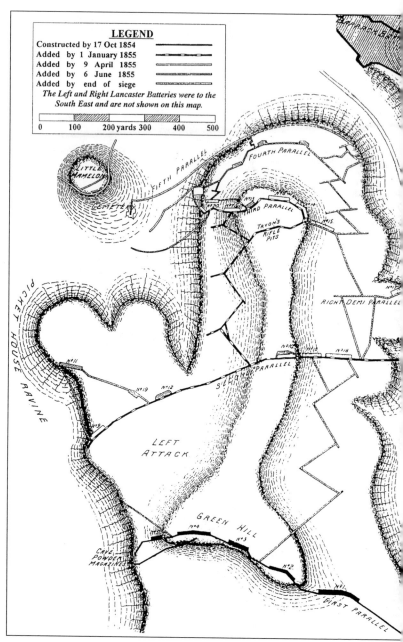

The British trenches and batteries outside Sevastopol

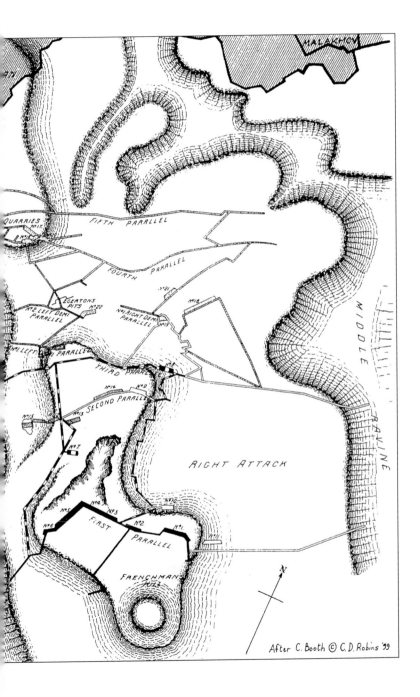

MALAKHOV

FIFTH PARALLEL

QUARRIES
No 25

FOURTH PARALLEL

No 21

EGERTONS PITS   No 22   No 18

No 2 LEFT DEMI   No 1 RIGHT DEMI
PARALLEL   PARALLEL   No 13

No 17 LEFT PARALLEL

THIRD PARALLEL   No 8

No 14   No 9

No 15   No 16   SECOND PARALLEL

No 15

No 7

MIDDLE RAVINE

RIGHT ATTACK

No 5   No 4   No 3   No 10

No 6   FIRST   No 2   No 1

PARALLEL   No 11

FRENCHMAN'S
HILL

N

After C. Booth © C.D. Robins '99

xix

Preface

Background

In 1998 the staff of what is now known as the Fusiliers Museum, Lancashire, in Bury (the Museum of the Lancashire Fusiliers until the formation of the Royal Regiment of Fusiliers), feared that the museum might no longer be able to occupy free accommodation in the barracks. They might have to move and, if so, they would need considerable funds to prepare and fit out a new museum building. While they considered fundraising measures, preparations were made for a move. Old cupboards were turned out, and in one was found an uncatalogued bundle of papers which may well have lain there unexamined for over a hundred years.

It was a miscellaneous lot: various papers relating to the 20th Foot (the regiment's title before 1881) and several sets of papers relating to the Crimean War. The latter included letters from Lord Cardigan, who led the Light Cavalry Brigade in their famous Charge, to Alexander William Kinglake (author of the monumental eight-volume history of the war); correspondence between Lord Hardinge, the Commander-in-Chief at Horse Guards, and Major General Richard Airey, Quartermaster General and effectively Chief-of-Staff to the Commander-in-Chief of the 'Army of the East', Lord Raglan; and a journal written in a dilapidated notebook. Correspondence found with the papers suggested that they had been loaned by Kinglake to Lieutenant Quartermaster Ben Smyth while the latter was preparing his *History of the XX Regiment, 1688–1888*, the first edition of which was published in 1889. Presumably, when he reached the Crimean part of his narrative, Smyth wrote to Kinglake asking to borrow any papers on the war, and Kinglake simply bundled up and sent whatever came to hand, relevant or not. This proved to be their salvation.

Kinglake had spent the first few weeks of the Crimean War at Raglan's headquarters and, after Raglan's death in June 1855 was asked by Lady Raglan to write a history rebutting the considerable criticism of her husband then current. When this became known, Kinglake was supplied with many documents, official and private, English and foreign, relating to the war. The result was *The Invasion of the Crimea*, eight volumes covering the Crimean campaign up to the death of Raglan, published as volumes were completed between 1863 and 1887. After Kinglake's death in 1891 the archive of documents in his care disappeared. It had for long been assumed that it was destroyed.

The Lancashire Fusiliers' Museum thus found itself in possession of part of the Kinglake archive many years after it had been given up as lost. The regiment now retained those papers relevant to its own history and put the others up for auction. Understanding the importance of the documents, the Curator took steps to have them microfilmed first. Alerted by national press comment on the find, I hastened to contact the museum, and was allowed to visit and examine the documents. I was given a set of the microfiches for the Crimean War Research Society (CWRS) and was granted permission to publish them. In due course the museum received a substantial sum at auction for the original papers from an anonymous buyer.

David Kelsey, a member of the society, agreed to help me with the transcription of the microfiches, consulting other expert fellow members of the CWRS as necessary. The papers relating to the 20th Regiment were found to contain some detailed accounts of its actions in the battle of Inkerman, as well as letters illustrating the efforts of Colonel Horn, its commander, to care for the welfare of his men. The letters from Cardigan to Kinglake, which had received most attention from the press, shed no new light on the events of the war, but well illustrated the conflict between Kinglake and Cardigan as the latter strove to ensure that the printed account of his conduct in the Charge of the Light Brigade would show him in the most favourable light. The Airey–Hardinge correspondence reflected the tensions between Whitehall and the generals in the field as the public at home grew increasingly concerned about the conduct of the war during the hardships of the first winter. There were also some notes made by Kinglake, a few individual letters, and even a copy of Raglan's 'third order' annotated by Airey. The item which proved to be of the greatest interest however was the journal in the notebook.

This was written by William Govett Romaine, Deputy Judge-Advocate to the Army of the East, the most senior civilian in Raglan's headquarters, called 'the eye of the army' by Raglan, quoted by Kinglake as his source for the chronology of the actions in the battle of the Alma, and regarded by the editor of *The Times* as a better source of information than the official despatches. His journal was clearly a find of the utmost importance. Unfortunately it began in early 1855, after the invasion and the three major battles of Alma, Balaklava and Inkerman, but it contained a tantalising reference to an earlier journal for 1854. That had not been found among the papers.

However, while the CWRS group was working on the microfiches, I discovered that Cambridge University Library had acquired 'papers collected by Kinglake for his history of the Crimean War'. I arranged to see the papers, and found that they were – with but one original item missing – the very papers from Bury which had been auctioned. It appeared that the anonymous buyer had wanted only an autograph of Cardigan, and having extracted that had passed all the other papers to Cambridge, replacing the retained Cardigan letter with a photocopy. An archivist helpfully referred in passing to 'the other Kinglake papers' that the library owned. These were produced and to my joy contained many letters from Romaine to three friends at home, all men of substance: Lord Mulgrave, MP for Scarborough and the eldest son of the Marquess of Normanby; Charles Jasper Selwyn, a fellow lawyer, later to be knighted and made a Lord Justice of Appeal; and John Harvey, whose family had held the manor house of Ickwell Bury, Biggleswade, since 1680. Romaine was clearly on close terms with all of them, and his letters to them are frank. I transcribed these, again with help from other members of the society. A particularly valuable aspect of the letters is that they cover the whole period of the war, compensating for the absence of the 1854 journal. Further searches in other quarters brought to light other correspondence from Romaine, some relating to the Crimean railway, and some with Raglan.

It is sometimes supposed that the Crimean War has been fully researched and that nothing new remains to be said or written about it. Some modern authors still rely upon the re-working of old evidence. The war is indeed extensively documented by contemporary reports and personal accounts, but manuscripts and journals continue to be found, many containing something new. It is only relatively recently that the important naval campaigns in the Baltic Sea have been properly recorded. Examination of the battlefields, especially outside Sevastopol, leads to discoveries still – the latest being work on the trenches of the British 'Left Attack' currently in progress. A hitherto undiscovered mass of contemporary letters and journals in family attics and dusty regimental museum cupboards is slowly coming forth. Romaine's letters and journal are a major example of such newly emerging evidence.

The documents

The result of combining the letters and the journal is a fascinating complete account of the war seen through Romaine's eyes at the headquarters of the Army of the East – first when Raglan was commander, and then as Generals Simpson and Codrington succeeded him in turn.

Only three or four senior officers and officials served continuously in the Crimea from the landing on 14 September 1854 to the Treaty of Paris in March 1856. One of them was Romaine. Born in 1816, he was the second son of the Reverend Robert Govett Romaine, vicar of Staines, Middlesex. Robert had changed his name from Govett, adding Romaine, and his second son followed suit, though his brother Charles retained the single surname Govett. William graduated from Trinity College, Cambridge (BA 1837, MA 1859). He was entered at the Inner Temple in 1834 and was called to the bar in 1839. After practising his profession in the courts for fifteen years, latterly on the Oxford Circuit, he was eager to be appointed Deputy Judge-Advocate[1] to the Army of the East and wrote to Lord Raglan to ask for the position.[2] In due course he was appointed and he landed in Constantinople on 8 May 1854, remaining with the army until the end of the war. He was to distinguish himself in several capacities. For example, after the battle of Alma he attended to the Russian wounded on the battlefield, and as a skilled administrator, he was soon involved in matters beyond his judicial role. It is recorded that it was owing to his advice that the Crimean Army Fund was set up. Raglan relied on him for correspondence with the Sanitary Commissioners, and when he made suggestions to Quartermaster General Airey for improvements to the organisation of the Land Transport Corps and the running of the railway, Airey promptly turned their implementation over to him. Samples of railway letters which give a flavour of this largely routine correspondence are in Appendix 2.

Throughout the war it seems that Romaine kept both a diary and a notebook, the former a review of the day's events written up in the evening in his hut, the latter carried in his pocket for on-the-spot notes of events as they occurred. After the war he copied these two sources into a single combined account which he passed to Kinglake. The volume covering 1854 appears to have been lost, but that for 1855 survived as described above.

Romaine took a keen interest in all aspects of the Crimean campaign, touring the field of operations and recording significant events. He was on familiar terms with divisional generals and with headquarters staff, and recorded their comments along with his own observations. His letters include his sometimes savage judgement on the conduct of the campaign and on the quality of individual officers. Some of his views came to the notice of government ministers and the press. A leading article in *The Times* of 6 November 1854, critical of both the speed and content of news from the Crimea, suggested 'Let someone at headquarters – why not the Judge-Advocate, a most efficient penman? – be charged with the duty of preparing intelligible bulletins'.

After the war Romaine suffered some early disappointments. He was not immediately awarded the Order of the Bath which he felt was his due, and he was defeated when standing as Liberal candidate for Chatham in March 1857, ending his dream of a political career. In April 1857 he was appointed as second secretary to the Admiralty and eventually got his long awaited 'Bath'. In 1861 he married Frances, a Miss Tennant after whom he asks in some letters. Later he served four years (1869–73) in India as Judge-Advocate General, and subsequently held appointments at the Egyptian Treasury, progressing to President, and then to Comptroller-General of Finances. He retired in 1879 and died in England in 1893 at the age of seventy-six.[3]

Romaine's account of the war based on his letters and journal has not been published before. It adds a most interesting view of events to those written by participants during or soon after the war. If something was going on: a planned attack or a sortie by the Russians, Romaine was there to see it, sometimes under fire as he watched. He bears the discomforts well but seeks to improve his living conditions, at first in a tent and then in a hut. He was clearly a member of the 'inner circle' of young staff officers at headquarters and their friends. He talks to young officers, of whom one at least had a premonition of death which was realised in the next day's action. He records the details of bombardments and assaults, of burials under truce, of casualties and damage, and also the gossip and rumours, the inside accounts of how decisions were made, and the old generals' reminiscences of Wellington and Waterloo. He is not slow to praise or criticise the various commanders, and his judgements are usually those now accepted, even when they differ from the opinions which were current as he wrote. The journal and the letters are occasionally illustrated by Romaine's own pen sketches.

Throughout he is frank and forthright, and new light is thrown on many aspects of the war. I believe that the papers are of the utmost importance to the study of the Crimean War.

Acknowledgements

The first and major debt to be acknowledged is to the Fusiliers Museum, Lancashire, in Bury, to their Board of Trustees and to Tony Sprason, their Custodian. They discovered the original journal and kindly passed copies to the Crimean War Research Society so that they might be examined. The Chairman of the Trustees of the Museum, John Kershaw, has kindly approved their publication in this way so that they may be made available to a wide audience.

I cannot overstate the value of the help and skilled advice given by Kathleen Cann, until recently an archivist at Cambridge University Library. The letters placed in her care were a mixed up pile of papers until she sorted them into chronological order (not easy where dates were unclear or did not indicate the year), marked and then photocopied them. Her help and encouragement were invaluable. I am also indebted to the Archivist, Dr Patrick Zutshi, at the University Library for negotiating permission for their publication. All the originals, both journal and letters, are now held and owned by the University Library, Cambridge, and are published by kind permission of the Syndics of the Library. Dr Mark Nicholls, Librarian of St John's College, Cambridge, and editor of the *Journal of the Society for Army Historical Research*, gave the original clue about the existence and whereabouts of the letters and provided the first valuable link to Miss Cann. Mrs Catherine Twilley, also of St John's, helped with guidance on information sources. Jonathan Smith, Librarian of Trinity College, Cambridge, where Romaine and Selwyn were pensioners before graduation, responded kindly to enquiries about the two.

The late Brian Cooke, author of *The Grand Crimean Central Railway: The Railway that Won a War*, kindly passed me the correspondence on railway matters, and Dr Alastair Massie, Head of the Department of Archives, Photographs, Film and Sound at the National Army Museum, helped in identifying and providing copies of the relevant parts of the Raglan papers held there. I am grateful to the Director of the National Army Museum for allowing their publication. Similarly, I am obliged to the Director of Library Services, Wigan Metropolitan Council, for permission to include examples of Romaine's 'railway letters' and to Philip Butler for his help with this.

Romaine and one of his principal correspondents, Charles Selwyn, were barristers and much helpful information has been given by G. F. Holborn, Librarian, and Mrs F. Bellis, his assistant, of Lincoln's Inn Library; A.S. Adams, Senior Librarian, Middle Temple Library; and Miss Theresa

Thom, Librarian of Gray's Inn. Some of Romaine's letters were written to the then Lord Mulgrave, elder son of, and later himself, the Marquis of Normanby and the present Marquis has kindly responded to enquiries.

The Crimean War Research Society has, of course, been very much involved with the project. Several members helped in transcribing the journals and letters, but an outstanding contribution to the finished work was made by David Kelsey. Not only did he lead the team transcribing the journal and help me with the transcription of the letters, but he also helped with this Preface, section introductions, the glossary and the endnotes. He also helped prepare the sketches for publication. Others who helped to transcribe the journal include Rodney Robinson, W. S. (Bill) Curtis, Michael Hargreave Mawson, John Barham and Mike Hinton. Any errors in the transcripts remain my fault.

Finally, I gratefully acknowledge the encouragement of Professor Ian Beckett, Chairman of the Army Records Society, and the help given by Dr William Philpott, Secretary of the Society, Professor Andrew Lambert who read the draft text, and Mrs Annie Jackson, whose editing was skilful, firm but always tactful.

Method

As far as possible the original words, spelling, and punctuation of Romaine – including use of superscript and the ampersand – is retained and editorial intervention has been kept to a minimum. Square brackets [ ] indicate such editorial intervention, including comments such as [*sic*], [blank], [illegible], etc.; words or parts accidentally omitted by Romaine but needed for sense; and words which have been inferred where there is doubt over the original due to obscure writing or missing torn paper (words in this last group are also followed by a question mark).

Romaine's spellings of proper names are used throughout, as are his transcriptions of the Cyrillic, but in editorial matter names are spelt correctly and Cyrillic names are transcribed according to accepted modern rules and practice. The division into sections is not Romaine's but for the convenience of the modern reader.

So as not to disrupt the narrative flow, the 'Raglan' and 'railway' papers are contained in the Appendices. Only those endnotes absolutely necessary are included and instead there are full biographical notes of the persons mentioned by Romaine, a glossary of military terms, and maps showing the places mentioned.

Colin Robins, Bowdon, July 2004

Introduction and Part 1

Going to War

The long peace ends

After the defeat of Napoleon in 1815 the Congress of Vienna established a balance of power in Europe which resulted in peace for almost forty years but it did not address the so-called 'Eastern Question' which had become relevant as soon as the Ottoman Empire had passed its peak: what order could, or should, replace it as it crumbled?[4] And so, until 1853, boundaries remained broadly the same. Neither Germany nor Italy was yet united. The major powers were France, Turkey, Russia, Britain, Austria and Prussia.

In France, Buonaparte's nephew, 'Prince' Louis-Napoleon had been elected president and had then, supported by loyal generals, declared himself Emperor as Napoleon III. He was keen to restore to his country the influence lost on the defeat of his uncle, and was ready to go to war to do so. The Ottoman Empire, under Turkey, was in steep decline. Many of its former provinces, including the Balkan principalities of Moldavia and Wallachia,[5] had obtained varying degrees of independence. Russia, under Tsar Nicholas I, was seeking to expand its frontiers, and wanted a passage for its Black Sea fleet to the Mediterranean. Nicholas eyed Constantinople and the Bosphorus greedily. Britain was concerned that the increasing strength and ambition of Russia threatened stability in Europe, and might interfere with the overland route to India. As ever, she wished to maintain the balance of power. Austria and Prussia were alarmed at the prospect of any armed conflict on their borders.

In 1853 the custody of the keys to Christian shrines in the Holy Land was awarded to the Roman Catholic Church by the Sultan of Turkey. Russia had urged the claim of the Orthodox Church to receive them, and Nicholas now seized on this quarrel to exert pressure on the Sultan and claimed the right to protect Christians throughout the Ottoman Empire – a demand with which he knew Turkey could not comply. It refused and Russia increased pressure by invading the Principalities of Moldavia and

1

Wallachia, ostensibly to protect the Christian inhabitants. Encouraged by French and British envoys to expect their nations' full support, Turkey declared war on 5 October 1853. On 30 November 1853 Russia destroyed much of Turkey's fleet in harbour at Sinope on the northern coast of Asia Minor and the world reacted in horror at this 'massacre'. Crowds in England clamoured for Russia to be punished. England and France called on Russia to withdraw from Turkish territory and when it failed to do so declared war (against Russia) on 28 March 1854.

Turkish troops resisted the Russian invaders who had reached the River Danube while Britain and France sent warships, and then soldiers, to the East to support them. Britain also prepared a fleet for operations in the Baltic Sea. When the expedition was announced Romaine sought the position of Deputy Judge-Advocate, and wrote to Raglan about it. (This correspondence with Raglan, and later letters between the two, is in Appendix 1.)

The expedition sets forth

Early in 1854 the British and French armies set out, some at first to Malta, and then to Gallipoli where defences were prepared across the peninsula in case Constantinople fell.

On 22 April 1854, in a first show of force, a combined British and French naval squadron bombarded Odessa, damaging its defences and sinking a number of Russian warships.

When it became clear that the Turks were holding the Russians on the Danube, the allies were moved forward, the British to Scutari, opposite Constantinople, and then on to the port of Varna in modern Bulgaria, in reach of the fighting on the Danube. Some of the French went straight to Varna, marching through European Turkey to do so. However it soon became clear that it was impossible to supply the British army if it moved far from the port for they had no transport and no proper administrative support. Medical arrangements were rudimentary, and there was no organisation to supply troops in the field. Economies had led to the disbandment of the Wagon Train which had served Wellington well. Commissariat officers, under the direct control of the Treasury (and with economy as their main aim), were recruited and instructed to buy most of the army's needs in the country where they were deployed. No one had known if there would be supplies there to purchase. Romaine, a lawyer with no experience of war, saw that the transport difficulties were huge and needed solving.

So, incapable of moving to support the Turks fighting on the Danube, the allied armies remained largely inactive for more than three months in the spring and summer of 1854, declining in discipline, morale, and health as cholera thinned their ranks. An exception was the so-called 'sore-back reconnaissance', when Lord Cardigan was sent by Raglan with a detachment of light cavalry towards the scene of the fighting to see if he could find the Russians and establish what they were up to. After a gruelling ten days Cardigan returned, having established nothing of any value, with the men exhausted and most of the horses crippled with sore backs – some so severely that they could serve no more.

In the face of determined Turkish resistance, and under huge diplomatic pressure from Austria, in June the Russians withdrew from Moldavia and Wallachia and as negotiations continued in Vienna the Allies' task was, to all intents and purposes, complete. The British expected to return home, but under the pressure of public opinion which demanded that Russia be 'punished' for its actions, the government gave Raglan a wishy-washy order making it clear that they would like him to invade the Crimea unless there were 'insuperable impediments' to doing so.

Raglan did not know how many troops the Russians had, nor where they were. He consulted Sir George Brown, commanding the Light Division, another Peninsular veteran. Sir George considered what their old leader, the Duke of Wellington, would have done, and concluded that Wellington would certainly not have attacked without knowledge of enemy dispositions. He added, however, that it was clear that the government was set upon an invasion, and that if Raglan did not comply with their wishes then he would be replaced by someone who would. The French had been told to do what we did. Raglan consulted his French counterpart, Marshal St Arnaud, and invasion was ordered.

The landings and the battle of Alma

After several weeks assembling pontoons and other small boats, the 'landing craft' of the time, from as far away as Constantinople, building jetties and practising embarkation of horses and guns, the force was ready and sailed in a huge fleet towards the Crimean coast. Surprisingly, the landing place had not then been decided and while the force was at sea there was a hurried reconnaissance, and Raglan selected Old Fort Bay, some thirty miles north of Sevastopol. The force began to land there on 14 September 1854.

The landings were watched by Cossack scouts but unopposed. As the Allies moved south towards Sevastopol their first encounter with the enemy was the 'affair of the Bulganak' (19 September), a brief clash between the main body of British and French troops and a small Russian force which, after an exchange of gun fire and the first Allied casualties of the campaign, promptly withdrew.[6] Some 40,000 Russians, under Prince Menshikov, opposed the advance at the River Alma. They had prepared formidable defences on the heights overlooking the river and were confident that they could hold out for at least three weeks. On the afternoon of 20 September, after a fierce conflict which lasted about three hours, the Russians retreated in disorder though the battle had not gone as the Allies had planned. It seemed that the British and French armies had each been left with a different idea of what the plan was, and what its army was supposed to do. The British thought that the agreed plan was that the French, on the right, near the sea where defences were non-existent, would scale the hills, outflank the Russians, and then 'roll them up' along their defensive line while at the same time the British assaulted straight ahead to the strongest part of the Russian defence. The French seem to have thought that a simultaneous assault would be made, with the British outflanking the Russian right flank with a large 'left hook'. However, very soon after the French had begun to move forward they appeared to lose their nerve and a liaison officer rushed to Raglan to beg an immediate British advance 'or the day is lost'. Although the Russian centre was unshaken, Raglan ordered an advance into the teeth of the enemy guns and small arms fire. This assault was, after many casualties, successful and the Russians were put to flight. It was felt strongly by the British staff that the brunt of the fighting had been borne by the British; the French seemed to be conscious of this and inflated the casualty figures they reported by including all the cholera deaths suffered since the landing. It is interesting that the plan for the initial assault to be by the French appeared to Romaine to be the obvious way to conduct the battle.

Now an opportunity was lost as forceful pursuit of the Russians would have turned their withdrawal into a rout. But Raglan and St Arnaud, who was dying, could not agree and the armies paused for two days to gather up casualties and regroup.

The flank march

Menshikov fell back to Sevastopol, ordered the naval forces there to block the entrance to the harbour with scuttled ships, left the manning of the guns to sailors and a small force and withdrew the bulk of his army to the interior. This manoeuvre was not without incident as the advancing British column 'bumped' the rear of the Russian army, and as the cavalry who were supposed to be leading had got lost in thick woodland,[7] Raglan himself emerged in sight of the Russian train.

When the Allies reached the hills overlooking the town, they could see the inhabitants still frantically building defensive works. It was decided not to attack from the north.[8] The Allied armies marched around the town and the British took the small harbour of Balaklava, about six miles to the south.[9] This became the British supply base, while the French used the neighbouring natural harbour of Kamiesch. Lord Cardigan's behaviour while camping overnight during that flank march led Romaine to comment critically about him.

Another opportunity, even more glaring than the failure to follow up after Alma, was now lost. Desperately ill, St Arnaud could not decide what to do, and Raglan dithered. Instead of assaulting at once while defences in many sectors were virtually non-existent – as advised by some, including notably General Cathcart – the commanders decided on a formal siege operation. This involved digging trenches and batteries for a preliminary bombardment which would be followed by an infantry assault. It took about three weeks to unload the heavy guns and move them into position, during which time the garrison and townspeople of Sevastopol continued to strengthen the town's defences, under the direction of Todleben, a brilliant engineer officer soon promoted colonel, and the overall command of a popular and inspiring leader, Admiral Kornilov. Meanwhile the powerful British fleet under Admiral Dundas cruised mainly well off shore, leaving only an in-shore squadron under his capable and energetic second-in-command, Lyons, to co-operate with the army, landing guns and sailors to assist the undermanned besiegers. During these preparations a false report reached London that Sevastopol had fallen, and church bells were rung in celebration. The army was furious when the reports were fed back to them.

First bombardment and the battles of Balaklava and Inkerman

The opening barrage on 17 October did not breach the defences sufficiently and the bombardment continued for a week, the Russians nightly repairing the damage that had been done by day. In this they were able to draw on the vast quantities of cannon and stores held in the town which was, of course, the arsenal of the Black Sea Fleet. Participation in the bombardment by the British and French warships was unsuccessful and nothing was achieved but extensive damage to the ships and many casualties.

Menshikov's strategy of taking his army out of the town now proved its effectiveness. He was able to move freely behind the besieging forces and the besiegers were themselves, in a sense, besieged. The first attack was on the British supply base at Balaklava. The battle of Balaklava on 25 October, during which the actions of the 'stand of the thin red line' and the charges of the Heavy Brigade and the Light Brigade took place, failed in its objective to dislodge the Allies. It was followed by two attacks by the Russians from the direction of Sevastopol: Little Inkerman (26 October) and Inkerman (5 November). These attacks were repulsed despite the superior numerical strength of the Russian forces. As the Allies settled down to a long siege some irritation with the French began to arise. Romaine, no doubt reflecting a general view at headquarters, notes that if the French had done their part properly, the British should have stormed Sevastopol on the second night of the first bombardment. He records that Raglan had an entire want of confidence in every statement made by the French, and describes their engineers and artillery men as utter failures.

Winter 1854–5

Almost immediately the weather turned. A great storm on 14 November destroyed tents and sank many merchant ships. The British in particular suffered gravely from lack of clothing, warm food and shelter. Deaths from exposure, malnutrition and disease were soon running at four times the number of deaths from enemy action. Romaine records the melancholy totals with up to ninety deaths a day from disease. Steadily the old soldiers who had landed at Old Fort were dying and the 'soft' new arrivals had not the character nor the physical hardiness to survive for long. The loss of horses was horrific and no mounted unit could muster more than a few animals. Romaine became aware of the problems the soldiers were facing over their rations and was clear that it was due to a failure of 'the heads'. (In passing one wonders why Raglan apparently remained oblivious to these difficulties.) The year finished with operations at a stalemate and the Allied armies, especially the British, cold, wet and hungry. There was worse to come.

I

Romaine to C. J. Selwyn

Constantinople
May 7th 1854

Dear Selwyn

We are just arrived in the "City of London" steamer and are anchored off the Scutari barracks. We had a very pleasant voyage as far as Gibraltar nothing but fine weather. There we stayed a few hours to coal & went on at night. About 2 AM 26th Ap^l we had a regular white squall which after 20 minutes of heavy rain settled into a gale of wind which lasted nearly 60 hours & so retarded our progress, that luckily we were obliged to put into Algiers to procure a supply of coal. We stayed there 24 hours and had a good opportunity of seeing how much the French are doing for their colony – They are laying out their money very well making beautiful breakwaters of huge blocks of concrete and that in places where there are 80 ft of water – making good roads forts theatres & handsome streets – They have embarked already 15,000 troops horse foot & artillery and will send altogether from Algiers 23,000 men, most of them are corps d'élite regts of Zouaves, Chasseurs d'Afrique &c.

We were very nearly run down the night we rounded the Capo di Gatta. It was blowing very hard a pitch dark night with the big black waves breaking in crests of phosphoric foam, when a light was announced right ahead – We put our helm to port according to rule, the other vessel a large bark put hers astarboard and as she was running before a tremendous wind & we were going four knots & had hardly steerage way, we could not get away from her – I was standing on the deck just about 12.30 PM [*sic*, meaning 'AM' – half-an-hour after midnight] when I saw her masts towering high up above me & the Captain who was close to me called out – "By God, she'll be into us right amidships." Passengers who heard that something was wrong came running up in their night shirts.

The vessel however luckily shot by our side so close that her yards nearly touched ours – The next wave carried her well clear of us. We had a second alarm of the same kind that night but not so near an escape as the vessel saw us a little earlier.

At Malta which we reached on the 2nd of May we found Marshal St Arnaud & orders to go on the same night in the City of London which was waiting for us. We have had the ship to ourselves, the Indian passengers & mails having gone on in the Ripon. We had a delightful voyage to Gallipoli which we reached last evening. There were three French line of battleships there – The 93rd Highlanders & Rifles were embarked in the transports for Constantinople while we were there in the boats of the <u>French</u> squadron!

We took in tow two large transports with stores & horses for Constanple. which we reached in 18 hours. –

We disembark tomorrow, the barracks and quarters are full and many regiments are in tents – I go tomorrow in uniform(!) for the first time to call on Ld Raglan and find out whether I cannot go into lodgings. In Pera[10] where we were they say there is not a room or a lodging of any kind to be obtained – There are 2 vessels close to us each having a regt on board who disembark & go into tents at once.

Our visitors say there is no talk of moving for 2 months but nobody knows yet.

They are fortifying the isthmus of Gallipoli about 8 miles out of the town. French & English work at job work. The English get theirs done some hours before the French.

The cold has been very severe but spring has now fairly begun though the trees are not so far advanced as in England. The cherry trees at Gallipoli being only just in blossom.

The French have shot four Zouaves for violent offences, but in general they behave very well though they are said to drink more than our men – I can give you no news until I have been ashore as nobody here cares for anything but tents, barracks, rations and uniforms.

We have had a very pleasant party on board Genls Airey & Buller Ld Wm Paulet. Col Maule & others of the staff. We are not at all anxious to get ashore as we bid adieu to comfort the moment we land.

You know of my disgust at leaving my horses to go by the Albatross, well it was rather increased when I found that there was room for eight horses on board the Ripon and that four horses were expected & prepared for – I had been told no particular hour to be on board the Ripon and found that luckily I had come by the train which had the Indian mail, in half an hour it was on board, the steam was already up and off we went. All the rest of the passengers had been at Southampton the day before and there were many speculations as to whether the Judge Advocate was coming & what he was like, nobody ever having seen a full blown J^e. Adv. the soldiers rather expecting to see him arrive in wig and gown –

We had a quiet rubber, myself and three of the elderly gentlemen I have named & wonderful to relate I have won two or three guineas by the operation.

I shall leave the letter open to let you know of my goings on tomorrow.

Tuesday.

I have only just got landed & settled in some rooms of a Turkish house with Col Maule. My horses landed safe & well from the Albatross – she arrived this morning just as my baggage was on deck to go ashore.

I have a Greek rascal who speaks French & Turkish & is I believe an escaped galley slave from Algiers but he is useful at present. Tomorrow I go to see the Genl in Chief & others but we have had such continual wet weather since Sunday aft^n till this evening that vessels with troops have not landed any one and we were willing prisoners on board. Knowing well that we bade farewell to comfort the moment we stepped off her decks.

I must finish this tonight as tomorrow early the post closes. I can give you no idea of what we are going to do. Captn Nolan went <u>yesterday</u> to try & buy horses in Syria. Every horse gun &c &c is landed here on the Asiatic side of the Bosphorus. I suppose because there is a barrack here, though 9/10th of all the world is under canvass [*sic*]. I sh^d think in a couple of months if we get horses that Head Quarters will be able to move. Till then I think only perhaps the Light Division will be got forward.

There are some Sappers & Miners but not a tool for them to work with.

Remember me to my pals at home.

My next letter will I hope give you more informat[n] touching public matters but here we hear such lies as –

1. French Revolut[n].
2. Cronstadt taken.[11]
3. Sir C. Napier lost 4 line of battle ships & 4000 men.
4. 14 Russian line of battle ships taken – &c &c.

The fleet did well at Odessa & what they did as it appears – but the Times reporter was there.[12]

Believe me ever y[rs]. W. G. Romaine

Send this to Banbury & any one else who can read it & wish to.

Cambridge University Library: Add. 7633/5/3

2

Romaine to Lord Mulgrave

[Holograph]   Varna, June 28th 1854

My dear Mulgrave,

As you don't seem to have been too much bored with my letters I shall send you one from this place. I have been here since the 21st. There has been no news since then except the arrival of the Cavalry and the 3rd Division. The latter are camped about a mile and a half out of the Town – the Cavalry at or near Devna – Lord Cardigan is out with some Cavalry to gather news of the Russians.[13] You will have seen by the papers that the Russians have raised the siege of Silistria after a final & severe struggle – Firing had been heard from the French outposts, two whole days & a night when suddenly they ceased to hear it. It was thought that Silistria had fallen. It was known to be very near falling as Omar Pasha had sent in to Gen Airey who commands the Light Division (while Gen Brown lives in Varna) to say that the place could only hold out three days longer – However on Saturday night the 24th news of the raising the siege came in – The Duke of Cambridge announced it to his Division on Sunday morning after Church Parade, as did Genl. Evans who said that he thought it would quiet the impatience of the troops for an advance & he thought that the Turks should have the credit of their gallant defence.

Calthorpe A.D.C. to Ld Raglan came in the evening before last & reported that as far as they had been the country was deserted, and that they believed that the Russians had crossed the Danube.

You at home know the reasons for this, I don't, it must be either that Russia & Austria have made friends & that this retreat is a concession to Austria, or the Emperor has withdrawn to save his army in consequence of expected hostilities in Gallicia or Silesia[14] – Whatever the cause, the men are furious at the retreat of the Russians without their having a blow at them, they are quite enraged at it. And this from a pure love of fighting, and I think a desire of distinguishing themselves by the side of their friends & allies the French.

It certainly is from no love to the Turks for there has been no attempt at fraternising with their sulky & morose allies of the true faith. The Bulgarians hereabouts hate us and our cause, though that may not be the feeling of those of them who have experienced the friendship of Russian Commanders & soldiers.

The Colonel of a Russian [*sic*, presumably intending 'Turkish'] Cavalry Reg^t encamped near the Light Division told Gen Airey that he was ashamed to give him the warning but that he thought that he ought to tell him that the men should not be allowed to go about the country singly – that the villagers put a very low value on human life and that they thought no more of killing a man than a sheep. Every man even the shepherds & herdsmen go about armed, either carrying a gun or pistol & dagger.

The villagers fled from our camps at first but now they are abundantly supplied with good milk poultry eggs bread & cherries – The rich men get butter at about two shillings a pound.

It is a beautiful country but covered with a thorny jungle over a great part of the surface, though the soil is admirable & with only a year or two of rest & no manure, bears excellent crops of barley –

The town is wretched & the shops naught, the few English or French articles purchased out of the transports being retailed at enormous prices, for instance a small box of English biscuits weighing about a pound – costs 35 piastres nearly seven shillings here.

What we shall do depends of course upon the distance the Russians retreat – It had been intended to make an expedition to Kortendje in rear of the left flank of the Russians, but now if they are across the River it w^d be useless.

I believe we could take Sebastopol, as we are now a large army here, but of course nothing will be undertaken, till news comes from Vienna.

The curse of this country is the character of the sovereign who shuts himself up in his harem with fifty times too many wives and too many bottles of Champagne – He is kept in entire ignorance of what is going on & when he has taken too much "Sherbet" alias Wine, he commits such freaks as making an Admiral of a Soldier &c &c.

He is surrounded by a set of Ministers who are every one of them villains of the basest description from Ruschie Pacha & Mehemet Ali downwards. I believe the best thing that could happen to the country would be that some unprincipled energetic rascal like the latter should succeed as he once nearly did in ousting his Imperial brother in law from the [illegible]. A vigorous arm aided by the French & ourselves for a year or two might make a Kingdom of the country that would make itself respected, but such a contemptible effete wretch as Abdul Medjid and the base wretches around him can never make themselves or the country respected –

The country & climate are magnificent. The sun on a clear day is no doubt much hotter than in England, as we are now about 10 degrees further south, but a person who lives temperately & drinks little or no wine can be out all day without any inconvenience – Every day there is a breeze except when one of our thunderstorms is brewing when it is sultry enough for India –

Lord Raglan is much better here than he was at his house at Scutari – If he is only half as good a general in the field as he is in the closet he will be a rare soldier. He is extremely popular with every one who has anything to do with him – However much burdened by work he treats every one with the same unfailing attention & courtesy – So much so that it is a pleasure to have to see him on business. I always make my visits as short as possible that if he does not see me with the same pleasure that I see him at all events he may not consider me a bore.

The troops are altogether behaving extremely well. I have had very few General Courts Martial and the number of District & Garrison Courts M[l] have been singularly few for the size of the Army collected in a strange country.[15]

The health of the Army has been good hitherto as seems likely to continue – I heard yesterday of a case very like Asiatic Cholera in the Fus Guards but the man has got over the attack & is doing well. Drinking is the great vice of English soldiers which no punishment will ever put an end to – No soldier is now allowed to go into the town without a pass – the French have moved to hills some three miles off and Prince Napoleon's Div[n] two leagues beyond them and the Cavalry in advance of all.

The Zouaves fraternise very much with our Highlanders and when drunk bestow their company upon them & invest their camp even at night to the great annoyance of the officers.

Varna and the camps are something after this fashion – [see Figure 1]

The forts are low works of the same description as those which have given the Russians so much trouble at Silistria. My house is within 50 yards of a battery which is now & always firing salutes. My horses are close to it and are learning to be under fire, they now hardly lift their heads to a shot – when they have anything to eat particularly –

I was rather anxious when I came here to go at once into tents, but I found a house had been told off for me on the sea wall, so I took possession and am very glad I did, for after a few days the grass in a camp gets trodden through and then the dust is very unpleasant as it gets at everything & helps to thicken the soup &c & what with open windows & sea breezes the houses are very comfortable – in summer – for in the winter they must be very cheerless as none of the windows fit – The house belongs to a

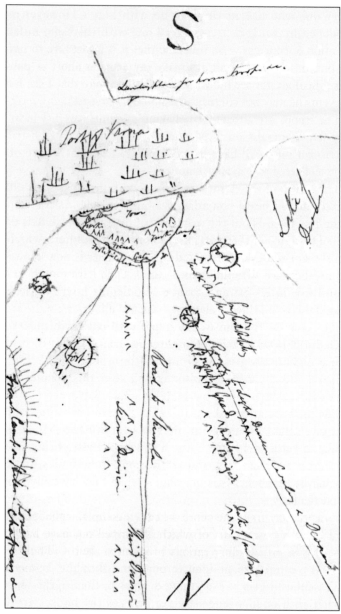

Figure 1. The camps at Varna (from letter to Mulgrave dated 28 June 1854).

Greek family who were in great tribulation when I came in, the poor woman crying dogs howling &c. But now that she finds she can sell me her eggs & milk above market prices & no question made she is quite happy & shows her contentment by sending presents of cherries which I return by sending her a quantity of coffee, a much prized luxury which is now exceptionally dear, but which thanks to the liberality of the Government at home we get very good & cheap –

I was delighted to hear so good an account of Lady Mulgrave's confinement, what is the young heir's name – My love to little Laura. I shall expect to hear great performances on the piano & in singing when I come home I hope she will have inherited a good voice –

I will not trouble you about a servant it is too far to send one and I must get on as well as I can with those I have –

I don't understand the Times abuse of the Ministerial changes as only on the 9th June they were speaking in praise of the very appointments that were made. The Duke of Newcastle for War & Sir G. Grey for Colonies – There must be some private pique or fancied slight at the bottom of such ill natured articles –

I have just come in from seeing a review of the 2nd Gen Evans Division. They are in first rate order. The exercise ended with a line of the whole division the artillery on the flanks and the whole line charged & cheered in a most hearty manner – The line was admirably tight. They are in perfect working order & are only longing for an opportunity to show it – I hope there will be a field day of the combined armies before we separate – The 1st Division were to have moved to a camp some miles off, but I heard just now that there has been a countermand & that there is not transport to feed them away from the shore. I heard a complaint that the Head Quarters Staff some part of which is camped out have had great difficulty in getting their rations brought to them – The French have sent out some dismounted regiments, but unless the men ride some of the ten thousand cats that infest my neighbourhood I don't know what four-legged animal they can cross. [?]

Some Turks marched in from Silistria this afternoon; but they know nothing of the Russian movements – But I believe even they report that the place must very soon have capitulated without help – which we could not have given. It may turn out that the Russians retreated, fearing that the rising of the river would oblige them to fight the combined forces with an impassable river in their rear. Whatever the cause it is a great triumph for the Turks & they have a right to be proud of it. Where are we to look for the million & a half of men in arms that Russia has been frightening the world with. In spite of the Baron de Munchausen & all his work it looks as if half the Russian armies did really exist upon paper only – If the post does not go out tomorrow I will send you any further news I may pick up, if not farewell.

I sh^d tell you that the Russians carried away their guns & broke down all the bridges behind them as they went. No doubt their rear was covered with clouds of Cossacks for no certain knowledge of their movements has come in. I still fear as I have all along, some treachery on the part of Austria. They have run with the hare & hunted with the hound so long that until they are committed, by some actual hostilities I shall not have any faith in them.

We are in a very bad way for transport. I reckon it would take a thousand bullock wagons to carry a fortnights [*sic*] bread alone for a fortnight for the army, as each wagon only carries 8 cwt and such wretched things are they that it would be almost unsafe to trust the food of an army entirely to them. Then you have to find carriage for ammunition & Ordnance Stores – Omar Pasha sent us 500 wagons, oxen & drivers but 400 deserted at once – We could not have moved to save Silistria – I have just been told that the post closes this morning early so I must conclude – A French steamer with pennant flying has this minute got aground under my window & appears to stick fast, but as the water is smooth I suppose he won't be damaged.

Remember me very kindly to Miss Grant, and to any of my friends of the Travellers whom you may see. Comyn, Fitzherbert, Greville and Cork.

And believe me Ever

Y^{rs} very sincerely

W. G. Romaine

So you are going to batter Cronstadt with gun boats? etc. That is
the only way to take it –

Cambridge University Library: Add. 7633: 5/4

3
Romaine to Lord Mulgrave
[Holograph. Incomplete. Probably started 8 Aug 54]

. . . has proved impossible to obtain labourers there at any wages –
many even of the shopkeepers who were making fortunes have left
many are dead & many sick. The 50th Reg[t] which was kept camped
near it to provide fatigue parties in loading and unloading vessels
&c lost at least 6 men in one day, it was then moved up here and
the 38th sent down, the next morning, two were seized & one was
dead – In the Head Quarters camp nearly every one has been sick
but we have had no deaths from Cholera as yet. The natives say
the Cholera ought to cease on 7th Aug[t] but I am afraid being a
Greek country, the Cholera reckons by the Old Style[16] which
would postpone his departure till the 19th. I am greatly afraid
we shall carry some of it in our ships with us and as we shall be
very crowded and be nearly two days on board, the results may
be very serious – We can't reckon upon more than 4 to 5 miles an
hour for the slow ships being towed at sea & as all must arrive
together, the slowest regulates the arrival – It is only 200 miles
across to Sebastopol –

Aug[t] 9th. Omar Pasha has sent in an A.D.C. to announce that his
army is occupying Bucharest this will lessen the danger of our
absence, unless he is foolish enough to fight a battle in the plains
between Bucharest & the Danube & gets beaten –

We are busy making wharfs and shipping gabions and fascines.
The troops are being collected close to the port. The Light
Division & part of the French embark at Baltchik Bay where the
fleets have so long been at anchor – I hear that they do not
estimate the Russian force at Sebastopol as more than 50,000 and
the Crimea containing only 200,000 inhabitants will not support a
very large army besides the army [*sic* – meaning obscure] so that I

17

should think since their regular supplies by sea have been cut off they must have been somewhat crippled for provisions – I see by the map that four miles from the place of landing there is a river marked with two bridges, here I suppose they will fight if at all, outside of their fortifications – They have been making a large entrenched camp in front of the star fort on the north side, our object will be to take the star fort as from there the town & fleet can be shelled and the batteries of the harbour commanded – They were at work at the entrenched camp when our generals reconnoitred and no doubt the delay in our attack will have given them time to finish it – Gen Brown had not returned from Constantinople last night. The Coldstream lost six men yesterday – The men are getting alarmed and if our inaction continues we shall lose more men by disease than by attacking Sebastopol – I tried very hard to get Ld Raglan to allow me to act as his extra A.D.C. at the landing & attack,[17] but with many civil things he refused. I will show you his letter some day, if —

All the army has been amused with a Memo – from the Horse Guards about shaving, <u>two inches</u> to left from the moustache to the corner of the mouth to the whisker & <u>two inches</u> from the chin to the beard! as if every body's face was the same size and that what would look proper for one man w^d not be ludicrous in another – They had much better have said nothing about it, as such a concession is simply absurd – The Royal George[18] has allowed the Guards to wear moustaches for a long time – In the other regiments you see many of the men going about with pieces of plaster covering the whole under lip, so burnt are they by sun and drinking wine & rum – I have not had the letter promised by Lady Mulgrave. I hope all the children have been well. do [*sic*] they go to Mulgrave – Pray make my best compliments to Lord & Lady Normanby when you see them – I don't know whether I shall get leave after the campaign, but I have my passport in case of accident – Goodbye, Y^{rs} very sincerely

W. G. Romaine

4
Romaine to C. J. Selwyn

[Holograph]   Camp on the Alma River
                                               Crimea. Sept. 21. 1854

My dear Selwyn,

I have not much time to write, but no doubt a line from this place the day of the "Passage of the Alma" will be interesting – You will read the details in the Times. I had a book & a watch the whole time of the battle saw a great deal & made notes – such as an excited horse w^d allow.

The Russians had intrenched the ground above the fords and had been there 15 days. Genl Menschikoff who commanded fled & lost his carriage & papers and it appears that he had said & written that the position w^d stop us 3 weeks – But the battle was over & the last shot fired in 3 hours.

The Russ^{ns} occupied the heights above the Alma R^r commanding the fords and had measured the distances to the principal points.[19] The French turned them by the right & Bosquet with the Zouaves drove them through the gardens & vineyards near the river to the right of the village which they set on fire just before the attack & which masked their position – The Turks were in reserve we had the right [*sic* – slip for 'left'], in front of which was what I call the great centre redoubt with 12 guns in position and 4 below it.

The Russians were 55,000 – 42,000 infantry & gun^{rs} – rest cavalry. They left none but the sick in Sevastopol – While the French were making their attack our troops slowly advanced to the burning village, when the Russ^n batteries opened upon them, our gunners being unable to see the enemies [*sic*] for the smoke for nearly half an hour. When the heights were taken our troops advanced to the river crossed it and the Light Division & guards & Highlanders had to take the batteries & heights above them. The regts stormed the battery having to ascend an open glacis of three hundred yards and so deadly was the fire that two regts were obliged to retire to the shelter of the river bank, when the Fusilier & Gren^r Guards came up & had a concentrated fire with their minies the effect of which was terrific. Sir G. Brown told me this morning that he rode into the battery himself, the first, his horse had severe wounds.

The Highlanders stormed the steep hill to the left of the Battery & found a heavy body of troops there advancing upon them. The Highl[rs] halted to take breath, formed line & then fired, swept the enemy away & advanced, driving every thing before them. In the rear of the battery they attempted to form with cavalry for their support, but the cavalry had seen our practice the day before & did not like it. And retreated getting some shells and shot from the French on a mamelon on their left flank.

The Russ[ns] then descended into a gorge & attempted a rally which lasted only till some Artillery arrived when after suffering heavily they retreated again – While this was going on the French after crowning their heights & driving the enemy out of the gorges occupied by them found themselves in front of a heavy body of troops & artillery & were checked for a moment, our men came up on their left and they drove the enemy off but not in such disorder as they retreated in front of our army.

I think our great mistake was charging the Centre redoubt before the French were forward enough to assist us – If I had time I'd fill pages with details, but I cannot do it now –

Our loss is just made up it is 1800 – killed wounded & missing – The French 1400[20] – Turks none, they were in Reserve.

The Russ[n] loss is put at 6000.

We have, three large brass guns, one is a 24 lb howitzer, a Major General & other officers & soldiers. The officers have suffered heavily. The Fusilier Guards have only 6 officers left unwounded. I found the smoke of the burning village so thick in our front that I went to our extreme right where we joined the French, saw Bosquet's attack & looked down the valley behind the smoke. I was so close to our rt. battery at one time which received so much of the enemies [sic] attention that I moved off a few yards to the right to an open space, which attracted fewer balls. For the round shot bounded along so thickly & the shells cracked so rudely overhead as to be very unpleasant. L[d] Raglan & all our officers behaved splendidly. L[d] R was too rash in exposing himself. The troops cheered him lustily as we returned after the pursuit & well he deserved it for a gallanter and more courteous man it would be impossible to find – I cant write any more so good bye – The Russians have retreated into Sebastopol and not stopped on the Katcha river & so perhaps we stop here tomorrow. I hope we go on –

Y^{rs} ever faithfully
W. G. Romaine
Head Quarters. Army of the East.

5
Romaine to C. J. Selwyn

[Holograph]   Balaklava
Sept. 29th. [1854]

My dear Selwyn,
I sent you a letter the day after the Battle of Alma which I hope you received. A detailed acct of it I c^d. not pretend to give, and since then we have had no rest and generally camped after dark sometimes, with^t. tents or rations and always without candles as they are not to be bought and are not served out. I had one bit wh. I used to light me to bed when I had one. To go on with the day after the battle – After I sent off my letter to you I had a horrible task to perform – An officer of the Quarter Master Generals department[21] came to me & said there were more than 500 seriously wounded men brought in prisoners & laid by the bank of the river, that they had had nothing to eat or drink since the day before, & many had been wounded as early as two o'clock the day before. He wanted a volunteer to go & feed them so I went with Kinglake (Eöthen) at 7 pm, took a cartload of biscuit & two pails and cups. Kinglake was so blind that he c^d not venture to go near them for fear of treading on them it being night & only starlight – So I and Sankey had to feed the whole of this frightful mass of wounded. The dreadful sights & smells of that night are not easily to be forgotten. Few were slightly wounded 3 only could stand upright, several were dead & made no response to the touch, many of them took my hand & kissed it & crossed themselves uttering words of prayer – It was necessary to harden one's heart & not think, to be able to get through with it.

The soldiers on guard would not assist except one of them who fetched some pails of water – the reason was that a Highlander passing over the field of battle after giving some of his small ration of rum & water to a wounded Russian on the field of battle had been shot dead through the back in sight of his companions who dashed out the Russians brains with a flintlock. Many men had been fired at or stabbed by the wounded, who it appears had been told that we sh^d murder them all. I have been told that we have over 1900 wounded prisoners – none of whom saw a doctor till the 2nd day after the battle, but our own men were not much better off, so few doctors were there.

Saturday 23rd Septr. We marched to Katcha River a beautiful valley full of smiling orchards & vineyards & pretty villas all of which had been much damaged by the retreating troops – Many of the Russians had slept here after the battle but at midnight a panic fear seized them and they fled to Sebastopol or elsewhere. The routed mob of troops reached Sebastopol late the night of the battle – The whole army is utterly demoralized. The next day we went to the Belbec River still unopposed though within 2½ miles of Sebastopol.

The next day we made a flank movement a masterly manoeuvre to avoid the numerous forts & entrenched camp North of the forts & harbour.

While going along & just emerging from the forest, we who were riding with Ld Raglan suddenly came within 50 yds of Russian soldiers. We turned our horses & slowly walked them back into the wood, sent for the 8th Hussars and Lancers who galloped by us in single file along the narrow lane, then part of a reg^t of rifles and then a troop of Horse Artillery was sent out. Presently cannon was heard close to us and to our surprise no crashing of trees followed, though artillery had been seen which was the reason why Ld Raglan & staff had been recommended to retire off the road till the troops c^d come up & form outside the wood. We were in a pretty fix if the enemy had known it & had had any courage or enterprise as two or three batteries of artillery were jammed up in the road with no troops to support them & the whole of the Gunners and –

I must stop as news is just come in that the Russians are coming up to fight a battle and all the staff are galloping out – a post goes out at 2 P.M. It is now 1½ P.M. My horse is saddled so

Goodbye

Y^{rs} ever

W. G. Romaine

Cambridge University Library: Add. 7633: 5/7

6
Romaine to C. J. Selwyn

[Holograph]   Balaklava

Octr 1st. 1854

My dear Selwyn,

I cannot remember where I left off in my last letter to you when it was suddenly interrupted by an alarm just as post was going out. On getting on horseback I found that the rumour was that 60,000 Russians had come out to fight us. The army was ordered under arms but to stand fast where they were and Ld Raglan went on to reconnoitre. He had the start of me but by hard riding I came up with him and found him with a small staff as most of his suite had been absent at the moment. Canrobert & Bosquet were also out with their staff. But the whole thing resolved itself into some 6000 Russians who were plundering in the villages from 5 to 7 miles off – This and the blowing up of the acqueduct[22] [*sic*] and some ammunition captured & destroyed on the road had given rein to the tale of heavy guns heard & large bodies of Russians moving on our rear. So we returned to camp. I had left my letter with the Times correspondent who was to put it on board the mail steamer at the last minute – He was going on board when I found him & wrote "false report" on the outside in pencil.

I think I have given you a description of the pursuit of the Russian division which is said to have been escorting Prince Menschikoff from Sebastopol – Some of the prisoners said that they were going out to form a junction with 40,000 Cossacks coming from the North, but it immediately struck me that they must be creeping from Sebastopol from the position in which they

23

were, and I thought that the state of fear in which we knew they were precluded the idea that they were intending to operate on our flanks. We returned after the pursuit to the main road on which we had turned to the left towards Bakschi Serai instead of Traktir, and in the evening reached Traktir five miles from Balaklava. There was a narrow gorge after leaving McKenzies farm on the Traktir road which [see Figure 2] was blocked up with abandoned wagons & munitions of war these were plundered & thrown over the precipice by the road side by the sappers, the ammunition blown up – The delay caused by the pursuit had caused the French army to cross the line of march of our HQ^r baggage & rear guard which had to stop and Ld Raglan & staff had no tents & no food –

We slept in a tolerably dry ditch close to a cottage in which Lord Raglan lay, and on the banks of a small river the Chernaya or Black Water – Some of the French & the English rear guard did not reach water that night & halted without it. It was a cold night but by great good luck I had purchased of a soldier from the spoils of the Russian general a large cloth cloak lined with fur which made me a bed and tent & all. Lord Cardigan was camped close to Genl Estcourt & myself, Kinglake & others. I have come to the conclusion that he is the most contemptible individual & the worst

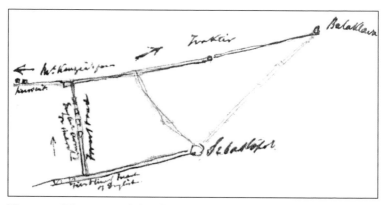

Figure 2. The route of the flank march (from letter to Selwyn dated 1 October 1854).

officer in the army. We all arrived on the ground after dark, and
De Morel, Estcourt's A.D.C. produced a bottle of Champagne
spoils of the Russ. General of which Ld Cardigan took two large
cups, soon after the whole baggage & tent of Cardigan appeared &
his supper was made ready – He never invited any one to eat or
drink or offered Estcourt the Adjutant General of Army a corner
to sleep in, but turned in majestic solitude as he had eaten. In the
morning he came & talked to us of the splendid mutton chops he
had for breakfast, but to our consolation he said he had no appetite
to eat a mouthful – He saw the Adjutant General eating hard
biscuit & very hard at that & drinking cold water with a long days
work before him & never offered him or any one else a cup of
coffee. The rest of the exhibition was when the cavalry was drawn
up ready to march. His Vet. Surgeon appeared with a report to
whom he s^d in face of two regts. "Damn you Sir & your horses &
reports too. Cant you see" then turning to the Cavalry "Threes to
the right march" meaning that the poor Vet^y. Surgeon sh^d see that
a General who had to attend to so important an order as threes to
the right, march must necessarily have his great mind so occupied
that he c^d attend to nothing else. He has quite destroyed the
regimental feeling of the cavalry by taking the command of them
himself cursing & bullying every officer, even the Colonels at the
head of their men – That everyone of them hates him and the
service [–] many long to go home. He & Lord Lucan only speak
by orderlies even when a few yards off each other –

We had only five miles to go to Balaklava the army moved at 7
and we at 8.30. We overtook the rifles at the little hills inland of
Balaklava which is a little landlocked bay shut in on E & West by
high hills which decline towards the North leaving a good road
winding among the rocky spurs of the hills on the East &
vineyards & farms on the West [see Figure 3].

The rifles were sent to occupy a little hill on advance of the
town, they fired a few shots & halted on the summit. The rest of
the rifles ascended the hills on either side of the road, some
Greeks came out, said that the soldiers had left that there were no
guns near. So we rode on to the spot where the road reaches the
bay by some trees at point A in plan scratched on last page. Some

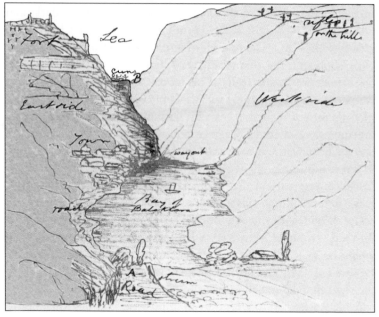

Figure 3. First view of Balaklava harbour (from letter to Selwyn dated 1 October 1854). Romaine's inscriptions (Left to right, top to bottom): Fort, Sea, rifles on the hill; guns, B; East side, West side; Town, way out; road, Bay of Balaklava; A, stream; Road. (Points A and B are mentioned in the letter.)

men were seen on the Fort at the place marked B and just as the staff reached the trees a shot was fired from B and a shell struck the ground by the trees but did not explode. A second followed throwing up the mud & water close to us. Ld Raglan finding that he had advanced incautiously too far, turned back a little way round an angle of the rock out of sight, but the fort had got the range and the shells exploded in the air just over us and fell in the soft ground of the vineyard exploding there & luckily doing no damage. As we could see nothing where we were & were in danger of losing half the staff by one unlucky shell, we moved off the road a hundred yards or more to the rear, our 24 lb howitzer came up & fired shells at the fort. The ships too came round & began firing, but both our howitzer & the ships guns so mistook the range that both were obliged to retire a little as their shells fell near us and ours near them. In the mean time the 77th & Rifles were sent to crown the heights & they ran and got under the walls of the fort, which hoisted a flag & ceased firing – The troops went in & came down with prisoners, arms &c and joined us at the town to which we proceeded when the fort surrendered. Directly after a tiny steamer came in, and in the afternoon other men of war and transports and then the Agamemnon was brought in by great skill as the entrance was very narrow & winding.

The staff distinguished themselves by running after cocks & hens & ducks in the streets.

The dandy Jim McDonald on the Royal George's staff getting off his horse capturing a duck and slaying it with his drawn sword. Leicester Curzon having his horse held while he potted some ducks for Lord Raglan's table. The vineyards are considered fair game by all and are speedily covered with soldiers when a halt takes place. They eat to excess of all kinds of fruit & die of cholera – We had a terrible sickness in the fourth Division, arising I have no doubt from their being kept camped on a narrow strip of land between the Putrid Lake & the sea. The day we marched, after the battle of Alma there were 60 cases of cholera in that division alone – The army are now camped on the hills in positions in front of Sebastopol and are getting very healthy though they have not had their tents till today since landing in the Crimea. They had them one night soon after landing as it was hoped there would be transport enough but it was found impossible & after carrying them 4 or 5 miles one day the poor fellows had to carry them back to the beach the next.

The French have had their full share of sickness and the day before yesterday some four hundred of the worst cases were brought down to the ships & embarked.

They tried a mean impertinent trick the other day, they sent men with materials to lift & carry away the four beautiful brass mortars which we had captured on the fort and would have succeeded, but that Adm[l] Lyons saw it from the deck of his ship & sent them away & had them removed on board – They had no shadow of pretence of a right to them as not a French soldier was within miles of the place when we took it. It was exactly like their sending horses to our camp at the Alma to take away the heavy guns we had captured – I had secured a drum belonging to the band of the Imperial Guard, which I intended sending home to Harvey for his hall but the French cut it off the side of the wagon & made off with it –

The army & navy are now very busy landing guns ammunition &c, and nobody who has not seen the detail of such an operation can imagine the amount of labour which is required to do it. Each gun requires a platform of solid teak beams for it to work on and it would require 6 or 8 horses to draw the platform for two or three guns, ten horses to draw each gun & then come picks spades shot shell powder &c and this has to go 8 miles. The weather and roads are good but one days rain would cause enormous delay by spoiling the road.

Octr 2nd. We have received the Constantinople Gazette and the French account of the battle, which makes us merely come up to pursue the routed enemy. But there never was a battle in which two combined armies had their separate work so entirely cut out. The enemy in front of us were in position in batteries long before constructed & admirably placed. The only fault in the battle on our side was the attacking too soon the great battery, but this was hastened from two causes, from the fact of our men falling from the fire of it before our 9 pounders could be of use, against the 32 and 24 lbs guns of the Russians, and from the French sending to ask us to hasten the attack. Twice later in the day did the French send to Lord Raglan for assistance, once to ask for some battalions on a point where they were hard pressed & could not make head – and again to ask to have the guns near them turned on a particular which which [sic] the officer said his men had three times failed to pass. Both times assistance was given, once by a battalion and the other time by turning the guns desired on the place indicated. I have little doubt that the truth of the battle will ultimately be known though I have no confidence that St Arnaud will be the man to publish it – Canrobert I believe will, he is now Commander in Chief as St Arnaud is gone home, they say dying of Cholera – Canrobert said "That all he asked of fortune was to command the

English army for three weeks now" – The second day after the battle I spoke to him at his tent, he spoke of his wound as slight and said "that we had attacked a terrible position 'rudement' in the manner which characterises our nation." One of the superior French officers said to Gen¹ Burgoyne that none but English soldiers could have taken the battery in the way our men did – the numbers of slain shown [*sic*] where the deadly struggle took place – The Russian prisoners put their dead wounded & missing now as high as 13,000 men. The French loss was said by the French Admiral to amount to 1350 <u>including cholera</u> – our loss of dead & wounded was 2100 men –

The French have landed here 8000 men we have landed 600 men infantry & 750 Cavalry horses & men at Balaklava, besides 500 Marines camped on the hill above the bay to protect the harbour. Dundas is now landing a thousand men and heavy guns from the ships. But he has taken the guns from the line of battle ships in spite of Sir E Lyons protest, instead of taking them from the frigates – so that the line of battle ships will be useless in the attack – There is no end to the obstruction he has put in the way of operations. Yesterday he wanted to send away & in fact ordered away the Sans-Pareil <u>steam line of battle ship</u> to carry a hundred prisoners to Malta! Sir E. Lyons by an energetic protest prevented it. Adm¹ Dundas remains anchored some five or six miles off and has never landed since we left Varna and refused all aid from his squadron which is the largest part of the fleet so that the inshore squadron under Lyons has had all the work – Though what use any squadron can be, that is not an inshore squadron it would be hard to say, as there is no enemy at sea to protect the fleet or army from. Delane of the Times who was out here has gone home furious & Layard who is living with Lyons in the Agamemnon will I know bring it before Parliament next session. His mean jealousy of Lyons has led him on till his acts amount almost to treasonable neglect of duty & refusal of aid & assistance. – The navy are mad with rage and I am sure if he gave an order and Adm¹ Lyons gave another contradicting it, they would to a man even in his own ship disobey him & obey Lyons, But this is a state of things that should not exist.

Our divisions & the French extend now from the East end of the waters of the harbour to Kamish and Arrow Bay where we & the French are landing guns & stores. We have taken the light-house & light it every night. We have cut off the aqueduct which supplies the harbour and another which supplies the town and as we know that before this was done water was selling at 10 silver roubles the barrel they must be much straitened

They had ordered all the people in the neighbourhood to come in and assist in the siege & the place was full of women & children, but the effects of want of water were shown yesterday as numbers of families were seen leaving the Town on the North side. They have collected some say as many as 40,000 men on the Belbek river, they remain there I suppose for the water, as many of them c^d be profitably employed at the works they are carrying on.

They had made enormous preparations for us on the north side of the harbour thinking we should come that way, and they have considerable fortifications & earthworks commanding the landing place at the mouth of the Belbeck River where we had intended to land siege train &c –

Our flank movement was I think a masterly one we crossed in face of the great fortress & army and established ourselves on a new base of operations & now we have a secure harbour in place of an open beach and this without the loss of a man or a wagon. This entire abandonment of a base of operations in sight of the enemy is quite unique as a manoeuvre, and I believe that in truth it was General Burgoynes idea. He has the whole charge of the siege and says he means to have us by bowling first to get at least 100 guns into position in one night and overwhelm the defences with a storm of fire for 24 hours & then they talk of an assault –

They are preparing some hot shot furnaces for the ships which constantly even now fire at the divisions. On Saturday I was out with Lord Raglan & staff to see what was doing and to find places for the batteries & divisions of the army – we were told not to crowd him too much when we were within range, but as soon as we appeared on the crest of the hill, a 56 pounder was fired at us and fell about 100 yds in his front – No horse or man moved so they thought it had not been far enough, & presently after from another place came a shell which burst in the air still further off – The angry rushing sound of a very large shot is very peculiar and the "thud" with which it came to the ground, gave a great idea of its weight & power. Many of the French soldiers who were standing by threw themselves on the ground when the shot was fired – I heard them say "Ah they don't shoot at the canaille[23] it is only when the staff come." Having been under fire five times in about ten days I have acquired some of the soldiers philosophy about bullets & billets – Kinglake at the battle of Alma was the only travelling gentleman with the army and acquired immense kudos by his coolness under a heavy fire. As severe Lord Raglan said as anything he ever was in except a part of the field of Waterloo. One or two other Peninsulars say that at part of the battle of Salamanca the firing was equally severe.

I received your letter of Sept 8th yesterday. You will see that all agree in your abuse of Dundas but he alone is to blame – The navy & Sir E. Lyons are burning to distinguish themselves and they are to be allowed to land guns & fight them though Burgoyne says he does not know where to place them to be of any use.

Some of the trenches are to be begun by the 4th & second divisions this evening I hear, but they will probably not continue after daylight as the others have not begun yet. These are on the right of the position & have a new white tower to batter & some earthworks to drive the defenders out of. I am sorry to say we had 6 deaths by cholera here last night in the Town – I had hoped it was leaving us –

Forward my letter to any one you like who cares to puzzle through such a length of scrawl – You may read it in Vacation time but in Term I won't send you anything so lengthy.

Y[rs] ever faithfully

W. G. Romaine

7
Romaine to C. J. Selwyn

[Holograph]   Camp before Sebastopol
                                                   Octr 22nd. 1854

My dear Selwyn,

So the most successful hoax the world ever heard of has been played off upon Europe in these days of Electric Telegraph. It must have been managed by some Greek House at Constantinople & very closely managed too, as it appears to have deceived every one including Omar Pasha, the Duke of Newcastle & the "Editor of the Times". It has caused great mortification to the army as they think it will detract from the value of their victory. I was standing by Ld Raglans side the first day our guns opened, & in rear of our left attack, when the mail bags were brought & opened & he pulled out a Times Octr 3rd with "Fall of Sebastopol" in large letters. With full particulars how 18,000 prisoners & 22,000 were killed &c &c. He was greatly annoyed I c^d see – The result whatever it be must fall so far short of this monstrous fiction – Since Tuesday we have been hard at work every day, but the French engineers and artillery men to every one's surprise have been utter failures – Their batteries were enfiladed, their magazines blown up three times, their men killed & wounded & dispirited & their works stopped for two days at a time. Their trenches have been insulted by repeated attempts of Russians in broad day & at night to enter & spike their guns. The French made prisoner a Russ. Officer & we took some prisoners & deserters & their tales agree sufficiently well. The Governor Genl or Ad^l Korniloff was killed the day before yesterday. Menschikoff & Gortchakoff are outside with 1000s of men on pretence of attacking our rear and taking our base of operations Balaklava – We have had two sham attacks which are called in derision the Battles of Balaklava. I can only afford you a half sheet of paper as my stock is very nearly exhausted & I have not yet got my baggage left on board ship near Eupatoria. My letter of 3rd Octr. must have shown you our state up to that time – The "Own Correspondent" is now about again[24] & his letters give a very good penny a line description of what occurs in camp & he really has many facilities given him for picking up good information. Yesterday was the day I had fixed in my own mind for being in Sebastopol, & if the French had only done their part as well we should have stormed the second night – We hear that their killed & wounded amount to 3000. The wounded were all burnt in their Hospital the day before yesterday. War is a horrid business when you look it in the face, but it is very difficult to keep away from looking on at the batteries doing their fearful work – Every day supplies a vast number of curious incidents of warfare, but lying here on the ground with lack of paper & in discomfort I cannot pretend to write them to you. I keep my note book in my pocket and it contains some things interesting already. We have some comrades here who keep their hearts & eyes always on the rear & how we are to get home, but though they are high up some of them, their words pass by Ld Raglan as the idle wind – He is very rightly & on good grounds possessed with an entire want of confidence in every statement made by the French. They were to have opened with 60 guns – They began with about 24 small brass pieces and by 11 o'clock were silenced the first day. They were silent 48 hours. Then they were to have opened from batteries within 600 metres. They made the trench but put no guns in it & were silenced again. The Russians have beaten them hollow. We committed a grievous mistake against the common sense view of every non professional man – We had Lancaster guns in position for days & yet never interrupted the work of the enemy who put up guns faster than us, and all for the sake of the effect to be produced by our opening. Why the Russians made twice the crash & with as heavy guns & their despised earthworks have proved admirably made & hard to destroy & when one battery is silenced another springs up. Our men & officers have behaved splendidly & done their work in the batteries most manfully. We have not half enough artillery men engineers sappers or Doctors – In some cases Doctors are doing the work of five men, where five men w^d. be amply employed, you may imagine how sick men have suffered in consequence. The artillerymen are so worn out with incessant labour that today they have been obliged to get 300 sailors from the fleet to help in the batteries. The soldiers [have] been terribly worked too. There is no drink luckily & no suttlers [*sic*] booths and there is no crime & the men are the best soldiers in the world and eager for the assault. I would we had 60,000 of them instead of 40,000 Fr and 20,000 Engl. Yesterday the Fr. wanted us to direct part of the fire of our guns against the batteries in their front, although we have as many guns against us now as we have ourselves in position – They want that determination under difficulties which our men have. I believe Canrobert wants the storming parties to be of English and French mixed – I have no doubt we shall take & destroy the place but I give six weeks now for its complete destruction & then a month for our removal if we go away – What do they say in England are we to go or occupy the Crimea – if we stay we must have clothes & houses for the men for the cold in some winters equal to 20 Reaumur.[25]

(Evening) The French batteries have done nothing again today nor ours made any further impression. New parallels are to be begun tonight, Menschikoff has 40,000 men to attack our rear. We want more horses & wagons warm clothing, & forage for horses or they will all die when the cold & wet come. We have had no rain since the day of landing – Our horses are now skeletons from half food & double work. Yesterday an officer died of cholera & Lord Dunkellin was taken prisoner. If Menschikoff will come & fight it will make things pleasant but I think they are playing a waiting game & look for bad weather to help them.

Good bye,

Ever yours truly, W. G. Romaine

Cambridge University Library: Add. 7633: 5/9

8
Romaine to C. J. Selwyn

[Holograph]   Camp before Sebastopol
Nov[r]. 18th 1854

My dear Selwyn,

Still dating from the old place. So you have been puzzled about the numbers of the French army. Whether purposely or no their numbers have always been a mystery even to us living by the side of them – At Varna I believe of all arms they really had nearly 70,000

Say	70,000	
Take	20,000	Cholera & other diseases }
		which is not one too many }
	50,000	
	24,000	landed at first
	26,000	
	9,000	landed since
	15,000	
	6,000	lately landed of infantry
	9,000	
	3,000	cavalry
	6,000	to be accounted for

Now the 5th Division which landed here not long ago had the Cholera when it left Varna & brought it here. How has our original army wasted, when of the 30,000 we landed we had at one time before drafts came to us only 16,000 rank & file under arms –

The hurricane of the 14th will have helped with the battering of Fort Constantine to dispose of some of the ships about which you enquire. The fleet has been composed of an inshore and offshore squadron. The former commanded by Lyons has done all the work nearly & the squadron commanded by Dundas in person has always been as far away as possible from the scene of active operations. The navy has in fact been grossly mismanaged, having such a scheme of making war as allowing Odessa Cherson Nicolaieff all to be remain [*sic*] hostile & uninjured places the head quarters of all the reinforcements which we have had to fight and all places which could be destroyed by the fleet or made to pay large ransoms in contributions of food &c for our army.

We had news yesterday that we were to be attacked front & rear today, but I did not believe it as we had not heard of the arrival of reinforcements. Now the two conditions precedent to a battle are fulfilled. Lüders has arrived with 12,000 fresh men & tomorrow is Sunday so I daresay we shall have a fight. They will take them to mass at 3. AM give them a skinful of brandy and set them on. An officer who has deserted from them says that they had 15,000 wounded men come in to camp. We can account for 5000 buried dead and we have about a thousand wounded & unwounded [?] prisoners. The French have now a very strong army but we have an enormous position to hold & occupy with troops, in a rough shape thus [see Figure 4].

Two landing places to protect one at each flank of our position and a first class fortress to besiege with a cunning [?] army equal if not superior in numbers to our attacking force. They have arsenals of greater capacity than Woolwich & Portsmouth put together and they can shelter the greater part of their men at night.

Novr 20th. While I think of it, if you see Kinglake will you ask him if he has sent my watch to Mr Massey the maker in the Strand.

21. Novr. Yesterday a Polish deserter came in & said that we were to be attacked in the night in front of Balaklava, but if there had been such an intention the heavy days rain would have prevented it for six hours rain quickly makes a quagmire of this tenacious clay. We have now dry cold weather & calm. If we only had the warm clothing lost in the Prince! Yesterday 26 men died of cholera. The 97th Regt of 1000 men is arrived, but war consumes men very fast. Of the three splendid Battalions of Guards I saw reviewed before they sailed, there are but few left, and worse than that, none of those that come in their places will be the men they were, fine thoroughly disciplined old soldiers – How they fought the other day. They really saved us from a disaster caused by our own negligence in not destroying the road by which the Russians came up before, & not making up a

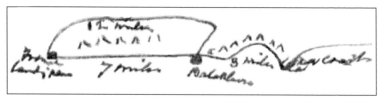

Figure 4. Allied positions south of Sevastopol (from letter to Selwyn dated 18 November 1854).

breastwork to house [?] those noble fellows. For most of them were lost by not knowing when to stop in their charge & being overwhelmed by columns of men on their return whom owing to the nature of the ground they had not seen.

I send you my note book, which you are at full liberty to read if you can, but I had rather it be not lent to any one. Will you do me this favour and put it in one of your drawers as I am afraid of losing it out here. We are to have heavy guns & mortars & try to shell the Russians out of the part of the town opposite to the French attack – We were to have assaulted on the 9th of Nov[r]. but the battle of Inkerman came on 5th & we were for several days overwhelmed with our own wounded & the terrible numbers of Russian dead & wounded. It seems we shall never come to the end of the Russian dead. Only the day before yesterday the sharp-shooters came on a place where lay 60 festering [?] corpses and in another place they found a dead Englishman & 12 dead Russians but all in such a state that they c[d]. not be moved to be buried so there they remain. We have great flights of vultures & hoodie crows flying over us. They were not here when we came but have scented the battle afar off – Last night the rifles had a sharp skirmish to dispossess the Russian sharpshooters of some holes they had made. We lost Tryon the officer commanding the party 10 men killed & 14 wounded, and have taken possession of their pits & are using [?] them very much in return. Biddulphs map and view give a fair idea of the position of the troops generally, though the Divisions are wrongly placed. But the view gives a most incorrect idea of the appearance of the place. We have made up our minds for a winter campaign & I have written for water proof ankle [?] boots long stockings and a consignment of good things from Fortnum & Mason, to be labelled "Law Books" for Judge Advocate Gen. I think that won't tempt the rogues, who pillage our baggage en route. I am gradually becoming a person of intemperate habits and drink very often nearly two glasses of wine per diem & am the better for it – I was a teetotaller all the hot weather & escaped even a passing touch of diarrhœa. If you take in any newspapers which you throw aside when read, stick them in the post – they come here some day or another & serve to enlighten me as to what people think at home. Never mind its being an ignorant Tory publication I shant see your blushes. Commend me to Follett & tell him to send me such another companion as Kinglake.

Y^{rs}. ever

W. G. Romaine

Cambridge University Library: Add. 7633: 5/49

9
Romaine to C. J. Selwyn

[Holograph]   Camp before Sebastopol
Decr 1st 1854

My dear Selwyn,

I have been up since daylight waiting on a sick servant who was taken suddenly ill with cramps in the stomach but thanks to a pill sent by the Doctor & my hot bottles & brandy & water he is up again & as I am cold & waiting for breakfast I may be supposed in a happy frame of mind to give you a description of this continually raining miserly spot of earth. First let me give you my opinion of our prospects – Don't believe any of the newspapers notions of an immediate assault or the claptrap about "les [illegible]" which appears at warm dinner tables. We have now determined that the place is to be besieged by force [?] – That has been only finally acted upon for about a fortnight. Before that there was a vague idea of storming the place and the 7th Novr was to have been the day. The battle of the 5th prevented that and when we had time to look about after that, the great men did not like to face another bloody day immediately & diverted themselves to fortifying our position & sending for more guns & powder – It was the same feeling that prevented our entering the place the day after we arrived. The minds of the Generals had hardly recovered from the storm [?] after the slaughter of Alma and they hesitated to order their men against stone works – It would be hard to blame them as one can easily imagine what a storm of indignation would have been raised by the "know nothings" in the event of a repulse. Now the place is ten times stronger than when we began to attack it.

That is, in the matter of earthworks & cannon. We have proved by our attack of artillery that they can beat us in number & weight of guns and having failed we are now waiting for heavier mortars & new guns, the old ones being worn out, and the firing from our batteries has ceased for weeks – In answer to our new erections of earthworks the Russians are busy making new batteries & arming them and when we & the French begin again I fully expect that they will have five guns for our one. We are going to fight another artillery duel, having previously ascertained that it is the weapon they are more abundantly supplied with & use the best. I fear it will cost us dearest in the end – Our army is suffering fearfully from cold and exposure from too hard work and insufficient clothing. The clothing did not reach us till the 14th Novr instead of the 14th Octr and then was all lost when the "Prince" sank in Balaklava Bay – We have the cholera again worse than ever it was at Varna. The adjutant of the 44th told me yesterday that he had lost 20 men in 24 hours & that the doctor said there were 20 more who must die and that the hospital was filling as quick as the dead were carried out – These were hardy soldiers who have not seen a roof since March not soft new arrivals, who perish like flies. The constant wet has killed down all our artillery & cavalry horses so low that I do not think there is one division that c^d move its guns and ammunition waggons, the 3rd Division c^d not move its guns two miles – The Heavy Brigade of Cavalry c^d. barely furnish 200 men for a charge of a mile and w^d have to return at a walk. The worst of the matter is that our carriage has failed us and the men do not get all their rations regularly and when they return wet through as they always do from the trenches, there is no wood to cook with & a long way to get water. They now have to dig laboriously with pickaxes among the rocks for the roots of the bushes they cut down when they first came – They have no change of clothes & their great coats are like cobwebs. There are now some jerseys & socks at Balaklava, but no transport for them and they don't or can't send the soldiers to the rear to get the clothing that is ready for them – so the men are wet for days & nights together get diarrhœa & cholera go into hospital & are dying at the rate of from 70 to 90 per diem. With all this the men though ragged & dirty are always ready for fighting and perfectly able to maintain their ground against any number of Russians that may come against them. They are longing to have a try at Sebastopol. I have heard them say "I only hope I shall live long enough to see the British flag on the walls of that town" – I omit the expletives – an attempt now would be attended with a huge slaughter if the Russians stuck to their guns. They have three lines of entrenchment full of cannon. The army of Liprandi in front of Balaklava is hutted. But they have their miseries which I believe surpass ours – Three deserters who came in from him yesterday say that they are short of provisions & the troops wretched & discontented – Not a murmur of discontent has yet been heard from our gallant fellows. The Russians have their bread baked at Bakchi Serai & brought in waggons – The wet has made the clay road deep and almost impassable, the difficulty of feeding their army may therefore be conceived. The French have blown up the causeway & cut all the roads leaving by Inkerman and the head of the harbour to Sebastopol and we & the French have now established & armed three redoubts far in advance of the 2nd Division of our army & which look down upon Inkerman & the head of the harbour – The consequence immediately has been that the steamers which in the battle of Inkerman threw shells over the whole field of battle have been obliged to move to a place of shelter & cease to fire, and all stores for the beleaguered Southern side of Sebastopol must cross the water & the defenders too must feel themselves shut up in case of an attack & must either die or surrender, as vessels could not carry them away in any numbers. The enemy are represented to us as discouraged & heartily sick of the siege. With them no place is quite safe as our shots which miss one object must do some damage to the rear, whereas if theirs miss the trench they are fired at they expend themselves harmlessly in the rear – They also have to contend with a fearful amount of disease, and they have not even a Scutari to send them to – Yesterday after a week of perpetual wet we had a fine day – Today it has set in black with pouring rain and I fully expect tomorrow to hear of 100 deaths by cholera. As the "Times" said every thing takes our "heads" by surprise. They w^d do nothing to make a road though all the world knew it w^d. be a slough directly the rain fell, which always falls in Novr. They made no efforts to bring wood to hut the army till horses & men died by scores a day from exposure. Now a ship load of wood is come & has already been a week at Balaklava because there is no means of carrying it where it is wanted. They refused me leave to have a little on the ground that the horses wanted it most as the army w^d cease to exist without artillery cavalry or transport for Commiss^t. This appeared reasonable enough and I said no more. Now a week has gone by, but not a horse is under cover nor has a step been taken to cover them that I can see.

With all the wants, discomforts & miseries you would be surprised at the perfect feeling of confidence which exists as to the final results and this confidence I fully share. I believe that we could if necessary go & capture every gun & Russian in Sebastopol. The men from being so constantly under fire and so uncomfortable in quarters are perfectly reckless of shot & shell. They go into the trenches & take down the sand bags which protect them to sit upon. Four times have the officers been obliged to report them, so many casualties having happened from their doing this. The Russian marksmen too fire so well that our sappers c^d not repair some damage done to a battery though the enemy's sharpshooters were 1,000 yards off. The French keep a profound silence in their trenches for fear of the storm of bullets, grape and case shot which follows the least noise being made, and they allowed yesterday that the Russians had the advantage over them in the musketry fire from their works upon the French advanced trenches. The Muskovi however have been a good deal cowed by the stern reception they met on the 5th. when they were repulsed in their attack & left nearly if not quite 5000 dead besides wounded & prisoners. We have repeatedly been told by deserters that we were to be attacked in front of Balaklava by Liprandi, but it has never come off. We have also been alarmed by moving of troops, but nothing further has come of it. That fearful charge of the Light Brigade was not wholly thrown away. The article on that affair in Times of 13th Novr was well & truly written & expressed my ideas of it admirably – Layard saw the fight as well as myself and I have no doubt wrote to Delane, but his letter was put in the form of a leading article as

Layard had complained of his letter about Alma being put in, without careful supervision by Delane to see that names were not ment^d. which had better have been omitted – I hope you received my last letter and its enclosure, my note book, not my Diary which I keep distinct. The notebook containing only the history of days spent away from the tent & pen & ink – Read it yourself if you can & will but don't let it get away from your custody. I shall be very glad to hear that you have received it as I sh^d not like to hear of its being in strange hands – I am still in a bell tent such as the soldiers had at Chobham. I might have a marquee but I preferred two bell tents as by that means my servants have a dry place to work in. They have besides two small patrol tents to sleep in. I have a Genl. C^t M^l. on Tuesday & another on Wednesday & was to have had one today in the 1st Division, but I found a District C^t M^l would do as the man c^d not be convicted of the graver offence – Very lucky I am as it has not ceased raining since daylight and I sh^d have had to have gone in scarlet coat & epaulettes & cocked hat some 3½ miles on horseback through the slippery mud.

We have three months more of winter before us, to be spent in tents and if not in fighting in readiness to fight day & night. Yesterday I was up at my favourite lookout place behind our "left attack" or "Chapman's battery" and I could not after a careful search see the large Russian army which are [said] to be encamped on the Inkerman heights near the Star Fort. I believe that they have moved away nearer to Bakchi Serai & Simpheropol to be more easily fed and I think the movements of troops in the Chernaya Valley which were supposed to portend an attack on us have also been in the same direction and that the force in front of us is greatly diminished through the impossibility of feeding them so far from their resources. The great body of cavalry is certainly no longer in sight in front of Balaklava & I think they too have had to move away in search of forage. They were quite useless against our fortified positions as long as we remained on the defensive & did not attempt to follow our enemies into the plain – If you have a map & know the positions of the armies & read through this long letter I think you will have a more correct idea of our position & prospects than most people have.

We have a sufficient confidence in the French and ourselves to feel that we can beat any number of Russians that the Czar can send now or in the Spring if only we can get covered & fed & have reinforcements sent us to replace the loss of life which a winter campaign must cause. A new outfit in guns is on its way & partly arrived but our animals [?] failed to bring even one mortar to the front & we wait for frost or dry weather to begin firing in earnest again. Now our batteries fire about a half hour during the day time for forms' sake to show we have not struck work – We have some advanced trenches into which guns are to be placed and we have also advanced trenches for sharpshooters very close to the place which annoy the Russians much in & in front of these there is often some hard fighting, but our men always hold them. The French are fortifying the extreme left of the position to restrain any assault on their lines. Tomorrow 2nd Decr is Anniversary of Austerlitz and they had intended to have opened their new batteries but I fear the "men of Austerlitz" won't shine & certainly they will not be ready for 8 or ten days then probably will wait for us. The idea of our engineers is that with our heavy mortars we can make the town too hot to live in & destroy it I doubt. I think the Russians have not the same superfluity of skills that they had & perhaps having the sea open if we were well supplied with land carriage we might use them up in the long run as it would be a hard task to feed their army & supply their guns from Odessa by the bad roads of the Crimea. Be confident of one thing that we are firmly established here nothing short of a repetition of the disasters caused in the hurricane of the 14th could give us any uneasiness as to the security of our footing in the country. Let Banbury have this letter to read & tell him to write – I don't touch on general politics as you must be wearied to death with articles headed "Vienna" & "Berlin" –& the news which is interesting from this place is what the army is saying & doing here – I wish you w^d also remember at home that you have chosen to invade Russia in almost her strongest corner and that you must worthily support the army you have sent out to die by sword & disease or there will be a fearful tale to tell by the Spring. Our sick & wounded are now 10,000 – here & at Scutari. There will be very few men or officers actually engaged at Alma or Inkerman who will appear to wear any decoration that may be given for those battles. Goodbye

Ever yours faithfully

W. G. Romaine

Cambridge University Library: Add. 7633: 5/10

10
Romaine to Lord Mulgrave

[Holograph] Camp before Sebastopol
Decr 6th 1854

My dear Mulgrave,

The least I can do in return for my Lady's forethought is to send back her sheet of paper with some record of our position here – I was very glad to hear so good an account of your own household – I had seen in the papers the death of Lady Strathmore and I guessed that she would have been staying at Lord Normanby's. I am very glad the parcel arrived safe at last as the things sent by Maule have acquired a value which I am happy to say mine haven't as yet. I find your letter was sent on 14th Novr my papers from England arrive [?] only 4 days later – They had only received the telegraphic despatches of the Battle of Inkerman of 5th Novr. It was a more severely contested action than Alma. Their force engaged outnumbered us many times and but for the desperate fighting of the Guards & 2nd Division they would have succeeded in forcing our position. They had brought gabions and fascines to establish a lodgment in the course of the night, but as the prisoners said, they had passed three times over the corpses of the attacking columns which had preceded them & all having failed they had nothing left but retreat. Our men since then have escaped being seriously attacked, but they have been overworked. The weather has been constantly wet & cold for days together with over a week 10 or 12 hours of sunshine. Wood has become almost impossible to obtain & the men have even burnt the handles of tools & the woodwork of the platforms of the guns in the batteries. Our baggage animals have died off so fast that now constantly some of the divisions are not supplied with their daily rations of meat or bread or rum, so that the men on coming cold wet & hungry from the trenches have often not enough to eat and still oftener not fuel to cook it and eat their salt pork raw. The consequence of this has been the most fearful mortality among the Divisions in front of Sebastopol which find guards & working parties for the trenches. The deaths have the last seven days been 82, 81, 84, 85, 75, 72, 63. Ten days giving as many dead as the battle of Alma. We have had a black time and the Ravens of the army have been croaking desperately – I hope and believe we have seen the worst. We have now had 36 hours of almost dry weather. We have received reinforcements, & have got some supplies of warm clothing, charcoal & hay and hear that huts for the army & stores are on their way out. If only the soldier had a dry warm place to sleep in, he would not perish as they have lately, like flies in cold & damp weather. You would not know the Scots Fusilier Guards or rather the remnant of these brave fellows, in their torn cobweb like coats dirty trousers, unwashed bearded faces & hollow gaunt cheeks. But every man of them on the 5th fought like a hero – The Brigade of Guards after the 5th were not 1500 men though they had received drafts before then. The siege has been at a standstill for a long time. The assault wd. have taken place on the 7th but for the battle so the Russians gained something by the fearful loss they sustained in that conflict. We buried 2400 dead Russians. The French 1400 and the Russians had two burying parties busy for two days burying those that fell beyond our lines. A deserter from one of them said his party had buried 500 making 4300 dead – the usual calculation has been 5 to 1 wounded to killed – though our own experience is 6 wounded to one killed in our battles. But 5 to 1 would give 21,500 put hors de combat. Some prisoners & deserters put their loss at 25,000 we reckon about 20,000. I believe no one ever saw so small a battle field with so many slain upon it. In some places they lay so thick you could only walk by striding over one corpse after the other. We ought to have had someone with the [illegible] of Fuseli[26] to depict the horrors of that scene just before night fell. When the Russians were driving off their last guns the two batteries of the enemy were beginning to throw shell on to the field thick as it was with their own dead & dying. They are a brutal enemy. Two days running did they fire on our parties burying their men though they also had parties with a priest engaged in the same work near enough to see that our men had no arms. But you will hear all the details better in the columns of the Times. This is a standing excuse in every letter that goes to England, and I fancy must be accepted as a valid one for you must be all bored to extinction with Sebastopol & Crimea & the true dispatches & the lying telegraphs. I suppose you have begun to put some faith in the St Petersburg Gazette. It gave a very tolerably true account of some of the minor affairs reserving all the powers of lying for the despatches of 5th Novr making it begin at 1 PM instead of day break and purposely confusing the attacks in the different parts of the position so that no one could properly understand what had really happened.

Today we have gained some of the fruits of our patient endurance. Liprandi's army has totally disappeared from its position in front of Balaclava. Starved out I have no doubt by the impossibility of transporting provisions along the deep clay roads from Bacshi Serai & Simpheropol. This morning at daylight the huts they have been so long constructing from materials obtained by destroying every house in Cammara [*sic* – normally transcribed as 'Kamara'] were all burning and not a Cossack vidette was in sight. Our great guns & mortars which are to do such wonders are only waiting a weeks dry weather and some live horses to appear in our batteries. The French batteries are nearly if not quite ready. So are the Russians and they will have about five guns to our one when the second act of the great artillery duel begins. But we are getting stronger every day & they are getting weaker – Every day now we shall be getting better clad better housed & fed & have more men to relieve the overtasked guards of the trenches. In less than a week the French will have 20,000 more men[27] – The plan I believe is to keep up a heavy fire with 13 inch mortars and every gun that can be brought to bear on one particular part of the town so as if possible to make it untenable by troops and then rush in. We have already cut all communication with the North side except by water, so the defenders of the Town West of the Dockyard

Creek will either fight or surrender if they can obtain quarter, as there would be no possibility of carrying them off by steamers in face of a victorious assaulting army. I hear the assault is to be made by 40,000 men of the combined armies, a force which in the reckless humour the men now are [in] must be irresistible spite of the three lines of entrenchment & batteries to say nothing of mines which the Russians have prepared. I fear more the effects of the heavy fire of the heavy artillery of the forts which can play upon the town after we shall have entered. I am still in the bell tent I had when we landed at the Taltscha,[28] one of those tents My Lady which no doubt you thought so picturesque at Chobham when arranged with flower pots & dwarf firs and the other amenities of a camp picnic. It has been now so long in the wet that all the part which touches the ground has rotted off. I got so starved with cold that I was obliged to dig a hole in my tent and burrow under the outer edge of the tent & so construct a flue with a chimney, 3 feet high outside. By great skill in the engineering department it draws admirably. I enlarged the hole inside till it looked like the grave of a monk of La Trappe. I have put my chair in it & now my feet are warming over a fire made from some of the oak of the noble ships that perished in Balaclava Bay at the very time you were writing to me at Florence – One ship alone went down with 168 persons (The steam ship Prince) with 200,000 pound in money 30,000 great coats 50,000 flannel drawers 50,000 woollen socks 30,000 jerseys &c &c &c, another had 15 days hay for all the horses in the army, another had siege ammunition another minié ammunition –

I find myself on capital terms with every body here and Lord Raglan especially treats me every day with more & more confidence and consideration. I rarely deal with him less than twice a week, though he receives few guests as his house party is 14 or 15 and he has only room at his table for about 16. I hardly know however whether it is worth while to hang round here; I have seen much of what I wanted to see the post is valueless as regards money and position and it leads to no promotion that I can see in any business. How will politics turn out next session will there be General Election. I fancy not. I hear from Chatham occasionally. Where matters seem to go on favourably for the

Liberal interest. The good folk there still seem to look to me in case of a vacancy. The details of an army in the field in time of pestilence and constant fighting are horrible enough to sicken anyone of war. Our cavalry have just been declared unfit for service and are gone into Balaclava for shelter. The two Brigades could not furnish 100 men & horses to make a charge of one quarter of a mile at a gallop & return at a trot. When they moved a large proportion – even of the splendid Scots Greys – had to walk & lead their horses. Not one Division of the army could move their artillery & tumbrils to action with the enemy. I have been very fortunate with my cattle my two English horses are both each in fair condition though I doubt whether Mrs Anderson would recognise them as their coats are like a winter Buffalo robe. My four original baggage ponies are also alive & well & now very useful as they bring my forage & wood & stores. The Commissariat having long given up all attempts to supply us. Unfortunately Mr Filder though a wonderful man of business has always made war in a friendly country & has not yet got rid of his Spanish & Canadian ideas. The Chief of these unfortunately for the army was that the transport of the country was always the best. This did very well in a land of mules & [illegible] but here where we have no country but the ground we camp on and the carriage of the country if we could get it is execrable & useless when the rains begin such an idea is fatal and has caused the loss of weeks of valuable time and of hundreds of still more valuable lives. Canrobert and Ld Raglan get on admirably, there is something very frank about Canrobert & he has an openly expressed feeling of admiration of the English which of course prepossesses us in his favour. I believe if St Arnaud had lived a week longer we should have stormed & taken Sebastopol when we first arrived. I think the Emperor of Russia was neither prepared for our coming nor for our rapid success when we did come, nor for our delay in taking it after our success. But when he found he had time he made the best use of it & brought troops from Bessarabia in carts & artillery men by post to defend the place. The only safe plan now for you is to believe nothing but the dispatches from the Generals out here – The truth is generally a little obscured in the St Petersburg Gazette, but still allowing something for colouring there is generally a groundwork of truth in the news it gives of any operations here – I have scribbled till my hands are blue in spite of my fire, but it is no use to go to bed just yet as the wind is Northerly and the salvoes of artillery which [the] Russians treat us to every night have not yet come off. They make now desperate attempts on our advanced trenches several times they have caught our men asleep in their blankets & bayoneted them, the advanced trenches being only 150 yards from the enemy. Last night they got into our second parallel, some of them being killed there, but they killed 6 of our men & wounded 25. I have just looked with surprise at the seven or eight pages of gossip I have written. I hope to have my warm clothing & the rest of my baggage now in a day or two. Please my lady don't send such a large sheet of paper next time or I shall wear out the gold pen which has adhered faithfully hitherto to my waistcoat pocket. The Russians are beginning to fire, there they go and now the clatter of the muskets filling up the short pauses between the booming of the great guns so good night. After this noise is over we shall have it nearly quiet till the moon goes down or gets under the cloud, or there is a sortie upon our poor worn out sleepy brave soldiers. I declare when I woke at night and heard the rain pattering on my tent every drop went to my heart except those that fell on my face, thinking of our poor fellows in the trenches who have not been warm & dry for many days & nights. Six bells has just struck in the sailors camp behind the 3rd Division which means eleven o'clock PM. I send this to Florence because if you are gone my Lady will open it & send it on when read & if you are not you must write one word when you start for England. My love to little Laura & kind regards to My Lady. The cannon are now going off like file firing, goodbye. Pray remember me very particularly to the Marquis & Lady Normanby.[29] You told me nothing of the Iron Stone – how goes it. Yrs ever faithfully

W. G. Romaine

II
Romaine to John Harvey

[Holograph]   Camp before Sebastopol
                                           Decr 8th 1854

My dear Harvey,

The cheery times of the year as they come round remind me of the pleasant roof of Ickwell so I despatch a line which I hope will find you at Christmas & convey to you & Mrs Harvey the good wishes of the season. We have been suffering a good deal from the long continued wet and the mortality among the soldiers in the trenches has been terrible. 72, 71, 74, 85, 82, 63, 62 a day! from sickness alone – the battles of Alma & Inkerman were not so deadly. The roads have been impassable from heavy rain falling on the deep tenacious clay. The men in front could not be fed. We alone have not suffered, Liprandi has been obliged to decamp from the front of Balaclava, we suppose to get nearer to his supplies at Bacshi Serai & Simpheropol. The only advantage we gain by his absence is the use of a good road from Balaclava to the front of our position which his guns commanded – we have now got frost & sunny days, a week of it would enable us to get up our heavy guns to the batteries & begin the siege again. My own opinion is that in an artillery fight they will beat us and that the place is only to be taken by a complete investment by superior forces. They have any quantity of guns & ammunition which they have only to mount but all their bread comes from Bacshi Serai – this seems to me to point out the means of operating with success, but to do it we want another army. The French are sending one we hear. If they land in sufficient numbers & appointed in every way as a separate army at the Katcha or Eupatoria so as to act on the lines of the Russian Communications.

Decr 8th We have just heard that Ld Raglan is made a Field Marshal of 5th Nov. I saw him about 5 minutes after he had heard the news & on my congratulating him he s^d I hope they have not forgotten the army I sh^d be very sorry if I was the only one promoted.

I heard an hour or two ago that a battle is expected tonight or tomorrow as the Russians have been busy all day sending large bodies of troops across the harbour from the North to the South side. Their object no doubt being to try & cut the French off from their bay at Chersonesus.[30] They made a bold reconnaissance with two steamers & fired on the French trenches doing them no damage. They have also reconnoitred our position as if they meant to attack us but I believe the real attack will be agst the French this time. Having failed twice against us when we were unprepared they will hardly attempt it again now that we have made the batteries & redoubts we ought to have made at first. The French are very strong in numbers and I have no fear of the result. I think Liprandi has moved his forces from our immediate front to assist in the attack and also to be out of reach of a contre coup which we are strong enough to administer while the fighting was going on on the French left – our gallant fellows have been & are worked beyond human endurance. We have much too large a share of the siege in proportion to our numbers. The men have suffered in consequence. Last night in one division 3rd – 2 officers & 25 men died of cholera – our great want is a very simple one Carts & horses, and another Commissary General who has not been educated in the wars of Spain & Canada to believe that the transport of the country is the best. Our army never has been fit to move in an enemy's country. The French on the other hand have an army perfectly mobile, and although they have few ships but little brigs & schooners they have an admirably organized waggon train, besides the mule train & ambulance waggons. We have not transport enough to feed our troops 5 miles from the ships and our hardworked soldiers have often half rations, & sometimes a whole division gets no meat or no rum. The men have behaved like angels. If the officers & men could but live long enough to have a little experience of war, but unfortunately they are going fast. Some of our 13 inch mortars were seen walking up the hill today to the front many of the guns are already there so if the fine weather lasts we shall be at it again ere long. To counter balance this the same fine weather will enable the Russians to receive the reinforcements which we hear are en route. I think if we were to invade Russia & have a winter campaign we have just chosen the only spot where such an exploit could be carried out. I think here we have the best of the positions. If only we could have had the harbour of Balaklava North of Sebastopol we should have starved them ere now.

A safe harbour was no doubt a necessity for a large army with a hostile country & a siege to carry on but we gave up a great advantage for it. It is now blowing half a gale of wind from the S.W. and my tent is so full of smoke that I can hardly see or breathe. I had been so cold, having to write sometimes from dark in the morning till late at night that I was obliged to burrow a hole under my tent side and establish a small fire place, it looks thus outside [see Figure 5] and inside the floor is thus, F being the fire place, the shaded part being a hole [see Figure 6] something of the shape & size of the grave of a monk of La Trappe made in his cell. My chair for I have one stands in this hole and I can burn my toes over the fire as much as I like, a seat is made by the bank of earth left & being covered with a small Persian carpet is not unduly uncomfortable as people aren't afraid here of sitting on the ground in December. A tent is a weary place in cold wet windy weather. The perpetual flapping produces a frame of mind which I sh^d. think w^d be produced by living in the house with a scolding wife. Do you know I begin to think I could break a dog, a feat which I always consider required your patient temper. I have succeeded or nearly so in licking into a good servant a young blackguard who was sent me out from London. He began his career by getting drunk on a bottle of my sherry on the second morning I had him & then of course being impertinent. I tried to move him by rough usage but he turned sullen on my hands & I have tried the soothing system with marvellous success & I am very proud of him. I have to put up with something now & then, but I can't get another. He has signalised himself by making some pastry! Samples of which I sent to several tents and now all the servants come to him to learn this wonderful accomplishment – I wish you could see the den I am living in. But in spite of many little hardships & discomforts it has pleased God to give me amazing good health and I am as happy as possible & generally wake up with a sort of feeling that I could give three cheers on very small provocation – So I don't

Figures 5 and 6. Romaine's tent – exterior and interior (from letter to Harvey dated 8 December 1854).

think I am to be pitied – Since Kinglake went home I have not an intimate companion. Ld Raglan I think likes me better, he certainly treats me with great confidence & has employed me on many things which do not strictly belong to my department. I dine with him regularly twice a week and there is always a cheerful sort of family party there & rarely more than one guest besides myself his house party being 15. Send me a line & tell me of Ickwell & its doings – I have no thin paper left & cant get my warm things up from Constan^{le}.

Remember me to Mrs Harvey of the Green (Here I was fairly smothered & had to get out of my hole & open wide the tent) My kind regards to Mrs Harvey. I had a long letter from Mulgrave the day before yesterday from Florence where he seems to be enjoying himself very much. Lady Strathmore was staying in their house when she died which made them all rather mournful for a time. I hear news from Selwyn sometimes – Come out in the Spring if all is well & share the tent of

Y^{rs} faithfully

W. G. Romaine

Cambridge University Library: Add. 7633: 5/12

12
Romaine to Lord Mulgrave

[Holograph]   Camp before Sebastopol
                                                    Decr 22nd. 1854

My dear Mulgrave,

I sent you a long letter to Florence on the 7th of this month, as I did not then know of the early sitting of Parliament which will in all probability have taken you to England before it arrives – I have no doubt my lady will open it if she has not left Florence with you. I have just been told that the post goes out at four and as it is nearly three now I have time to send you a line. It is cold & wet and has been so for the last 30 hours. A wet night doubles the number of deaths in camp and increases the sick in hospital very rapidly – 600 were to have been put on board ship, the French having lent us 300 mules & cacolets to move them with – It has been terrible weather for it – We have now got the treatment of the sick & wounded under much better system. Lord Raglan having rebuked two of the Principal Medical Officers in General Orders[31] has had a capital effect. This wet weather is much against us but we have the satisfaction of knowing that it is much more detrimental to the enemy – All their bread &c is prepared at Bakschi Serai and has to be carried thence along the deep roads, the distance being nearly 20 miles. A Russian prisoner who was taken yesterday, says they are very weary of the siege & that we must take it, that they have plenty of ammunition but a very small store of bread. He is a Russian & not a Pole, and therefore anything he says against the Russians may be believed. We are getting up guns mortars and ammunition as fast as the bad roads & want of horses will allow us. They talk of being ready by the 1st of Jany. I hope if they send out navvies to make a tram road for us they will come with their houses ready to put up before they come ashore to sleep, or they will die off like all the new arrivals or go into hospital. Of the fine Corps of Mounted Staff Police numbering 52 when they arrived there are now only 25 fit for duty. Owing to a good road not being made to our front from Balaklava during the fine weather, the Commissariat & Artillery horses have died so fast that last week the men were obliged to go down from their camps four and five miles off to bring up their rations. Add this ten miles walk through deep & slippery mud to the fatigue of a night in the trenches in wet and cold with half cooked pork to eat, no dry clothes to put on a wet blanket for a bed and a wet tent for a house and you may form an idea of the causes of the fearful mortality which rose from 20 to 60, 70, 80, 90 deaths within 24 hours out of the small numbers of the Army here in the Crimea and this went on for many days together. I[t] then got as low as 20 and now I fear this cold wet weather will bring it up again, as the new regiments feel the exposure very much and the weakly men are used up at once. There is no shelter on the hills. I fear that when the houses arrive they will be useless as there are no animals to carry them up to the front. Yesterday Filder undertook by Mem^m. to Ld Raglan to feed the troops without the soldiers having to go to Balaclava for their rations, but he broke down & the rations did not all arrive. I am still in a bell tent and therefore in discomfort, but I cannot talk of my hardships when I think of our poor noble soldiers suffering as they do without a murmur – An officer has so many advantages which a soldier has no chance of, as long as it is pleases God to continue to me the good health I have enjoyed hitherto I shall be as happy here as in my pet arm chair at the Travrs.

I had a capital letter from Buchanan the other day full of good wishes & remembrances from my friends at Chatham. He says the Registration has been so successful this year, and places the party in a majority of 70 to 80, and that they are confident of returning me at the next Election – Sir Fred^k Smith and his brother the member have quarrelled with one another and the party about the expenses of the election, and an action is "going on" about them. He says that he thinks neither Sir Fred^k nor his brother will ever stand again for the place. I hope it is not true that Hayter is too ill to hold his office as he does the rather difficult work of it so well. If he does vacate it will they offer it to you and would you accept it if they did? Tell me whether Ministers are likely to go well through this Session. I think they will myself, especially if the news we have just got of the Austrian Treaty is true. I think the Duke of Newcastle is the best War Minister we could have had, plenty of zeal & energy and his heart really in it – A change of Ministry would be a real calamity now – For this year at all events I think a factious opposition in the House would be very ill received by all parties in the Country.

Send me a line as I want very much to know how my Lady has borne the journey and how all at home are. I will write you pretty often if you wish it.

Y^{rs} very truly

W. G. Romaine

We shall probably open fire on New Years Day.

Cambridge University Library: Add. 7633: 5/13

13
Romaine to C. J. Selwyn

[Holograph]   Camp before Sebastopol
                                                    Decr 28th. 1854

My dear Selwyn,

We have now been here just three months and the Russian batteries are at this moment pounding away as actively as if not a shell had been fired – On our side guns shot shell gabions fascines, platforms for batteries are going up to the front as they did nearly three months ago – No not as they did then for now all our horses are dead. The French have taken up nearly all the guns with their artillery horses, & the shells in their wagons and to day 1600 French men were carrying up shells by hand and Turks were carrying up gabions & fascines on their shoulders – We had 300 Highlanders also carrying shells up the hill – They have not had the same work in the trenches and the drafts they have received have made up their losses and they have been well looked after by Sir C. Campbell and are in a good state – The destruction of health & life in this wasting siege has been awful and will surprise the peaceful folks if ever the details are known. I could tell you of regiments that arrived less than a month ago, now mustering less than half their number – I go to bed every night that it is at all clear and frosty with the dread of some horrible disaster – A man who has lived as Consul here 13 years says in eleven out of those

56

13 years they have had 12 degrees (Réaumur) of frost[32] equal to our zero and this generally accompanied by high north east wind – He says if we have such a frost & such a wind no human being can exist in a tent

– Well houses are arriving fast at Balaclava they might as well be at Kamschatka[33] there is no possibility of their being transported to the front until the works of the siege are over – The wretched soldiers have many of them now to go down on foot through seven miles of the stiffest mud to bring up salt pork on their backs there is such a want of issuers in the Commiss^t. Dep^t that they frequently do not get back till dark. How fit a man must be after that to go on duty in a pouring rain for 12 hours in the trenches. No wonder the recruits become reckless eat a little food raw or none at all go to the hospital & die –

We have had some horses & mules landed – there is no person whose duty it is to look after the animals they are loaded immediately without food and in 60 hours 80 out of the 260 are dead.

Want of organisation & experience in the Art of War is costing us tens of thousands of pounds.

Heaps of all kinds of stores sent by the liberality of Government are arriving but there is no place to store them or land them & nobody to issue them.

I received letters from the Crimea Army Fund, from Denison at least whose brother is coming out. He asked me to help them in any way – I drew up a scheme for the distribution the great virtue of which was that it altogether ignored the Commissariat. I have received from the Quarter Master General his written approval of every part of the scheme and requesting me to let him know when I am prepared to take the next step. It is not <u>quite</u> in my department and I only sent him the scheme as it seemed to me a simple & feasible one – and lo! in this quiet way he shoulders off the whole affair on to my hands. However if I can do it I will & get well abused by every body into the bargain – I have now a good deal of writing on my hands besides riding about on business – But I keep in perfect health & spirits in the midst [of] a good deal of discomfort of my own and a horrible amount of sickness & death going on around. The Princ^l Med^l Off^r says there are now applications here & at Scutari for Medical Boards from 140 officers! & this constantly going on – The 7th Reg[t] has one Commanding officer 1 Capt[n] 1 adj[t] and a Paymaster – voila tout – We have only had two sharp frosts as yet & then the wind dropped but one of those nights 2 sailors were found frozen to death and we & the French had men frostbitten who will lose fingers & toes – I believe the Russians are calculating on the winter to do their work – Two thousand mules packsaddles & their drivers would save everything – give us houses food clothing and bring up our ammunition – We are absolutely in want of nothing but transport – With that fuel could be obtained and the men would be enabled to have their food properly cooked – The French I hear are more in dread of a lack of fuel than anything else – The trees & brushwood have long disappeared and there are not roots for much longer within any reasonable distance – I should suppose our sick now amount to twelve thousand and our dead to seven thousand – I have got a stove erected in my tent, small but a stunner for heat. And with my fur cloak I think I can tide it over any winter as far as keeping out cold goes. I have got an iron pipe from the Sebastopol aqueduct and am erecting it as a chimney for my servants tent. So I hope they will be as comfortable as myself. I am almost in despair about the packages which have been sent me from England – Those since 25 Sept[r] not one of which I have received – The officers parcels have been plundered in a shameful manner & chucked ashore on the beach at Balaclava by the Captains of Transports in a way most disgraceful. What the officers have suffered for want of good clean & warm clothing, boots &c is unparalleled. Most of them in the front men & officers are lousy there is no other word in the English language that I know of which is nastier to the ear but it is a true one. That fact is a better measure of what they must have gone through than anything else I could tell you. A few days ago I should have said & did say that we sh[d]. be in Sebastopol in a month – Now I hear they are going to begin a regular attack in form on the Round Tower such as the French have made on their side opposite the Quarantine Fort. The Round Tower works now contain 118 guns when we came 7 guns only were mounted there –

Tell me what your opinion is with regard to the chances of peace this year, my own I confess is that we shall have war – The army have had great promotions, I wish the regimental officers had had a larger share of it as they have had so much of the hard work – The Times has been very savage agst Sir R^d England I see I hope that we shall be saved from his commanding the Army. He is an incapable – He allowed a battery of Artillery within 20 yards of his tent to lose all its horses from sheer neglect and said not a word – This battery being attached to his own Division. This is only a small matter but it shows the man & the General – I was much hurt at Genl Pennefather's name being omitted altogether from the Duke of Newcastles letter to the Army. He was the General of Division who was in the thick of the fight all day, leading & rallying men with great skill and energy. Coddrington [*sic* – Codrington], a good fellow and a great friend of mine is consoled with for his wounds & praised. He was not engaged with his brigade & has never been wounded in the Campaign – So much for the justice of a dispatch – It was not Lord Raglans fault as he made mention of the 2nd Division being chiefly engaged at Inkerman & commanded by Pennefather. Pennefather was under Sir C. Napier at Meeanee^34 with the 22nd Regt.

Post goes twice a week so I will write again ere long.

Y^rs faithfully

W. G. Romaine

Cambridge University Library: Add. 7633: 5/14

59

Part 2

The Long Winter

Bad weather and overwork continue to take their toll

The wretched conditions of late 1854 continued into the following year and many British regiments were reduced by sickness and disease to a handful of men. The 46th paraded on occasion at around sixty strong, and the 63rd even fewer, though Romaine was too gloomy when he said they had paraded with only 'four men and a corpse'. One of the main problems was the lack of roads which made the movement of rations and other stores, including ammunition, from the port to the camps and trenches extremely difficult. The shortage of firewood for the soldiers to cook their raw meat ration got worse and worse as roots were grubbed up for miles around. There was huge pressure on Raglan and Romaine began to record more criticism of Filder, the Commissary-General.

In response to reports that the Russians had murdered wounded officers and men at the Battle of Inkerman Romaine suggested that a Court of Inquiry be held and this was done.[35]

Meanwhile there was a lull in activity on both sides due to the bad weather, shortage of ammunition and, in the Allies' case, the guns wearing out and needing to be replaced.

Some British officers, especially in the cavalry which had lost so many horses that it had virtually ceased to exist as a fighting force, now asked for home leave but to leave one's men was considered bad form by the British public and Lord George Paget was ostracised when he went home, though Romaine thought this unfair.

Disquiet at home

A new feature of this war was that in Britain the public were being told of the dreadful conditions the soldiers endured. Newspapers had correspondents with the army – William Howard Russell of *The Times* was the most famous but there were several others, and young officers wrote home to parents, some of whom had considerable influence. Matters were promptly raised in Parliament and the government was held to account. In January, John Arthur Roebuck MP moved for the appointment of a select committee to enquire into the mismanagement of the war. The motion was carried against the wishes of the government, Aberdeen resigned, and Palmerston succeeded him. Officers of the Army of the East followed events at home with keen interest. In Crimea, administrative arrangements slowly improved. Prefabricated huts arrived but there were huge difficulties in getting them up to the camps. It needed hundreds of men to move them to where they were desperately needed as regimental hospitals and accommodation. The Crimean Army Fund received huge support in England and raised a large sum which was spent on comforts for the troops but there were the usual problems in getting goods up from the harbour at Balaklava and issuing them to the men. Private parcels to the officers were also at risk of being plundered, and Romaine was convinced that his and others' parcels were being stolen by Turkish customs officials at Constantinople.

A joint operation with the French for a night reconnaissance in force to the east was planned but on the night chosen there was appalling weather and, as Sir Colin Campbell set out with his British troops, the French decided it should be called off, but neglected to inform Sir Colin in time and the British struggled through a blizzard for some time until the staff were able to find and recall them.

At last the arrival of spring with its much better weather and easier travel on the dirt roads brought further relief. An experienced and competent officer came out from England to organise the transport which was taken from Commissariat responsibility.

Another development which was to have a great effect was the Balaklava railway, nicknamed the 'Grand Central Crimean Railway'. When Samuel Peto, head of a firm of engineering contractors, read in his newspaper of the difficulty in getting supplies and ammunition from Balaklava Harbour up to the camps and batteries, he contacted the Duke of Newcastle, Minister for War, and offered to build a railway at cost price. The offer was immediately accepted. Within days Peto had despatched surveyors to the area and had begun to assemble the stores and recruit the men needed to build it. In a week or two they were on ships on their way to the east, and on 8 February construction began. By 19 February the line was open to Kadikoi, nearly half the way to the camps. Lord Raglan, seemingly believing that dealing with civilian engineers and navvies was not a military matter, turned to Romaine, his Deputy Judge-Advocate General, to liaise with them. (Examples of this 'railway' work are at Appendix 2.) Romaine was also required to draft replies to the reports rendered by the Sanitary Commissioners, whom he thought vulgar and unfair.

At long last the French, who had agreed after Inkerman to take responsibility for the extreme right of the Allies' attack, moved troops for this, but they were slow in doing so and the Russians were able to come forward and seize the Mamelon, between the two lines and dominating the new French positions. There were heavy casualties in correcting this error.

The Russians attempted to take Eupatoria but the Turks there under Omar Pasha held firm. Meanwhile at Sevastopol the siege was pursued intermittently and with little energy. Soldiers on both sides felt the effects of the bad weather, and devoted more attention to keeping alive than to fighting the enemy. Allied soldiers continued slowly and painfully to advance their trenches nearer to the Russian defences, and there were brief flare-ups from time to time when the Russians sallied forth by night seeking to destroy the allied works and kill or capture the working parties. The burden of duty in the trenches was heavy and Romaine was touched by the nobility of the British soldier. Officers, like their men, strove to improve their living conditions. At headquarters, the staff did the same, albeit with huge advantages over the troops huddled miserably in threadbare tents, increasingly worn out by duties which came round ever more frequently as their numbers fell. Drafts of new troops came from England, but they were mostly raw recruits. Disease and the desperate hardness of life in the trenches and camps swiftly reduced their numbers. Romaine spent much time improving his hut. His legal duties continued, and as Raglan's trust in him grew, he became more and more involved in 'civilian' affairs like the railway which were not within his real responsibility. He was made chairman of a board on the employment of Croatian labourers, and another on improvements of the harbour at Balaklava.

14

Romaine to John Harvey

10 P.M. Therm^r. 16° Fahr^t. wind North
H^d Q^{rs} Camp before Sebastopol
Jan 14th 1855

My dear Harvey,

Though it is not a very cheery day or rather night to write an epistle I must send you a line in answer to your friendly letter of Xmas day – If ever the hares come they shall be treated with due honour & your health & Mrs Harvey's solemnly drunk, if theres any thing to the fore warmer than icy water. I don't like to begin telling the state of things here it would make too gloomy a picture. I have just had a letter from Ld Wm Paulet [see next item] who says <u>since</u> the 17 Decr they have received 3000 sick at Scutari, that he does not know where to put them & that they are going to establish a hospital for 3000 at Smyrna. We can fill it with those now here ready to go – and then we shall be ready for another – don't follow the lead of the Times & lay everything to Lord Raglan – There are many things, for which he has officers given him to see that they are performed & to whom he has a right to look for their performance – The care of the sick is one department. The making of roads is another – & so on. Remember he has the whole correspondence with the French army & with all the Departments in England and diplomatic correspondence, besides having nearly everything that goes on here brought before him. He does not get above two or three hours sleep any night. Whether or no he is a great General is of course a question, but that we could have found another man with his knowledge and the same qualifications to be at the head of this expedition I very much doubt. He has an equanimity of mind & temper which to me is miraculous. Just for a moment think what a hasty word or note sent to the French General w^d do. And after all I look to the perfect union of the two countries after the war as being the great blessing to atone for this fearful amount of misery – No human being can judge of war without having seen the details of a campaign & above all a winter one with troops in tents within a few hundred yards of an active enemy. We have now two feet of snow on the ground & more falling. Although Sunday I had to turn to & dig out the snow from round my tent. My two English servants had to go in to Balaklava for forage & returned without either hay or chopped straw – My two good English horses are alive & well. One is covered partially with a few planks over his head the other not at all – None of the good things sent by the Crimean Army Fund people have arrived. I have received letters of introduction in favour of three of their people coming out & being asked to help them, I drew out a scheme, the chief virtue of which was that it ignored the Commissariat (Hang Filder) I got it approved by the Quarter Master General in all its details & had it cut & dry for the two men who have come out & everything is ready when the stores come – I found on looking to my log, that I wrote to you on the 12 Decr hoping you w^d get it at Xmas but I supposed it had not arrived when you wrote so it will probably come the day you shoot my hares. I hope they may arrive more safely than other packages sent me. I have had five dispatched since 23rd September containing all sorts of valuables clothing waterproof boots, even home-made plumb [*sic*] puddings, think how good they w^d have tasted, besides we have a renown for Xmas plumb puddings & mince pies – But not one parcel has ever reached me – Think of four large boxes of the choicest cigars sent as presents by friends being lost or smoked by vile Turks in the Constant^e Custom H^{se} for that is the limbo in which our goods are tossed. You must give me the credit of the bright idea of the Court of Enquiry into the treatment of our wounded on the field of battle of Inkerman. I told Ld Raglan that it was a question that ought to be set right one way or the other by taking evidence & I got my Court of three good men, the result has been the Emperors ukase ordering any soldier guilty of inhumanity to disabled men to be shot. Some body has said that my place is a sinecure one. I wish he had to dig out the snow from my tent to avoid being drowned when the thaw comes & then had to do a days writing for me. I dine alone generally & get most of my work done at night so as to have the day to move about in. I

have got a stove up in my tent! Think of that Master Brook[36] and I sit down in a damp hole in the tent just in front of it & am able to keep tolerably warm & write with the help of a pair of warm muffetees, do you remember those funny looking red ones with half fingers like a bunch of coral. Here they are with the smoke of Ickwell gunpowder on them at work scribbling away. What an unfortunate expedition you describe to Boulogne, poor Dr Roupell he is a great loss to all of you – He deserves a good nurse to tend him in his mortal sickness for a kinder hearted man I believe never lived – Oh for a thousand good mules packsaddles & drivers to get us some shelter & food for our men these dreadful nights. I look at the thermometer at night about 12 with dread, a drop soon to zero – not by any means an uncommon thing – would make a catastrophe – something like Carbul. We number now 11,000 bayonets without counting non commissioned officers & this after all our reinforcements. The 63rd reg^t paraded the other day four men and a corpse – But this is the only regiment that has lost heart & <u>despaired</u> – They lost their Colonel at Inkerman & have been good for nothing since – I approve of the Foreigners Enlistment Bill & so does every one here if it will send us soldiers of a ripe age. The boys sent out here as drafts don't stand a weeks work – two nights in the trenches finishes them, they all disappear. The 3rd Division which embarked 5000 strong & has since received two reg^{ts}, now musters 2000 men & this Division was not in either battle! I hope you will consider this worth the threepence postage as I am terribly in arrear with my correspondence & can't write more. For the siege news vide Times – I am fated not to carry home any relics. I had some medals &c picked up at Alma & Inkerman & Ld Raglan asked for them for Her Majesty who wished to have some small relics of this kind, & I was only too happy to devote them to such a purpose. I have never quite got over the loss of the drum which I had hoped to have seen at Ickwell. Good bye old fellow – My love to Mrs Harvey as you say "I doubt whether it's quite proper" but it is so far off, perhaps you'll forgive it & deliver the message of
Y^{rs} ever W. G. Romaine

Cambridge University Library: Add. 7633: 5/15

15
Letter from Lord William Paulet to Romaine

[Holograph]   Scutari Jany. 7. 55.

My dear Romaine,

I have sent your enclosure.

3,400 sick have arrived here since the 17th of Decr. I do not know what to do with them: they come so fast, and all of them <u>lousey</u>, and naked.

We are sending men to England, Corfu, and going to establish a large Hospital at Smyrna for 3,000 men.

This is a most troublesome and anxious command, and nothing but escaping the Winter in the Crimea would tempt me to keep it. However I must try and do my best.

L^d and L^y Stratford are most kind: and assist me all in their power, but it is a difficult job to organise so a [*sic*] large a Body, like this, which has been scrambled together without any System and an insufficient Staff.

I am nearly worn out and hardly know which way to turn.

Everybody talks of Peace, I doubt it; any body looking at the British Army at Scutari would wish it.

Remember me to Neighbour Pakenham.

Hoping you are quite well & can continue to warm yourself

Believe me always

Very truly Yours

W. Paulet.

My correspondence and interviews with people are enormous.

Cambridge University Library: Add. 7633: 5/16

16
Romaine to C. J. Selwyn

[Holograph]   Camp before Sebastopol
                                                Jan 18th. 1855

My dear Selwyn,

The letter writing humour has not been on me for a long while and even now I am only going to begin an epistle in the hope that some day it may be finished. We have been enjoying two feet or so of snow round our tents for some time and a N.E. wind at 16 degrees below freezing point, a temperature not favourable to superfluous writing in a badly closed tent. Besides whenever there is hardship & distress in the Army there is always an increase of crime and for some time I have been rather busy for a sinecure holder. Today a thaw began & till sunset the snow was diminishing in depth, now the stars are bright with a high wind and frost. Today is Epiphany for the Russian heretics and a manifestation of the Russians is expected during the night and the Divisions French & English have received warning to be more than usually on the alert. The Russians fear the cold more than our men, the greater part of them being much worse clad and infinitely worse fed – For some time since the roads became bad they have had only a pound of their black biscuit powder & no meat and like our men are overworked. We hear that they are also short of powder, certainly the last few days they have not fired half so energetically as usual and if we could only begin our bombardment at once "something might turn up" as Mr Micawber says – our guns are now parked in rear of the batteries and half the required amount of shot and shell is there also. We have got some horses at last and there really is a prospect our trying once more, to enter the city we have so long been looking at. I have lost much of my faith in big guns and engineers, but they all agree that they can make the South side too hot to live in. I hope in their calculations they have allowed for what the Russian batteries can do for they will have five guns to our one, whether they can find men & ammunition for them I can't say. The "wasting siege" has brought down our roll of rank & file to 13,500 men, but that does not include noncommissioned officers – None of the men are yet in the wooden houses. They will not understand in England that we have not transport for heavy goods, that a barrel of rum is too heavy to be moved to the front, and the pieces of huts are large & heavy. It takes 180 men to carry up a hut for 20 men – A few have been brought up for hospitals. But the men when they come out of the trenches have to seek wood – This wood being roots of brush wood two feet under snow & a very limited supply of pickaxes & a hard frozen stony ground to work in – Yesterday the fine orchard round Head Quarters was given up to the 3rd and 4th Divisions to be cut down for firewood. The roots of all the vines for miles round have long been used up – I am living in immense luxury I have dug a very deep hole in my tent got up a stove from Constantinople & put in the hole so deep that the pipe comes out below the fringe of the tent and I can warm my toes and with good woollen mittens keep my hands warm enough to be able to write – The water freezes in the tent at night but the fur cloak of the Russian General a prize of war keeps out the cold wind. At the present moment it is blowing so hard that my candle will hardly keep in. Our men are now pretty well clad if they had boots big enough to put their feet in. Every bodys feet have swollen with wet & cold and then when two pairs of socks are put on the ammunition boots are not large enough & many men go with their boots down & heel [sic] so get frost bitten – Besides this the boots when taken off froze as hard as iron in the tents and none of the soldiers had second pairs. They have suffered horribly for an army not on the march and within 5 or 6 miles of their ships – I have only heard of one reg^t being thoroughly demoralized. The 63rd paraded one morning 4 men and a corpse! They fought well at Inkerman under their Col who was killed but their officers must now be a set of shipwrecks. The men were recruited in a great hurry from the dregs of Dublin, men being taken who were refused by other regts. The Govt has done a foolish thing a most absurd piece of wasteful energy. An electric telegraph [paper torn, words illegible – 'from Balaklava'?] to Varna 350 miles of cable to end in Turkish post horses, when they are to be had. My bright idea of having a Court of Inquiry to establish the fact of the ill treatment of our disabled men on the field of battle by the Russians has resulted in a Ukase ordering any soldier to be shot who is guilty of inhumanity to the wounded. Lord Raglan consulted Canrobert Adm^l Lyons &c & made me put my proposition on paper before he would authorise it. I then got those good men Sir John Campbell, Col [the paper is torn – read Lt Col Cadogan, Grenadier Guards] and Col Egerton to form the Court and in two days presented my [paper torn, piece missing –

'report'?] which was sent home. By the bye Lord Raglan has offered to allow my letters to come in his bag. I will put the mode of address at the end of the letter. Besides that quite unasked he is going to represent to the Authorities that I am worse paid than any civilian out here. I don't know what will come of it & don't much care – At present I shall be about 300 £ out of pocket by the venture, but shall have seen a good deal for my money – I heard yesterday that my friend McMurdo is to organise a baggage train for the army. I hope he will, and come out with it, a man who had been Quarter Master General of an army for years of actual warfare under Sir Charles Napier should not have been left behind – Ld Cardigan tried hard to have him as his Brigade Major. Ld Hardinge refused him & then afterwards refused the same request made by Lord Raglan, why because McMurdo was of too high rank! He was B^r. Lieut Col though only a Cap^n in his own regt and was willing to pocket the loss of rank. I was very savage at the time about it but I don't think he could have lived with that brute Ld C^n And you are all crying him up as the Hero of the Lt Cavalry Charge! Wait till you hear what the Light Cavalry say of him. I sh^d think the truth must have leaked out since Ld George Paget went home. By the bye how ill you have behaved to him. Why sh^d not a cavalry officer leave after being in such a battle when there were not enough soldiers left in his regt for a Captain's command and now, not one soldier in the regt doing Cavalry duty – Is a man never to be allowed to sell out while a campaign is going on –

Gen Bentinck's case was very different. He was a regular malingerer, his wound was most trifling and was used as an excuse to get away from the fighting & get rewarded. There was a shout of indignation that such a man sh^d go & dine with the Queen & get the best appointment in England. He left a very bad report of himself here as to his conduct in battle. In spite of a long interruption I find I have filled a sheet and if I begin gossiping there seems no end to it. I wish my pen w^d write better. By referring to your letter I see you ask why we ever cease firing? The guns were worn out there were no others for a long time. When they came they lay for weeks at Balaclava because there were no horses to bring them up, and now that they are up it will be days before we have ammunition enough up at the front to begin our Bombardment. You cannot begin to bombard with less than 500 rounds a gun. The 13 inch shells weigh 184 pounds.

11.30 P.M. The Russian & French guns have just begun furiously but we are all warned & ready this time & if a sortie is made the Russians will get a severe drubbing – Harvey asks to see my letters to you – He says they interest him so perhaps you will forward them if you think of it, I wrote to him a few days ago, so perhaps there is nothing very new in this – Many thanks for the care you promise to take of my log book can you make out the meaning of the small sketches in it, here & there. Three of the Crimean Army Fund people have brought letters for me & I have drawn up a plan for their distribution which has been approved by the Qu^r Mr Genl & is to be carried into effect. Good bye, Y^{rs} Ever

W. G. Romaine

Cambridge University Library: Add. 7633: 5/17

17
Romaine to C. J. Selwyn
[Holograph. The letter is torn and a piece is missing.]

N°. 2   Camp before Sebastopol
Jany 19th. 1855

My dear Selwyn,

This letter is No 2 & will come by the same post as the one dated the 18th I forgot to tell you the address in the last. The letter itself intended for me shd be addressed to me care of FM Lord Raglan but sent to J. H. Ashe Esqr Ordnance Office who will put it in the bag for the Crimea. It makes sometimes a difference of two three or four days in the delivery here. So if you send by post to the Ordnance Office it sh^d be sent under cover to Mr Ashe – I hear the reason that Russell has been writing such angry letters against the Staff at Head Quarters & the Times such furious leaders is that Russell who wants to come back to Head Quarters has received an intimation that he is not wanted. Hence the anger. Such articles have a very bad effect in the army they tend to discontent mutiny & desertion. The position of the men is improving we have had now three days fine weather the snow is going and they are getting the large brown leather boots. Fuel is terribly wanted, the yacht Fairy which was to have brought Tea from the Crimea Army Fund is not arrived & I suppose will not cross the sea till she is towed.

Today there is a conference Canrobert Lyons Bruat &c at Lord Raglans. I hope they will en attendant the getting up of ammunition make a dash at a large body of troops across the Tchernaia. Their men are so badly off for food that they are obliged to send two battalions to Bakshi Serai every day to bring bread they return the next day – By making a detour we could get in their rear they have only two batteries of six pounders with them and a coup might be made. I have great hopes it will be attempted – One good result of the Times articles is that the Russians are so persuaded we can do nothing till spring that their army is scattered all over the country. If they have been preparing sleighs at Odessa to bring men & munitions South this thaw will upset their calculations entirely – I have not that I know of received one of the papers you have sent me. I take in the Times regularly, that is pay regularly & get it irregularly. I hear that Lord Lucan is going to write & publish a pamphlet about the Cavalry affair at Balaklava – If he does, send me a copy. I had to write a regular built legal opinion on a contract for laying down the Electric Telegraph from ~~Bucharest~~ Varna to Balaclava. Selwyn's N.P.[37] stood in great stead. We hear from Vienna that the Emperor of Russia has really made great concessions to the demands of the three powers – L^{d}. Burghersh hears from his father or from his mother every post. For my part I cannot believe in peace until his armies have been defeated. His great masses of troops have as yet not even seen an enemy but I think he will never have a fairer chance of making peace on terms which will leave his empire untouched in extent. From what I heard this morning from a very intelligent deserter I begin to believe that we can drive the Russians out of the town by bombarding it – He says that before during the fire there was no place safe from our fire that doctors were killed across the town while operating and priests had their heads blown off in the churches while performing mass. The

Emperor has ordered all communication between the North and South sides to be stopped when the assault takes place that the garrison may have no escape. This may cut either way. If our men once get in nothing will stop them. They will be desperate & will rather die than retreat to the old quarters where they have suffered so much. There are plenty of mines ready for us – and electric batteries sunk by the boom to blow up the ships when they try to enter as no doubt they will when we have taken the South side. I think & hope [a] decision will be settled today. The French allow no accounts of their state as to sickness &c to appear, but they for a long while had & now have from 2 to 300 sick a day. The Russians allowed no letter giving an acct. of Inkerman to go by the Post. An officer at the Post received & read every letter. They gave out to the world that they had [few?] wounded. A deserter a Russian who came in said there were 7000 in one place collected & that there were several other places for wounded. This same man said that our Minié balls all went <u>through</u> the battalions killing two & three men whereas an old ball if it went into a man generally lodged there. Nothing of any consequence that I have yet heard of happened last night though there was a great deal of firing at one time – Three nights ago the Russians got into the French trenches but were immediately driven back leaving three officers & 17 men dead, they carried away many dead and wounded. It appears they always have plenty of men who have humanity enough to go to the rear with dead & wounded – Remember me very kindly to Kinglake when you see him, also to Charles Roupell [?] Banbury & Nicholson – tell the latter that as he reads my letters or hears them over a good glass of wine, that I should hope he will send me a line again ere long. Murray I hear is deep in his fifth chin – The carrying up of shot ceased yesterday and today, the men being otherwise engaged, so the siege will not begin quite yet, to the great annoyance of the French who are so close and have to keep so sharp a look out every night against sorties. If the thaw lasts I hope to get a roof of wood over my tent, though rather late it will be better than never and it will do to use as a Room to hold Gen Cts M^l in. Having satiated you with gossip for a month I shall say goodbye Y^{rs} ever W. G. Romaine

I wish I had been in England to see the Bishop for whom I have a great admiration, I should like a cruise in his yacht what is it called "The Mitre" – Commend me to all the members of your family – How is the Chancellor Rolt?

Imagine my talents & "savoir vivre" I have managed to get a loaf of <u>white</u> bread of the size of a threepenny loaf in England every day from the Lordly oven at Head Quarters and it only costs me a shilling per diem – There's luxury –

Cambridge University Library: Add. 7633: 5/18

18
Romaine to Lord Mulgrave

[Holograph]
<u>Private</u>

Head Q^{rs}. Feb 9th. 1855
Camp before Sebastopol

My dear Mulgrave,

I have not time to write you a letter – I have been very busy lately and besides that I have been getting some planks put over my head in the shape of a roof in order to get out of my tent which was too small to keep the books & papers of my department & the books & correspondence of the Railway – It don't keep out the rain this house of mine & the mud floor is very wet – My principal object in writing is to settle what is to be done at Chatham in case of a General Election – I am very much inclined to take the advice which all my friends without exception have given me, which is to stay here and see the war through –

If so I wish to leave with you the power to announce to the good friends of the cause at Chatham that the place of candidate is vacant. I had rather they did not know this unless it becomes absolutely necessary as I hold much to the hope of representing them. I think I could make a useful and hard working member & should suit them. But I have here a position in which I believe I am useful can do some good and am well received and I think esteemed by the Chief of the Army.

The life out here suits my turn of mind very much and I should leave it with regret –

But I should not like to be thought guilty of a breach of faith towards a party which has shown so much confidence in me as the liberal party at Chatham.

I should not hesitate a moment in returning did I not know that by holding up their hands they can have five hundred better men in an hour. The loss would be wholly on my side. You see how I am situated and I leave myself in your hands, if I am wanted, I come, coûte que coûte,[38] If I can be replaced I stay here –

I will write again by next post.

My kind regards to Lady Mulgrave who I hope has recovered completely from her late illness.

Ever yours faithfully

W. G. Romaine

Cambridge University Library: Add. 7633: 5/19

19
Romaine to C. J. Selwyn

[Holograph]   H^d Q^{rs} Camp before Sebastopol

Feb 10 1855

My dear Selwyn,

I have but little time to write as post is just going out. I have not had a place to sit down in for the last three days for I have been getting a roof put on the four walls inside which my tent has been so long pitched that it was quite rotten.

The house was yesterday & last night like the pictures of the dropping well at Knaresborough[39] in the "Hundred Wonders of the World"[40] and it was a long time last night before I could find six feet of dry ground for my bed. But I slept well, though woe w^d betide the overseer or Constable who put a pauper or felon in such a place –

Today I have got some felt and a party of Zouaves are busy over head nailing it on & knocking snow & mud through to the destruction of the beauty of three official letters I am sending home.

The world here is very much excited by the news of 26th of Jan^y.

Ld Raglan told me yesterday that he had heard by Telegraph that the Queen had sent for Ld Derby – I feel sure he can't form a ministry which w^d have a majority in the House of Commons.

If there is an enquiry, Lord Raglan will come out of it very well. Some think here that De Lacey Evans has been manoeuvring to get the Command and Lady John[41] to be Premier. Johnny always has upset the Court.

I was glad to hear by last mail from Kinglake that he was recovering. Did you see in Times of 18th leading article that a "great authority" had said so and so. Kinglake unluckily writing to Delane quoted some words of a letter of mine & they were put in in inverted commas; luckily no one here recognised me as the "Great Authority" as it w^d not be considered correct for a Staff Officer to be writing home to the newspapers, though I was not stating an opinion but only a fact. I will write & tell you more of what is going on by next post. Things are looking much better. There is a good chance that by 1st March we may be in the town – The men are much better unluckily we have snow come back after 10 fine days.

Good bye

Y^{rs} ever

W. G. Romaine

Cambridge University Library: Add. 7633: 5/20

20
Journal for 18 to 22 February 1855

[Holograph]   1855, Private Memoranda & Diary
                                         Head Quarters Camp before Sevastopol

Jany. 18th. [Should be February 18th.[42]]

For first 17 days see Diary for 1854.

Report from B^r. Major Simmons attached to Omar Pasha's staff that yesterday morning a large force of Russians estimated at 40000 of all arms with 100 pieces of cannon and wagons loaded with scaling ladders advanced to attack Eupatoria – That the Turks under Omar Pasha aided by a flanking fire from the Sampson [*sic*] & [blank space][43] succeeded after a struggle of four hours in beating off the Russian army. The wagons of scaling ladders were captured, Selim Pasha was killed. One of the Russian Archdukes is said to have been there. At one time as many as 60 Russ^n. cannon were firing at different points of the attack. At 2 P.M. when the report left the Russ^{ns}. had retreated from 2 to three miles. An attack was expected again today. Sir J Burgoyne said that the occupation of Eupatoria was insisted on by L^d. Raglan agst. opinion of Canrobert and that if the occupation succeeds he not be entitled to the credit of the suggestion. Several vessels were being despatched with assistance shot shell &c. We had service at 12.30. And as I came out I met Genl. Canrobert & staff in the passage waiting for the conclusion of the service. He stayed some time. From what I have heard since I conclude that they mean to try to effect a diversion in Omar Pasha's favour by a strong reconnaissance under Bosquet. They will probably go out by the Baidar road & endeavour to get in the rear of & envelop their batt^s. left on the North bank of the Tchernaia – From the account brought in by spies & the account sent in by Mentschikoff, read clear [meaning 'deciphered'?], it seems probable that they have collected all their available infantry cavalry & artillery for this attack, and that the attempt on the lines was more than mere reconnaissance seems clear from their bringing their scaling ladders. In the present state of the communications they must have had great difficulty in bringing so large a force together and will have still greater difficulty in keeping it supplied beyond the few days for which they could carry food with them. The effect of this first repulse will have a good effect on the Turks, and must dispirit the Russians very much, as letting them understand that an army is firmly established on their communications. It is unfortunately now blowing a heavy gale from Eastward, and though Eupatoria is sheltered on that hand yet such severe weather must impede communications very much and the wind is liable [?] to chop to SW.

Monday, Jany. 19. 1855 [Should be Monday February 19th [44]]
Went down to Balaclava with T. Tower about the Crimean army Fund. They have arranged the distribution admirably on paper,

but they have an immense amount of goods and no means of either unloading their ships guarding their stores or serving them out. They have brought out one Clerk or Secretary Mr. Brackenbury and no issuers! and are to have & have now 11,00 [*sic*] tons of goods in great variety. I went to see Sir C Campbell but he was out. I had previously been with Gen Airey who offered to take of [*sic*] their hands a number of the light stores; but this w^d. not lessen their difficulties much. I then went to Mr Beatty and asked him to give them the use of the Railway. He said they might have the use of the trucks on Wednesday night from 5 P.M. till daylight. Glyn & Smith & the rest of them are to work hard to engage labour for that night & they are to try & unload their ship and get the goods up to Kadikoi by the R^y. Their ship the Parma [No ship of that name identified] is close to the R^y. terminus at Balaclava. Sir C. C. will help them at Kadikoi with a fatigue party early in the morning.

I told Filder that he c^d. have the R^y. on Thursday night to Kadikoi – but he seems to think it w^d not help him.

Dined at L^d. Raglan's, there they seemed to think that it w^d. help them in moving the heavy shot shells &c. Lord Raglan was very busy at dinner time arranging about Bosquet's reconnaissance. L^d. George Foley came in from Canrobert rather cold at 10.30 PM Was no rain or snow though the peculiarly distinct sound of the cannon shot foretells rain, wind E. Algernon Egerton was looking ill –

Tuesday Feb. 20.
Wood A A G of 3rd Div^n. called. He says they have lost 240 men of their division this month. But he says the men had decidedly taken a favourable turn but what effect this change of weather may have he cannot say. Last night the wind changed to NNE & blew hard with snow drift. At 8 AM the Therm^r. stood at 17° the snow drifting in at countless cracks. Last night at dinner there came in a report from Simmons from Eupatoria that the Russians had not shown again that only the usual cavalry posts were seen. The Turks lost 167 men French 9 Tartars 13. 76 Artill^y. horses, 67 being killed in one battery, 19 men and [?] all the guns dismounted

– The letter asked if the cavalry sabres promised to Omar Pasha were ready. The Russians will suffer tremendously if they are on the march such weather as this. It must also delay Bosquet's expedition.

Wood says they had orders last night to be on the qui vive in case the trenches were attacked when the departure of Bosquet was known.

Wednesday Feb. 21.
Therm[r]. 21. 8 AM.
The French Cavalry and our Cavalry Artillery & the four Highland regts. turned out in spite of the cold & the blinding "poudré" Sir C.C. marched as far as the Tchernaia and exchanged shots with the enemy's outposts. He reports 1400 men only there. After waiting some little time and seeing Bosquet thought the weather too bad for the expedition & did not move he returned – Our cavalry mustered 300 horses & though the men were 12 hours on their backs not a casualty occurred. Not a man of the Highlanders who went out went into Hospital on his return – Shute says in another 3 weeks they will have 100 more cavalry horses effective if they are not used for Hospital & Comm[ry]. purposes. Today the weather was fine & the sun quite warm though the therm[r]. never was above 28 in the shade – Tower came up again looking in great distress – The Crimean Army Fund find that they are like the departments here, overwhelmed with good things for the army, but powerless to distribute them. The good folk at home will have sent out 1100 tons of goods with one clerk or Secretary and no issuers! Their manifests are incomplete and incorrect, and they have many bales of which they can only ascertain the contents by opening them – They can only unload at the rate of 10 to 15 tons a day and that is as much as they can convey to Kadikoi. They came out here to supply the Army with things that Gov[t]. c[d]. not, and the first thing they have to ask for is Gov[t]. assistance. Labour is in such demand that Gov[t]. is paying sailors & others 5[s]. a day & artificers 7[s].6[d]. and can get very few at those prices – their services being demanded by their owners on board their respective vessels. I went with Tower to Gen. Airey &

got an order for 20 Croatian labourers till Furth^r. [?] Orders for the "Fund" – I then saw Captn. Peel of the Leander and he has promised 20 men for tomorrow. I told Tower to see Beatty & try & get him not only to lend some trucks which he had promised me he w^d. but get him to draw them to Kadikoi – The R^y. having received a number more of their horses. The mail came in after dark – letter from Mulgrave, Harvey & [illegible]. The night is still but cold. Thermr. 18. Sir G. Brown called on L^d. Raglan, but he was out. I met him at the door & he charged me to tell L^d. R. that the ships outside reported having seen 3000 Russ^{ns}. coming from the North across the Belbek R. The Inkerman heights are said to be filling with troops – The 5 deserters who came in yesterday report that there was great excitement in Sebastopol – They were afraid of an immediate attack. If they were camped out during the storm they must have suffered very much – Sir C.C. march will have had the effect of relieving Omar Pasha from pressure. A rupture between Prussia & France and Austria & England seems more than ever imminent and the preparations of Russia for war greater than ever & more urgent. The expense of the War on her is beginning to tell, as appears from the Ukase ordering an issue of paper money redeemable 3 years after peace – i.e. ad Graecas [illegible] [meaning 'at the Greek Calends', viz. 'never'?]

Russell the Times Correspondent came up to Head Q^{rs}. during the Snow Storm and lost his way & found himself at the Monastery. He got to camp half frozen – He shewed me a written order from Canrobert to visit the French trenches whenever he pleased.

Thursday. Feb. 22.
Somerset was over here and he tells me that he was round at 4 AM on Tuesday morning to go and recall Sir C Campbell if he had gone out or at all events to tell him that the Turks had not turned out. Foley had come over to Head Quarters having been sent by Canrobert to Sir C.C. & lost his way Somerset started with a Serg^t. & 3 orderlies & Foley With some difficulty in the blinding snow he found his way to C.C. nobody was in and no one knew

where he & his men were gone – Somerset had not been told & getting no news he rode for Genl. Vynoi's camp to tell him that Sir C.C. was out & ask him to get out his division. He found Gen. Vynoi just on the move. On the road he met L^d. A. Stirling [*sic* – presumably Lt Col A. Stirling] who s^d. he had lost his way and when Somerset proposed riding to tell the [?] troops across the plain Stirling s^d. the plain was covered with Cossacks & that he had been chased by them. However they went on & met a man on horseback who turned out to be Wetherall who had also lost his way & had been on a hill looking out. He said there were no Cossacks about & when Stirling appealed to his experience it turned out that Wetherall seeing Stirling rode at him to get some information as to Sir C.C. route and galloping & shouting had scared Stirling into the idea that he was being pursued by many Cossacks – They rode on and reached Sir C.C. finding him a long way ahead of his troops which were along the Tchernaia – The Russians had only 6 small field pieces & if Bosquet had turned out they w^d. have effected a complete surprise as it turned out it was a regular coup manque – Tonsky the Pole the head of the French Secret Intelligence Dept. insists upon it that the Russ^n. 8th Comp^y. of [illegible] Corps was at Eupatoria.

Somerset told me that L^d. Raglan was very strong against being here so late in the year and wrote home to that effect so that Govern^t. was warned. Gen. Tylden wrote to the same effect and insisted on having his letter recorded. Cator also was agst. it. Calvert wrote to say that it was impossible for an army to live in the Crimea in winter in tents. This was when we were at Varna. S. said that when Lyons landed at Balaclava immediately after its capture, he said to L^d. Raglan, now is the time to go in, they are not prepared to defend Sebastopol – That L^d. Raglan agreed with him, but said he must ask Sir John Burgoyne who was a man of such great experience But Burgoyne said only wait a few days till the battery train is out and you will walk in without any loss of men. S^t. Arnaud giving up the command there was no one to counteract Burgoyne & Canrobert and we waited for the siege train & the opportunity was lost – There is no doubt that the slaughter at Alma still weighed on the minds of every one &

disinclined the Generals to send their men so soon on another bloody assault of batteries – Now we have but 20,000 soldiers before its much stronger forts. [?]

Cambridge University Library: Add. 9554/4

21
Romaine to Lord Mulgrave

[Holograph]   Head Quarters
                                                              Feb 23rd. 1855

My dear Mulgrave,

It is not a very long time since I wrote to you but I want to send a line to acknowledge your letter of the 5th and to thank Lady Mulgrave for her kind letter of family & household news. I am sorry to say I have not yet received any one of my packages from England nor the package which you say Lady Normanby has been so thoughtful as to forward from Florence – I heard from a friend at Scutari today he says that the Custom House there is absolutely blocked up with parcels for officers & men and that at one time the buildings were so crowded that cases were placed outside uncovered in the mud – He says it will take months at the rate things are being done there to clear it. These packages contain many of these articles not only costly to purchase but invaluable to parties out here and they have been rotting in that Custom House for months – Things that were sent to me in September have never reached me: I have paid bills to the amount of £72:16 and not received one pennyworth – Write me as long letters as you can find time for as they interest me very much, especially political news at such a period as this –

We have winter upon us again. On Tuesday morning a well planned expedition was arranged and Sir C. Campbell led out his men, four Highland Regts 300 Cavalry and two batteries of Artillery to the Tchernaia and came near enough to exchange shots with the Russian outposts – But the French were daunted by the fearful storm of snow, a regular Canadian poudré and did not perform their part or they must have surprised the party. Happily not a man of the Expedition went into hospital on their return, nor was there a casualty among the horses – But it makes me regret more that the French hung back. The Russians had only 1400 men and six cossack field pieces – Their 2 guns must have been taken – It has had the effect of alarming them & bringing them back from Eupatoria & so taken the pressure off Omar Pasha – We hear from 5 Polish deserters who came in together that they are in great alarm in the town expecting our attack every day. They are very badly off for food, having nothing but biscuit powder and water. Hay at Bacshi Serai is 3 silver roubles the pound or about 10^s. for 36 lbs – Barley oats &c 8 to 10 times the usual price. Four regts of Cossacks are nearly dismounted & the 2 regts of Hussars which fought or rather ran away at Balaclava have few horses left – The artillery are best off but their horses are not fit for work. Sir G. Brown has returned & encamped with his Division.

There is one thing which I think might be done by the Authorities at home which would be a great convenience to the Army and would be a gain I think instead of a loss to Government – At present an officer wishing to remit money cannot send less than 50£ by a Treasury Bill and there are only two days in the month that Mr Filder will sign Bills – Now the sending out of gold here is expensive and of course causes a great drain of coin from home – Not long ago Mr Filder had no money left and the payment of officers was delayed. If a responsible man and a couple of clerks were sent to establish something like a money order officer for the transmission of money to England, he would receive all the spare cash of officers and men and pay it into the Commissariat Chest and pro tanto would diminish the amounts required from home. It would relieve Filder and his hard worked staff of one branch of their labours – The traders who come out here would I am sure be only too glad to get Government bills at par to send home in exchange for the goods which they sell at such enormous prices to us – Ask some man who is conversant with money matters – such as Mr Abel Smith if this suggestion is worth anything –

I am so glad my friend McMurdo is employed to organise the transport of the army – If that had been done when the Army left England instead of leaving it in Filders hands we should not have known distress of any kind – We could have spared horses to make roads, to put up huts &c &c. We are to give the French 30,000 articles of warm clothing instead of receiving 10,000 greatcoats as the letter writers in the Times stated. How such a story was invented has puzzled me. The Crimean Army Fund were up here yesterday in great distress – They have got their goods to Balaclava and find that they are just as near the army as when they were in London – They had fair warning for I wrote them word that they must be prepared to do everything for themselves and bring their staff with them – They have 1100 tons of goods of most miscellaneous nature which would stock two shops like Fortnum & Mason & Swan & Edgar & they have brought one clerk and two issuers! The two business men Glyn and Jervoise Smith go home on Monday & leave Tower & Egerton to eat their hearts out here – They have not the means of unloading their ships & carrying the cargo to Kadikoi one mile off – I managed to get them 40 men yesterday 20 from the Q^r Master General (a man by the bye most unjustly abused, for he is a clear headed energetic hardworking man, who will be obeyed) and 20 sailors from $Capt^n$ Peel of the Leander – I saw Mr Beatty the Engineer of the Railway & he promised them the use of some trucks to Kadikoi, to which place it was to be open today – Did I tell you that I had undertaken the correspondence between the Railway & the different departments of the Army at Ld Raglans request. I see by the Times of Feb 5th that they are ready to open their batteries upon us. I think Ld Raglan was "très fin" to use a civilian as manager – Luckily my skin is thick & I don't care a rap for the Times leaders – I only undertook it because L^d R wished it and I w^d do anything to oblige him – I only meant to have sent you a few lines and I find I have scribbled more than a sheet – Havent you had one run down to Mulgrave to shoot Overdale even – I hope the change of Ministers won't remove you from office – It came at an unlucky time for me as Ld Raglan had just written to say that my pay ought to be at least enough to cover my expenses but his letter must have arrived just as the house was on fire and so I suppose it was burnt in the General Conflagration of the Ministry – I am very sorry for Lord John as I had a very sincere respect & admiration for him –

Figure 7. Self portrait for little Laura
(from letter to Mulgrave dated
23 February 1855).

My kind regards to Lady Mulgrave and [best wishes ?] to all the children – Tell Laura as she gave me her picture I send her mine – I am very like what I was in India only no beard, so you must cut out this bit for her – [see Figure 7]

Some one has sent me by a French ship an enormous Parmesan cheese, no name, no letter. I thought it must come from a charitable person whoever he was who w^d be glad that as many as possible share in it – So I sent Ld Raglan a slice for his large table – The Adj^t Gen a slice, The Commandant, Doctor, Postmaster, a huge bit to the officers & men of the Hussars of the Escort another to the 68 Reg^t detachment which forms our Head Q^r guard, a goodly slice to some Zouaves who are camped here to help us build huts &c and kept a comfortable corner for self & servants – I shall write to My Lady & tell her all about my domestic arrangements.

I am nearly frozen – Goodbye –

Y^{rs} ever

W. G. Romaine

Cambridge University Library: Add. 7633: 5/21

22
Journal for 24 to 27 February 1855

[Holograph]

Saturday Feb. 24.

Therm^r. 28. 8 AM – N.

Very heavy firing last night on the right – Sent off some letters by the private bag the mail having started unexpectedly. Fine smoking day – Walked with de Morel to the Right Artillery Park to see Col. Dickson – He was recovering fast from his wound when by going out in the cold he had a relapse. He is now getting well. He was reconnoitring places for the new battery with Bizot and other French officers and had been recommending a place 600 Yards in advance of the present position, in the exact place that the Russians have now placed their counter battery and being upon the parapet was turning to come away when he felt a blow on his shoulder which he thought was only a contusion however the ball had passed along the shoulder blade & gone through with^t. injuring the bone – He told me of the repulse of the French last night. They had found it necessary to take the Earthwork which the Russians had begun and 2 batt^n. Zouaves & some infantry of the Marines had orders to seize it – They must either have been informed of the attack or else fully expected it for they were quite prepared The moment the French got near fire boms [*sic*] were thrown and the fire began – The Zouaves were supported by the Marines – The Enemy had a column on each side of their line of attack & fired into them in flank & rear. They got into the work & were repulsed three times and the Marines ran away and after some time the Zouaves followed them. The officers of the Zouaves must have sacrificed themselves most gallantly for they had 5 killed & 11 wounded out of a loss of 200 men – They were furious against the Marines.

Dickson told us of the good luck of Gambier who is now Col. of the Horse Art^y. in England – He commanded the Siege train, and never was in either of the two attacks during the whole time that the siege lasted. Dickson was in the R^t. Attack and Gambier made him believe that he was engaged in the left attack every minute he c^d. spare from attending on L^d. Raglan & he played off the same game with the officers of the left attack & for some time it was not found out. He was in the left attack trenches at 5 AM on the first day & at 5 min before the signal time for commencing he went away & never entered it again – He delayed as long as possible bringing up the two 18 pounders ordered by Ld Raglan at Inkerman, in spite of the pressing entreaties of Dickson & D'Aguilar – I remember being there & wondering why they delayed – His character was so well appreciated by the men that one day when two officers were seen approaching the batteries while a heavy fire was going on, and some one s^d. there is Gambier the men were heard saying, I'll take my oath without looking that it ain't the Col – He ain't going to show himself here while this fire is going on. He was wounded at Inkerman, receiving a contusion on the chest. Dickson met him supported by two Art^y. men & in asking what was the matter, he whispered a shell burst in my breast! But on looking inside his coat there was no blood. However he managed to get on board ship – then to Malta & then to England & arriving just in time got the Horse Artillery. He is known amongst his friends as the Great Impostor – Dickson says that Layard wrote to him to say that he had nothing to do with writing or forwarding information for the Articles in the Times against Lord Raglan – Went then to see Bostock – He & De Bathe were first going to start for the French advanced parallel to see the place of the fight of last night – We walked past the long rows of graves of the Russians & of the Light Division & then to the battery in front which is not armed. We met Lindsay & Drummond of Sc. Fus. Gds. & then crossed to the covered way close by where the working parties had made large mounds of earth gathered in the rocky soil to fill sand bags – We then entered the covered way & followed the parallel till we came to the advanced trench in which the guards were, there were officers of all kinds there Zouaves & their men Voltigeurs & officers of Engineers marking the places for guns. The Tirailleurs were firing away at the enemy in the pits in front of the Russian battery which was about 600 yards off. All this way of our descent nearly was under the fire of the Inkerman batteries, but they did not fire – The Minié balls whizzed about both while we were going down & while we were there. We stayed some time talking to the French officers & smoked a cigar there – Two men had just been carried away wounded, one died before they got him out of the trenches. I had a look through the sundry loopholes out of which our friends poked their rifles for the chance of a good shot at the Russian sharpshooters. A good many rifle balls whizzed over our heads as we returned but they were good enough not to fire any shells. It appears that the battery must be taken but it will be much stronger tonight. The ground is desperately bad & rocky & the cover every where very insuff^t. The Russians are much more economical of their shot & shell than they used to be or the white tower w^d. have been firing all day as it is only 800 metres distant. As we reached the plateau the French relief for the Guards of the trenches were going down, and a party without great coats or cooking utensils which looked like a storming party was in company. It was a melancholy sight to see hundreds of men going to kill & be killed to capture or defend a wretched earthwork – The dead of the fight of last night were lying out still in front.

They say that Gen Niel the Emp^r. A.D.C. is ordered out to the Crimea. They have a rumour in the Guards camp that Gen Airey & Col Gordon are recalled – Marsh has heard the same story that Denison wrote me word of – that L^d. Raglan was to be recalled to take the Horse Guards & supervise the Reorganisation of it. They say that there has been a cabinet Council on the subject. If that is so then the result certainly cannot be known yet.

Tuesday Feb. 27th.

Gen Canrobert was not satisfied that the Zouaves who fell in the attack on the Russian redoubt on 23rd. had been buried & sent in to Osten Sacken who assured him that they had. But as Canrobert was not satisfied a truce of two hours was agreed on from 12 to 2 PM today. The French and Russians towards the Quarantine Fort fired till 20 min past noon but at 12 all the other batteries had ceased firing and white flags were hoisted on all of them on both sides. The combatants of the different armies came boldly out to have a look at one another and the City swarmed with spectators. The Zouaves left behind only their supports & with their officers & men with stretchers advanced towards the Russian battery. They were met by a Russ^n. officer & salutations were exchanged The French did not advance more than 100 yds from the Russ^n. Batt. when they divided into two parties going right & left in search of the dead but found none. The French & Russ^n. were intermingled. Some sat & smoked others talked. No bodies were found. Before the truce had ended, both sides had withdrawn but the signal of a gun from the Russ^n. R^t answered by a French gun, and the white flags came down and the sharpshooters began their work again with great eagerness.

There was very little firing of cannon but plenty of musketry. Several of our men were killed & wounded today by a shell.

L^d. Raglan appears very much out of spirits to day, I fear he must have been much vexed by the attacks agst. him charging him with indifference to the distress of his men.

10 P.M. There is a sharp attack now going on somewhere on French side. – Therm^r. 10 P.M. 52.

Cambridge University Library: Add. 9554/4

23
Romaine to John Harvey

[Holograph, partly cross-written]

Head Quarters Camp before Sebastopol
March 6th 1855

My dear Harvey,

I am happy to be able to announce to you the safe arrival of the box per "Durham" contained an unascertainable amount of "preserved" not "potted" meats – My friend Col McMurdo who is to organise the transport of the army had just arrived post haste from England and become my guest, so in grateful remembrance of the Ickwell hares I sought out a pot of "Jugged Hare" for his refreshment and it was pronounced excellent. I gave my servants a feast of roast mutton & roast beef, that all hands might taste of your bounty. Now for your letter – Not "half the stories you hear of ships remaining loaded with stores for want of formal orders" are true but all the stories are untrue, utterly – They are bosh – We have suffered because you good people in England or your rulers would not give us transport fit for an army of 30,000 men, properly organised to do its work. What little transport we had was under the control of Filder who had enough to do looking after his eternal contracts for biscuit salt pork & rum – No doubt mistakes have been made here – The not strengthening the front of the 2nd Div^n and the not making a road from Balaclava are instances – Though much may be said in defence of the latter – When we came here after Alma, having landed 27,000 of all arms what with the battle & the Cholera which began the day after the battle – 60 men in one Division alone – we had not more than 24,000 to begin the siege and maintain a most entrenched position in face of an enemy more numerous than ourselves – After the 20th of Oct[r] when the "coup" had failed and a winter campaign was certain I think the siege sh[d] have been set aside for the purpose of making roads and strengthening our position and I think a Great General w[d] have done so – But I confess I speak with great doubts of my own opinion, when old soldiers thought & acted differently – I think though I expressed the same opinion to you several months ago with regard to the road – After the wet weather set in we were never strong handed enough to carry on the siege and make roads too.

The packages designed for the officers got into the Limbo of the Turkish Custom House in this way. Before it was certainly known in England that we were fixed here for the winter, parcels were sent to Const[l]. "to be forwarded" to the army & so were put in the Custom House. The Navy as long ago as May last got a seal from the Porte, so that their things being "plombéd" were easily rescued – Our seal was not procured till January, through a stream of objurgations directed by me upon the Q[r] M[r] Gen[l] & his assistants – Now the things are in course of clearing out and by July I expect my warm clothing – The same steady course of treatment produced a parcels delivery office here, though I had many fruitless fights before I c[d] get that established, luckily one day at dinner L[d] Raglan overheard the discourse & took my part, and two days afterwards I heard that the office had begun its labours – I was informed the other day that they received and sent out on an average 300 parcels a day. We have now had nearly three weeks fine dry weather, until today it has been cold, today the therm[r] was at 42 in the shade and very pleasant – did I tell you that Ld Raglan has asked me to conduct the correspondence between the Railway Engineers and other Army Departments. So look out for a leader in the Times against your unfortunate friend – I thought it very cute of the FM to pick out a civilian to bear the brunt of the abuse which may be expected, in case the Times finds its "only bit of blue sky" rather clouded – Two mails are in, but I hear that the bags are not to be sorted till tomorrow, so your letter will be finished

My dear Mrs Harvey,

It was very kind of you to send me a line. Letters from old friends are very cheering & welcome – You must know that I am enjoying the height of good living – I am in a house! With a roof – There are plenty of cracks in the roof which let in snow – & sun when it shines, but a close place is not bearable after living in a tent during the cold weather – The other day the East wind blew quite warm and the therm^r went up to 60. I could not eat my breakfast & could hardly finish my dressing with the door shut airy as my house is. Two days after the therm^r was at 18° at breakfast time. I have bought poultry and have fresh laid eggs every morning for breakfast. I have not yet established a whats his name for hatching em – Such a change for the better has come over the spirits of the Army with the dry weather – You hear the laugh and the song in camp now, instead of the dreadful pattering of the rain in the tent – the most distressing sound after a while, that I ever heard – The last new arrivals of troops have kept healthy, unfortunately the noble old soldiers who have stood through it all are dropping off fast – the men entitled to clasps for both Alma & Inkerman will be very few – Nothing to my mind can equal the heroism of the men who endured day after day & night after night the dreadful hardship of the trenches – Always wet through even in sleep, bad uncooked food, diseases, scanty rest & fuel nearly every stitch on them frequently frozen besides being wet, their comrades dying round them by hundreds from the very same sufferings which they themselves were still undergoing but few flinched from the sore trial "They thought it a shame to go into Hospital while they c^d by any means do their duty as it made the work harder on the rest". That was the reason given me by a soldier, anything more simple more noble or more touching can hardly be found – I have acquired an immense admiration of the British soldier – I wish spirits had never been invented and then he w^d be perfect – The papers have done all they can to spoil them and make them discontented. But the letters written with the greatest ignorance & in the worst spirit have come from the officers – You should all remember that the grumblers & croakers are the only men who write to the papers – The good officers do their work and hold their tongues – Something must no doubt be allowed to men who have really suffered a great deal – You ask if the French are much better off than us – There are very few of them hutted even now – Comparatively few have to this time had fur coats – None of them the warm clothing our men have had – It was a question some time ago whether we sh^d not give them 30,000 articles of warm clothing which we could spare. The story about the 10,000 French great coats was an impure invention – There was not even the grain of truth on which a lie is sometimes based – They were more numerous and their turn to be in the trenches came only once in five days. This made all the difference in their favour, and one quite sufficient to account for their comparative immunity from disease – Though their men went in to Hospital at the rate of 300 a day – The Russians have just received five miles of convoy – and last night kept up such an incessant cannonade as I have seldom heard since 5th Nov^r – Two Polish officers deserted to us today – There is a general expectation that something is to come off next week – The batteries are all nearly ready. The Russians have sunk more ships. I believe on purpose to leave only the number which the Western powers wish to restrict them to – So the Proud Czar might only have to agree not to <u>increase</u> his fleet in the Black Sea – which would not sound so humiliating as if he agreed to destroy them – You won't mind having your portion crossed I hope.[45] I saw young Teddy yesterday he is getting fat, and expecting to go home on promotion he is a very gallant and good officer and did his duty well at Inkerman which was a day to try anyone. The French failed signally the other day to take an earthwork which the Russians had thrown up opposite an intended battery of theirs. I have made up my mind rather to stay out here than come home even in case of a General Election. I have got a position which suits my tastes perfectly. So if the Times does not write me down incompetent, I think I shall stay with the army till Peace comes if I live so long. It is to be hoped you will have a wet day to read this in.

Good bye

Ever yours very sincerely

W. G. Romaine

Cambridge University Library: Add. 7633: 5/22

24
Romaine to C. J. Selwyn

[Holograph]   Head Quarters
                                                   March 11 1855

My dear Selwyn,

You seem to be in a state of war at home while we are enjoying peace out here. Things have taken a very decided turn for the better since the fine weather set in. That is as to the state of the armies both French and English – the young soldiers & fresh regiments no longer sicken & perish but improve in health & strength – The French met with a signal repulse some time ago in an attempt to take and destroy a Russian outwork which had been thrown up in front of one of their batteries – This earthwork of the Russians has now developped [*sic*] itself in the form of two very formidable batteries[46] –

Our guns have spoken at last though in a rather feeble manner. The first occasion was to shell a ship which had annoyed us – They managed though at a distance of 1800 yards to damage it a good deal & cause them to warp it away, the engine being apparently destroyed as it ceased suddenly to work – The other occasion was to day after church I heard that our guns were woken to drive the Russian working parties out of a lodgment they had effected on a mound in front of the Round Tower – This was effected by a few very well directed shots – But our guns were immediately answered by those of the enemy from several places & we ceased firing and the Russian working party actually returned in broad daylight. Since dark there has been a more than usually heavy fire both of musquetry & cannon – The grand attempt of the bombardment will certainly take place this week if word may be believed. I have no longer the implicit faith in engineers & great guns which I had when I came here and I think unless the supply of Russian ammunition falls short, that their fire will over power ours & the French too – I sincerely hope not as a failure would be disastrous in the present state of affairs here at home and in Europe generally –

My great friend McMurdo has been living with me since he came out & it is a great charm to have an old friend so thoroughly interested in the war as he is, to talk matters over with –

Thanks to good friends at home my Christmas presents have just arrived & we are living on the fat of the land –

I have all sorts of miscellaneous duties thrust upon me – Chairman of a board on the employment of the Croatian labourers, on a board about the improvements of the harbour at Balaclava and now I am to be Coroner at an inquest on one of the Railway labourers killed by a truck – The Railway will turn out famously & be of capital consequence to our operations – It is already most useful and in another fortnight will I hope have surmounted the dreadful hill – I should say General Simpson who is coming out is a muff if I may guess from a specimen of his conduct in letting off an officer who had been guilty of such disgraceful conduct in England & who if he had been there dismissed would have saved me the trouble of getting him cashiered as I expect to do this week. His reason for letting him off being a fear of what the public would say if they knew of such "blackguard" [sic] conduct – That is not the hard "man" that Layard has been asking for. Is it a Republic that the army is to return home to, with a Provisional Government like the French of 1848 formed of Editors of papers – Though we all think the Times has in many things deserved well of the country – That the sick & wounded owe them much there is no doubt but the Government is too much afraid of them & follows instead of leading & forming public opinion –

I suppose the turn of my little department will come when the Mutiny Act has to be passed. Though our proceedings out here have not given them many salient points for abuse. I have asked for some few alterations and sent them home an Act of Parliament I want passed, for the trial on the spot of crimes committed on shore by sailors & other civilians – They may do as they like with it, expressavi animam meam[47] as you or the Vulgate hath it.

If I have time I will write you another sheet if not goodbye

Y[rs] ever

W. G. Romaine

Cambridge University Library: Add. 7633: 5/23

25
Journal for 11 to 28 March 1855

[Holograph]

Sunday March 11th.

Today after Church I heard that the Russians had last night established themselves on a mamelon in front of the round tower and that we and the French were to drive them out by fire from the batteries. Went with M[c]Murdo to the Quarry in front of the 3rd. Div[n]. about two o'clock. Soon after a gun was fired from the rt of our 21 gun battery, and about seven were fired altogether on the large Russian working party. The guns were well laid and had the effect of making them leave the work. The Russians then fired from three or four embrasures of the Round tower works, from a ship or battery close to the arsenal, & from a battery below the Redan our guns having ceased firing after a short time the Russians returned & resumed their work unmolested.

At night there was a heavy fire. Burghersh has returned from Eupatoria. He says the place is now very much fortified, that there are both cavalry & infantry there that the ditch is a very formidable one. That there will be 70 guns in all mounted there. Calvert says that a Pole who swam the river Tchernaia yesterday & came in, & who was at Eupatoria says that there were 1500 men killed & wounded in the attack mostly his Reg[t].

Monday March 12th.

The French it appears were to have fired when we did, as only two of our guns bore on this new work of the Russ[ns]. At night it was arranged that the French & ourselves sh^d. each send a large party to work & make a large parallel to oppose the new Russ^n. work, but the Engineers staid [*sic*] so late with Burghersh talking, that they lost their way and the party never arrived. Our men were attacked and had to fight instead of working and instead of a long parallel only a bit of sap was done. The Russian work is so strong today that they are not to be driven out.

Omar Pasha is here in conference. The French Generals & Admirals are also here.

It is to be feared that the Russians will have guns in the work in a day or two which will throw shot through our camps & destroy our huts.

Thursday March 22

Having heard last night late that there was to be an attack on the pits in front of the French advanced works where they join ours in front of the Picket house of the Light Division I had myself called at 3 AM and got up to the picket house at 4 AM without losing my way much though it was very dark. I halted at the picket & while there Pearson came up & told me I sh^d. see nothing there & must come on to the work in front of our two mortar battery. On my way I met Genl. Brown & the rest of his staff who had come to see the fight. Then Gen Jones, Airey Estcourt &c came up. We waited some time – it became broad daylight we could see the French trench full of men and amongst them were some of the Imp^l. Guard – We began to think it was all over without a fight when a move took place and out of a boyau in front of the parallel B rushed some 40 Frenchmen There was no general leaping over the parapet as we expected [see Figure 8]. The Russians ran out of two or three of the pits & made off up the hill to the mamelon or for the pits just on the slope of it. They were fired at by the whole line of Frenchmen in the trenches. One or two fell but got up again & when all was quiet not a body French or Russian was on the ground. The Russians in the pits marked P.P. as some of the French came out of their cover stood up & I could see their heads over the sand bags & they kept up a heavy fire on the French The French however seemed to have done all that was wanted for in three moments they were all back again not leaving one man on the ground. While this was going on the Russians opened a very heavy fire from their batteries on the lines of French protecting their men very effectively. Our men in the advanced trenches also fired – Gen Canrobert who was on the hill did not seem satisfied for he got off his horse & strode rapidly down the hill past us. Nothing further happened. None of the pits was stormed. The Fr. will take the abandoned pits into their lines tonight.

Friday, 23rd. March

The Russians seem to have been emboldened by the mild nature of the attack this morning for about 12 last night a furious attack was made all along the advanced works of the allies. There was so strong a wind from the Southward that the Camp of the Division and in one case the officer commanding the guards of the trenches knew nothing of any[thing] unusual having occurred & Gen England told me that that was the report that was made to him this morning. The 20th. 21st. & 57th. & 97th. had parties in the advance works & were attacked & driven back. The 57 were at work & had to run some with their tools in their hands fought their way back to their arms & as soon as mustered formed & drove the enemy back. The same nearly happened in the other attack. A Greek (Arnaut[48]) Col. lead [sic] in men & wounded Gordon who was shot in five places. but the Greek was killed shortly afterwards. He was dressed in

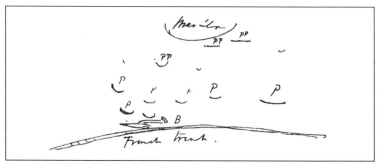

Figure 8. Plan of French raid on Russian pits (from journal dated 22 March 1855).

Greek dress had handsome pistols & [illegible] 40 Russ[n]. gold coins were found on him = to nearly 30£s. It appears that the Greeks had been swaggering about how they were going to take the batteries – Unfortunately 3 officers Hon C. Brown Vicars & Jordan were killed Col Kelly 34th. & another officer were both prisoner & a corporal & 15 men and 2 more officers Montague of Eng[rs]. & Gordon RE were wounded. Major Tylden took the command of our party & charged with them. 14 Russ[n]. dead were found in the advance battery of Chapman and there are 28 more corpses outside visible – They did no damage to the guns & not much to the works. It was all repaired before morning! The attack was preceded by a tremendous cannonade in which one of our guns was disabled. The French ground was easier of attack being on more level ground & the pits in front of them were occupied by the enemy. Some of the Russ[ns]. got into the trench but were all killed. This morning there were 150 corpses lying in a row outside the French trench besides numbers of French & Russian dead further off & near the pits. Two French penetrated a long way & lie dead on the side of the Mamélon.

The French allow a loss of 100 dead & 200 wounded. Unfortunately the 97 after skirmishing out in front on their return found a Fr. Reg[t]. had retreated to their lines & taking them for Russ[ns]. the 97 attacked fired into them & were fired upon & then drove the Fr. out of the lines with the bayonet, but not before loss had been occasioned. M[r] Aylet [sic – actually 'Aylmer'] 97th who was found wounded s[d]. I gave it to three of them & there they lie, his comrades went to look & found 3 Fr[n]. 2 bayoneted & one shot.

The Russ[ns]. in front of the 20th abandoned their muskets when they were charged & flew.

The result of this repulse was that the Russ[ns]. abandoned all the pits nearest to the Fr. lines.

In the afternoon I rode out to the Picket house & left my horse & with Capt Rosser of 10th Hussars walked down to Gordon's battery from which they were firing a 68 pr and a 13 inch mortar. We went down part of the way to the trench leading to the French advanced trench and taking off my cap I looked over through my glass. I c[d]. see a great mountain of Russian dead at least 200. Many were lying in a row outside the Fr. lines, more again about the pits which had evidently been hotly contested. Quantities of gabions were lying about. The batteries were firing on the mamélon in which the Russians were at work in spite of the heavy fire. A prisoner tells us that at least 100 men killed & wounded are carried out of it every day – A very intelligent Russian prisoner a "little Russian" said that they were afraid of us, and we afraid of them, but that whichever party went at the other in the most "friendly" way (meaning "determined") would win. He seemed to have no feeling of patriotism or fanaticism, nor to care anything for the old or new Emperor. He was a very ugly dirty looking fellow but gave a capital account of every thing that passed within his neighbourhood. In the afternoon there was a conference with Canrobert & others & I hear the French are to convert the pits taken into a parallel & gain 150 yards or so towards the mamelon.

Saturday 24th March

The Russian prisoner one of several taken has given such accurate information that with the assistance of the Polish Officer a complete plan of the Redan with its guns its ditches fougasses, magazines, galvanic wires &c has been drawn. Yesterday the town was on fire in two places from the mortars.

The Russians kept up a heavy fire last night and under cover of it all reoccupied all their pits again nearly up to the French. The Russian attack of the night before was made in heavy column lead [sic] by the Greek volunteers of whom many were killed at Eupatoria. Hearing that there was a flag of truce from 12.30 to 2 PM to bury the dead I rode with McMurdo to the advanced works & leaving our horses went amongst the burial parties – there was a line beyond which neither party was allowed to go. There were several Greeks lying dead. One of these rascally Greeks called out to me How do Cap[n]. The Russ[ns]. employed in burying were very fair men marked 12 on shoulder straps & 44 on the button.[49] The officers were well dressed & looked like gentlemen. The dead presented the same frightful spectacle, having stiffened in the attitude in which they received the mortal blow, or with their arms extended as in some convulsive moment of sudden agony. It was a ghastly sight when one of these bodies was put on a stretcher to see the arm waving aloft as the movement of the bearers caused it to have the appearance of life –

Parties of Russians collected the bodies in the rear of the great centre pit, others took them a stage further to the rear and a third party carried them behind the mamélon for burial. The R[s] during the night had made excellent progress in their work and nearly all the embrasures in the mamélon are finished neatly & well with sandbags. The pits are some of them with[in] 30 yards of the head of the Fr. sap which appears to have been destroyed. The Russ[ns]. have nearly made [?] their pits into a complete entrenchment though so close to their enemies & I have no doubt unless the Fr. are a little more adventurous tonight will have it completed before morning. While this burying party was going on the French cavalry were having their races – near their camp, but the front for once had the greatest attraction. It took the R[s]. till nearly 3 PM before all their dead were carried away. Gen Coddrington [sic] & a number of Engl. & Fr. Officers had a great talk with the Russ. of[rs]. until the flag of truce was hauled down. The truce was asked for by us from 12.30 to 2 PM but it lasted till 3. When the truce was nearly out the Russ[ns]. withdrew to their pits, the Fr. to their lines and after a pause of 5 min. the rifle firing began again very intensely and our Guns began to fire on the Mamélon. The guns from the place also fired on the Fr. parallel part of which I believe it enfilades.

When I got back to camp I found another consultation was going on at H[d]. Q[rs]. Col Kelly of 34 is dead of many wounds. We are making another battery for two mortars below the one in front of the L[t]. Div[n]. Picket House it is well placed to avoid the fire of the Mamélon & to look into the Admiralty buildings. The L[t]. Div[n]. will have it that L[d]. R. has monstrously ordered that these bldgs & the town are not to be fired at.

Sirocco wind. Therm 3.30 PM 66.

Tuesday March 27.

Went up to the front of the Light Division and watched the operations of the siege. The Russ[ns]. have connected their pits opposite the French advanced work in face of the Mamélon – The boyau of the Fr. nearly touches the R. line. The R^s. fired very well upon the line of Fr. and appeared to damage the work a good deal, the Fr. seemed to keep very clear of the part under fire. Gen Airey tells me that during the time it was proposed that the French sh^d. help us by manning our ~~batteries~~ trenches Canrobert said, "It is quite impossible that our men sh^d. occupy them. Our men must have a road to their trenches perfectly under cover the whole way & the trenches themselves must be as safe as their barracks or they w^d. instantly desert them." Nothing surprises them so much as to see our men quietly walking across the open where people are being shot at & where shells are falling & bursting every few minutes. I saw a party today returning from working in Gordons battery which had two very narrow escapes but they neither altered their road nor quickened their pace – Some men were wounded by the fire of musquetry today.

Captn. Hill of the 89th. was taken prisoner this morning while posting the sentries in front of Chapmans advanced battery. He had gone out to post the sentries when he was shot & wounded. He spoke to the sergeant to bring him in, but a body of 200 Russ^{ns}. came up, the 10 double sentries fired & ran & the Sergeant being alone had to leave him & the Russians carried him off. It was a still day & the bells of the cathedral c^d. be plainly heard between the booming of the guns. Some of our fuses are bad & the shells exploded too soon, one when only 50 yards from the mortar.

Dined with L^d. Raglan. After dinner walked for an hour nearly with him. He said that at Waterloo the Prussians were in sight a great part of the day, but did not come to the field of battle till late. He was wounded at 4 PM, when riding with the Duke along the ridge, the shot of a musket came from La Haye Sainte. His arm fell but he rode to the village where he had slept suffering great pain. The Doctor came to him and said "My finger is now in y^r. elbow joint, you must either have it amputated now or wait some days till the inflammation has gone down." Upon which he decided to have it done at once. The only great pain was when the bone was sawn through. He seemed to think the Prussians were waiting to see how the day went. But I do not think that Bluchers character makes such an idea probable.

Wednesday March 28.

Wind S.W. 56

There has been a lime kiln erected in front of 4th. Div[n]. to the left of Sir G Cathcarts tomb and the R[s] have been firing at it from Malakoff tower. General Barnards tent was struck and his table cut by pieces of one shell. He yesterday moved his camp. Today while I was at the front, near L[t]. Div[n]. picket house, they began throwing heavy shells at the lime kiln, one went just over my head & fell in the ravine below me. Two others went just over the lime kiln. I went to look at the place their range had been the same to a yard as to distance and they were only 20 yards apart, one had gone so deep that I c[d]. not reach the bottom of the hole with my umbrella – Ten more 13 inch mortars have arrived today. The artillery horses by the Himalaya have arrived. Settled an answer to D[r]. Gavin of the Sanitary Commission with Airey & Gen Simpson. I did not much approve the wording of it. Sir John M[c]Neil was here today to see Lord R. He is a fine intelligent looking man. Col. Warde R.A. said that some of the fuses were so bad, that he has been obliged to put aside those of 1798 & use those of 1801 & 1804 – ! The Fr. boyau in front of their advanced trench before the Mamélon does not seem to have advanced much though I know that they have 900 men working, & the trench seemed full of men. Their work seemed very good & very near the Russian pits & connecting trench, but at some moment they must meet & then one side or the other must jump over and have a fight for the trench – This moment neither side seems very anxious for. The Russ[ns]. have got a 2nd. line ready when the first is lost and a covered way to it from the mamelon and on the right side of the mamélon another trench & more pits. They made 5 more pits in front of the Fr. & 4 opposite us, but across the ravine. There was a very heavy fire on the mortar battery on our extreme left by Chapmans advanced battery. The Malakoff battery fired very regularly at any object Fr. or Engl. Dacres two days ago said openly we were to begin our fire next week, but we have heard it so often – A telegraphic message has arrived from Vienna, bringing it is said the result of the 2nd. days Conference, but no more has transpired & I have not been to H[d]. Q[rs]. to enquire.

Cambridge University Library: Add. 9554/4

26
Romaine to Lord Mulgrave

[Holograph]   Head Quarters
                                          Camp before Sevastopol
                                            March 29th. 1855

My dear Mulgrave,

I received your letter late last night from Lord Raglans bag, but our mail is not yet come up from Kamiesch.

I owe you many thanks for your arrangement of the Chatham affair – The good people there would be so greatly the gainers by it that I am sure they would be satisfied – Buchanan wrote to me to know how far the report was true, and I wrote to him by last mail, a letter which if the necessity should arise he is authorised to show to the Committee.

I mentioned in it that you have full authority to act for me.

But I really believe that we shall have peace and that the Mulgrave woods will see us with peaceful guns on our shoulders this autumn.

The French here say "we have got a good war at last, let us keep it so" – I begin to be of the old English belief that one Englishman is worth three Frenchmen, although I remember looking upon that saying as a vulgar boast.

The war has had one most comfortable effect upon me. I shall never again be in bodily fear of a French invasion, though I believe the French soldiers would receive an order to invade England with very little real ardour. There is not even a Zouave who does not give the "par" to our soldiers for fighting qualities.

Our soldiers are not to be matched in the world, next to them come the Russians. There are not the men in the world who would work under fire as they do except our own. Our batteries are ready to open whenever the politicians give the order – As long as this comparative quiet lasts we shall go on increasing our works. Ten more 13 inch mortars arrived the day before yesterday. The Railway has reached the top of the hill so that we shall be able to keep the batteries well supplied, as long as the stores at Balaclava hold out.

Yesterday the Russians were shelling the 4th Division from Malakhoff tower a distance of two and a half miles. They did no damage and the men seemed to think it a good joke. They are awfully noisy fellows these big shells, I was out in rear of Gordons battery & they all came over my head. It is wonderful how accurately you can tell where a shell is going to fall, after a little practice. These large shells are very harmless to men but very destructive to buildings guns earthworks &c.

The French have been working away at an advanced trench which now for five days has been close to a similar one of the Russians but they don't seem to like the last step, which must lead to a serious fight – I went down to the advanced works during the truce for burial of the dead on the 24th. It was a very curious scene, but as the "Times" was represented there, you will have read a good description of it. The loss on the part of the Russians is calculated to be nearly 3000 men in all.

The whole of their batteries in & around Sebastopol are said to contain 1000 pieces, of all sorts – I have written a long letter to Lady Normanby thanking her for the bag of most valuable articles for a campaigner – I have previously written to thank her for the Gigantic Parmesan.

The only trophy of the war which I shall carry away is a large fur cloak which was captured with the baggage of a Russian General, my medals &c were begged of me by Lord Raglan to send home I think for her Majesty. The cloak I hope will keep me warm in some winter journeys to Mulgrave –

We are infested with a tribe of Commissioners amongst them is a vulgar dog of the name of Gavin who has written a report on Balaclava which it would be a real pleasure to have the right to cut up and ridicule – The mixture of fine phrases misapplied, of bad English & spelling would amuse you very much. He says (not in his report but in private) "the public voice of England has spoken – and he shall demand this that & the other" –

Sir John McNeil seems a thorough gentleman and I only hope he will carry that insufferable Filder the evil genius of the army, away to England with him when he goes. The dysentery from which the army suffered so severely has entirely disappeared. The cavalry are smartened up & look as well & as clean as the day they arrived –

You cannot imagine the consternation with which the news of Lord Cardigan's appointment to command the cavalry was received –

His going away caused his soldiers the same sort of relief that the death of the Emperor did to Europe. My opinion of him is that he has not one quality of a soldier. There is not one officer out here for him I have contracted such a profound contempt as for his Lordship –

If you see any one of the Light Brigade in England just ask him whether my Lord deserves to become an object of Hero Worship for his charge at Balaclava – He rode a very fast horse and wore a very smart coat –

Lord Raglan I am happy to say is in good health, some time ago he was not very well. I think he felt a good deal the severe attacks made on him in England.

I cant understand why no one in England ventures to state in public the actual numbers of troops here in the English camp. We keep reading speeches in which the words disgrace disasters and dishonour occur in connection with this army. Do they think that three battles are to be fought and two great victories gained that a winter campaign is to be endured and six months of open trenches and no loss to be suffered. I believe the French loss will have equalled ours, and that two fifths of either army has been placed hors de combat.

But I have written you an unfair quantity of gossip for a Senator to read.

I was so glad to hear such a good account of My Lady and the bairns – Pray thank Miss Lewis for the mittens they are packed up against a cold day. Warne has not yet delivered himself of the other things you announce. When they come I shall write my Lady a budget of gossip, all about my farm and how I have fowls and a goat and had milk for breakfast and pancake for dinner.

I send her some violets picked up behind Gordons battery within range of the "doomed City" of the Times of Oct 1854. I shall expect to be repaid with a double violet "in the good time coming".

Ever yours faithfully

W. G. Romaine

General Simpson the new Head of the Staff gets on capitally with every body.

This paper is part of Lady Normanby's thoughtful budget and as in duty bound I inflict three sheets on you.

Part 3

Preparing to Attack

The second bombardment

As the weather improved so did the supply of food, clothing, and replacement tents. Huts were erected, first for regimental hospitals, and then for men and officers. The railway carried more supplies and large quantities of ammunition. Convalescents returned from hospitals at Scutari. Morale improved. Even the criticisms from the Sanitary Commissioners seemed more reasonable and Romaine was made responsible for correspondence with them.

Omar Pasha arrived outside Sevastopol with 10,000 Turkish soldiers – fine men, not the 'despised wretches' of the Battle of Balaklava.

On 9 April 1855 the second bombardment began, watched with eager anticipation by many of the staff. It was intended to be followed by an infantry assault, but each night the Russians repaired the damage suffered by their works during the day. After four or five days of intense firing, the Allies were short of ammunition but the Russian firing continued unabated. Moreover, when the Allied guns were damaged or became worn they could not easily be replaced, whereas the Russians had an ample supply from the fleet arsenal. The siege settled down to occasional forays by the French as they tried to improve their approaches to the town, and regular sorties by the Russians. Romaine began to doubt that success was possible.

The electric telegraph became operational and the delay in communication with England was reduced from weeks to hours. (The generals, especially the French, did not necessarily see this as an advantage.) Romaine refers to the use of a 'numeral cypher'.

Minor operations by the British included a reconnaissance of cavalry and horse artillery towards Chorgoun, and the capture of rifle pits at the cost of the life of a popular commanding officer in Egerton of the 77th.

Lord Stratford de Redcliffe arrived to hand out awards, and Romaine's legal duties continued with courts martial and inquiries, including one into the accidental shooting of his erstwhile *bête noire*, Doctor Gavin, and another into what to do with the Englishman, Upton.

The Allied commanders began to consider operations elsewhere in the peninsula. Turkish forces left for Eupatoria where they were to be very successful, and an Anglo-French expedition under General Brown set off for Kertch. Romaine feared that Brown would make a mess of it, and regretted that Sir Colin Campbell had not been appointed to command. It was recalled before it got there on the orders of the Emperor. Pelissier replaced Canrobert and was immediately more decisive. The expedition was sent again, was a spectacular success and was extended to Yenikale and Anapa. Sardinia joined the alliance, and a contingent of her troops arrived in the Crimea.

General Simpson arrived from England, charged with finding fault with Raglan's staff, but found them satisfactory and remained as Chief-of-Staff. In Vienna, diplomatic moves to halt hostilities failed.

Meanwhile, the French 'nibbled' ever closer to the Russian defences and made some gains but at heavy loss on both sides as the Russians counter-attacked with determination. British forces behaved well against regular Russian sorties by night. The French and Sardinians now moved forward to the Chernaya river, reclaiming the land lost on 25 October 1854.

Mr Fenton the photographer visited, but sadly Romaine does not seem to have been a subject. A report criticising Filder, the Commissary General, which Mr Beatty, the railway engineer, had sent to London brought repercussions.

Third bombardment and the fall of the Mamélon

Meanwhile ammunition had been stockpiled ready for the third bombardment, which began on 6 June 1855. The British attacked and captured the quarries, and the French took the Mamélon. Preparations were made for a fourth bombardment, the stockpiling of ammunition now transformed by the railway. There was keen anticipation among officers and men as the end of the siege seemed to be near.

27

Journal for 4 April to 1 May 1855

[Holograph]

Wednesday. Ap^l. 4th.

The cold wind has done blowing and the weather is very pleasant. It appears quite true that the Turks are to come from Eupatoria, leaving enough men there to defend the place. Walked out to the lookout in front of two mortar battery in front of Light Division Picket House. There was a heavy fire going on between the two batteries on the Sapoune the Mamélon & the French 15 gun battery. M^r. Filder came up for a minute or two. The Turks were bringing in gabions to make traverses in Gordons battery. The inside is being revetted with sandbags. Yesterday evening Bainbrigg [*sic* – Bainbrigge] RE was killed. One Sapper had his head blown off by a round shot & his head struck agst the jaw of another Sapper & broke it. There is now no firing agst the French left. We had at one time a good many officers in the lookout and the Russ^ns. sent first a shot which only just rolled up & then a shell which burst just in front of us, one bit just skimming over my head which I have picked up. Lord Raglan was down at Gordon Battery & walked back to the Picket House & then came with Genl. Jones to the Lookout. He had been sitting he told me on 68^pr. in the battery when a shell came through & covered him with dust.

Soon after he came in to the lookout a shell was sent up which burst just beyond us, one bit falling within a few yards which Gen Jones picked up & took away for a friend who is going to England. There was by this time a great crowd at the picket house as L^d. R. had ordered the 13 inch mortars to fire. The first shot was well pitched into the tower, They returned with a shot at picket house which moved the people a little, then one which came well up but did not burst. Then there was a pause. Some time after L^d. R. went there was a pause I went to the picket house to look for my horse, and put the bit of shell in there for my servant to bring back. I had just left & was on the road when a big shell came up & fell into the picket house enclosure, rt [?] on the hard ground & bounded a few yards and I thought was not going to explode when I saw every body lying down & immediately it exploded I threw myself down, one bit knocked down a French soldier by the Telegraph tent where I had been standing the minute before. I walked on a few yards looking at the crowd when a second came in just the same line but further down the road, & burst but did not harm any one. Several horses broke away, but the whole affair was received with shouts of laughter in spite of the wounded man. The garden battery threw some shells up to 4th. Div^n. and some other battery threw 2 shells up to the Windmill.

Mr Gavin has written a better sort of a letter in answer to last, He came to Lord R. & was shewn a very insolent letter written by Mr Newlands but he took it & tore it to pieces – He said "Your Lordship is much mistaken if you think I have come to make difficulties. I have come with the full intention of doing every thing to assist you."

I have another letter of his to answer but it is a very sensible affair & all will go smoothly. Gen Airey wants carriages on 6th. to bring up 300 of 71st. Reg^t. to work at batteries to strengthen them & he wants them taken back at night. It w^d. be too slow a process the bringing them up.

Sold my little Horse to McMurdo. The old Horse, late taken ill. I believe the Pole "Yan" gave him water when he was hot.

Thursday. Ap^l. 5th.
Went out to the front where a heavy fire had been going on. Went to the look out place. They were firing the big mortars just behind me. The Russians were throwing their shells into our trenches from the round tower & mamélon. Col Warde RA told me that they had lost a second 32^{pr}. out of which not a shot had been fired. This was by the fire of the mamélon – and all because they leave the embrasures open. Saw several more wounded by the Russ^n. shells in Gordons battery. Sold McMurdo my little thoroughbred horse my saddle &c &c. He gave me an order on Cox & Co.[50] which I have crossed to Lond. & West^r. Bloomsb^y. Branch. McMurdo

was in the trucks carrying in water barrels, from a suggestion of mine – I had seen how the poor fellows suffered from thirst last time. M^c was nearly floored by a round shot. There was a sharp fight which I hope was the taking of the pits in our front. He says there was a good deal of cheering. The Russians have been throwing many [?] shells right in among the Divisions again today. He thinks they have done no serious damage. Three came up from the Garden battery Four came up in the afternoon just as I had passed by on my way home.

Saturday. Ap^l. 7.
Saw L^d. R. early about the Railway accident.[51] Saw Gen Estcourt. Went to Balaclava & saw Col Stirling and Sir C. Campbell. He showed me the report of [a] deserter who had come in from Karales. He says there are 10,000 men at Mackenzies Farm & 10,000 at each of the three places called Karalez. That the Greek legion is at Tchorgoun, 300 Cossacks towards Baidar that a division of artillery is near but owing to the great losses among the horses there are only 32 guns instead of 64 to the Div^n. he says that Prince Gortschakoff reviewed all the troops & told them that he was bringing 80,000 men from Circassia to help them. He says also that the whole army talked of nothing but the attack on Balaclava which was to be made after 12 at night on 8th. Ap^l. in fact on the morning of Easter Sunday which feast of the Greek Church falls on the same day as ours. We attacked Odessa last year on Easter Sunday & they are to have their revenge. I do not expect it myself, because they made a great stir about an attack being made on so holy a day – Then I do not think a body of troops large enough to have a chance of succeeding against Balaclava could be concentrated in one night near enough to begin an attack soon after midnight or indeed by morning. There must be an attack on the heights on Sir Colin's extreme right. The Greeks may be bold enough to come & do that unsupported by artillery but I doubt it. Sir Colin is confident. He says unless his men run away he does not see how they are to get into his position. The Russians succeeded before on 5th Novr. in putting off the attack by fighting a battle. They know we are very near being ready & may think it

worth while to try & cripple us again in the same way. But now we have troops enough to hold the position – 8000 of Omar Pasha's soldiers have arrived at Kamiesch. Every preparation is made to receive the Russians if they do come. They have prepared an entrenched camp near the Tchernaia to retreat to if they are beaten. They were very quiet this afternoon in their batteries, which is generally a sign that something is brewing for the night. They however fired on the French 15 gun battery from the Mamélon & round tower.

I cannot help thinking from the great number of batteries which they have erected and are still erecting to overlook the battle field at Inkerman, that they intend a combined attack on the French batteries there by troops from the town and the North side, the attack to be perhaps made when Balaclava is attacked or a feint made to attack it. Balaclava in its present crowded state would be a great prize to take or burn. Stirling has written a comical letter in answer to Russell's letter about being chased by Cossacks within the lines. Calvert I hear is inclined to place some faith in the deserter. I see by L^d. Lucan's evidence or rather speech in the House of Lords that the day before we were attacked at Balaclava, 25 Oct^r , a deserter came in & announced it. This deserter is a Tartar who has been 11 years in the service of Russia. It was a warm day on the heights but a cold heavy fog was blowing into Balaclava all day. This if it continues w^d. enable the Russ^ns. to get up very close unperceived, but w^d. make it very difficult for columns to find their way & form for an attack whereas our men have been months in the same place & know the bearing of every gun.

The Guards landed a reinforcement of 200 men convalescents from Scutari, today. And yesterday & today 450 convalescents came up for the diff^t. divisions. The men seemed in good health & spirits –

April 9th.

McMurdo slept at my house and the Sergeant of the Guard called us at 4 AM. We rode up to the front and arrived at the Quarry [marginal note: "5.30 AM"] of the 3rd. Div^n. a few minutes after the fire began from the French. The English batteries took it up and the firing soon became very active along the whole line. The Russians were apparently taken by surprise and did not return the fire immediately. There was a heavy fog when we arrived and rain had fallen at intervals during the night & in the morning. The effect of the fog & smoke was entirely to obscure the town. The wind blew in the face of the Russ[ns]. it being nearly SSW. At 6 AM. an explosion near Quarantine F[t].

At 5.45. The fog cleared away and the town was visible, but the wind got up and the rain began to fall heavily. At this time the French fire was very heavy on the town and was well returned by the Russns. from the Central Redoubt (or Square Tower) the Bastion du Mât the Garden battery and the flank of the Barrack battery which bore on them. Things continued in this state a long time.

At 7.25. The Round Tower which had been hardly firing a gun began to return the fire from three or four guns on the side facing us and from some guns facing the French 15 gun battery towards Inkerman. The Redan hardly fired a shot, but the flank of the Barrack battery fired vigorously on us, as did the Garden Battery the Wall batteries the road batteries and the battery at the Head of the Arsenal buildings. The Mortar battery on the flank & below the Round Tower also fired. The Mamélon soon gave up firing more than one or two guns at considerable intervals. The fire of the redoubts of Volkynia & Selinghinsk on the Sapoune ridge seemed to be nearly silenced by the French fire.

I went to breakfast with Messiter & Keith at H[d]. Q[rs]. of 3rd. Div[n]. returning in the rain & mud to see how things went on.

The Garden battery fired well all through the day and one angle of the Bastion du Mat.

The Central Redoubt seemed to be silenced or was silent in consequence of the place being too hot for the defenders.

At 12.45. The batteries from the inside the town surrounded with houses to the North of the Hill & Flag staff on which the Governor's House was s[d]. to stand began to fire. Some of our shells had been seen to fall in the town. But the low fog & smoke all blowing towards the town made it impossible to see with any accuracy what the effect had been.

The wind veered to nearly due West but the heavy rain continued to fall.

The general opinion is that the Russ[ns]. are in want of men to man their extensive line of defences. The fleet was under weigh off the town, threatening the sea defences, but very wisely did not come in to attack.

The points most weakly defended by firing upon us, are just those which we know to be strongest in resisting an assault by their being provided with ditches abattis and mines. There is certainly as yet no sign that the Russians intend to evacuate the town in consequence of our fire. Our loss as far as ascertained is not heavy.

The very slack fire of the Russians from the Redan & Round Tower has taken every body by surprise, and is very puzzling. The shots that did come from them were very well directed.

Wrote an opinion on the Mule Contract of Major Fellowes who has had a dispute with Samary & Oglon &c [?]

Col Dacres RA who had been charged with getting 6 guns into an advanced battery prepared for them, had not succeeded owing to the entire darkness of the night.

Ap[l]. 10th.

The rain continued to fall during the night at intervals, the firing except on one occasion about 12 did not sound very heavy –

10 AM. Col Dacres who has just come in says he does not see much difference in the state of things as compared with yesterday.

Lt. [blank space[52]] of the RN is killed and Lord J Hay is severely wounded in the jaw by a piece of a shell there are 20 sailors killed & wounded.

I saw L[d]. R. who sent for me before breakfast to write ~~an answer~~ letter to the Sanitary Com[rs]. who have taken upon themselves to order houses to be pulled down, which are occupied by officers of the Com[t]. at Balaclava.

Rode out to the 4th. Division to enquire into the truth of a story which had been brought to L[d]. R[n]. of 33 deserters having come in. It turned out to [be] without any foundation. I then went down to the look out in front of the 3 Mortar battery which was firing towards the buildings of the arsenal. The two Russ[n]. batteries at head of creek of S^ت George fired occasionally at the French 15 gun battery, and the other French batteries at Inkerman were being fired at across the head of the harbour.

While I was there a new battery from that side opened, but the range was very great. The Mamélon had its embrasures masked and was quite silent. The Round tower fired but seldom but a mortar battery at its foot fired occasionally and two guns on its left flank fired on the French. The battery at the Head of the Arsenal the Redan and its continuation to Dockyard Creek fired regularly & sometimes severely on Gordons & Chapmans Batteries. The latter was much engaged also with the garden & wall batteries and guns on the road above the creek and in the interior of the Town.

I then went to the 3rd. Div. Quarry from which the Redan could be seen well. It appeared to me that our batteries though much less fired on than the Russian had suffered more than theirs. The Embrasures of Gordon were much knocked about. We had had 10 guns dismounted, but only 3 disabled.

Col. Dacres failed last night in getting the 6 guns into the advanced batteries.

The sappers were hard at work preparing a battery for 3 heavy mortars to right of Gordons battery but within the advanced trenches.

The Russians have never moved out of the advanced trenches & rifle pits held by them, to the right of middle ravine in front of the Mamélon.

I went afterwards to the observatoire near the Maison D'Eau. The Russian boat bridge which unites the two sides of Dock Yard Creek has not been injured by the French fire. The face of the Bastion du Mât has been destroyed & no embrasures are left. The Barrack battery appears uninjured. The Garden battery fired repeated salvoes on a Fr. battery which annoyed it. The Wall batteries appeared uninjured. The battery & its flanks about the [illegible] square tower still continues to answer the much reduced fire of the French. Vico tells me that the French have diminished their fire to economise shot & shell, but keep up enough fire to continue the superiority which they consider they have obtained. The fleet hovered off the harbour but out of range.

After looking over the whole front I came away with the impression that we shall fire away all our stores, if we continue in this way, and in the End be no further advanced. If the object is to destroy the defences prior to an assault, we have signally failed. There is not one point upon which an attack could be made with greater chance of success now than before the bombardment began. The silence of the Round Tower has puzzled every one. I believe they have very wisely kept their men under cover & saved their ammunition for the event of an assault. They cannot be seriously damaged by our horizontal fire & their firing w^d. not protect them against the vertical fire of our mortars. This fire is often very bad from the wretched state of the fuses. Numbers of shells never exploded & a vast proportion burst in the air, before it reached its mark.

The firing slackened on all hands soon after dark. Omar Pasha dined with Lord Raglan, he sat & drank of the best.

Wednesday Ap^l. 11th.

They tried very hard to get the 6 guns into the advanced battery on the left, but with 300 men to a gun they could not go ahead. Several of our guns have recoiled off their platforms & the artill^y. men have been unable to get them in place again. Last night there was a slight fire in the town and the allies did all they could to encourage it by firing rockets & shells close to it. Gen. Simpson sent letter from Sanitary Comm^{rs}. denying Com^y. Gen. Filder's Memo about their having ordered houses to be pulled down. I had to send them an answer & request them to send their report which they say is ready. Lord R. sent me over despatch from L^d. Stratford approving of the course taken with regard to the trial of the Croats. L^d. R. said to me in evening "You seem to have just fitted him." I received today a question to answer for Lord Raglan as to his power of attaching an officer of the East India C^o. service to a reg^t. I thought not.

There did not seem to be much difference today in the appearance of things in front. Our embrasures in Gordons & Chapmans batteries are a good deal knocked about. I saw a large convoy of wagons laden with gabions descending the hill towards the port yesterday which does not look much like an intention of evacuating the town. The shells do not seem to have sensibly damaged the richer part of the town and only one has gone through the roof of any building of the arsenal.

While I was walking with Vico in the vineyard near the well, Lord Raglan came up & said that Gordon had been with Canrobert when the death of Bizot the Chief Engineer was announced to him. He had been shot in the advanced trenches where our rt. & Fr. left join near middle ravine. The ball entered at his ear & went through the head coming out at cheek. Dined with L^d. Raglan. Vico came in & said that Bizot was only wounded & not necessarily mortally.

Thursday Ap^l. 12th. –

4th. day of bombardment. It seemed to me that the French fire was really overpowering the Russian front line. The four guns of our advanced battery which were got into position last night have been very useful agst. the Upper garden battery, which has annoyed us much. The French have been keeping up so heavy a fire agst. the Enemy and their fire has been so backed up by Chapmans Bat^y. that I think they really mean to make a lodgment in the Bastion du Mât. I hope they won't be forestalled by the Russians making an attack on their Inkerman batteries & using the store of gabions I saw yesterday to lodge themselves firmly on our rt. This w^d. be a contre coup with a vengeance.

Rather stormy & showery at night & very dark. 100 mules sent down to carry shot & powder into the trenches.

Mail came in, news from Vienna rather unfavourable. The Consideration of the 3rd. condition postponed.

Today on the parapet of the Flagstaff Battery a Russian officer stood up facing the French fire walking over the embrasures & gesticulating to his men and to the French. This looks as if they require more than ordinary encouragement.

Friday

Walked out to the front. Very heavy fire on the six gun battery in advance of left attack. They had a sergeant of artill^y. and two men killed and 7 more wounded two of the guns disabled & the parapets & traverses were very much knocked about. I could not observe much difference in the fire on either side. The nearest firing was on French right (old attack) and our left (Chapmans) I therefore expected that the Fr. intended to attack at night. They were attacked three times last night apparently only to hinder them working at their sap. And it had the effect desired to a great extent as the Fr. only seemed to have made a few yards.

I rode up again in the afternoon to the Maison d'Eau.[53] It was singularly clear. Sir G Brown was there, he had I think come to see the destroyed or rather silenced battery – There are enough guns apparently in the arsenal to arm all the batteries once again. The Russ[ns]. opened two new batt[s]. in the town today. It appears to me that they are making a sort of citadel after Fergusons plan[54] in the centre of the town, that is one tier of guns over another. The round tower & Mamélon were both firing. We then rode to see the camp of the 10,000 Turks of Omar Pashas army who have camped overlooking the valley of Balaclava in rear of Turkish old camp & along the line towards Vynois camp. They are fine looking men with a very different air & gait from the poor dejected animals who were here in the winter. They marched by to the most detestable music. In the Evening at 10 o'clock hearing that the gun boats were to shell the town I went with Burghersh & Maxse to the Maison d'Eau & got up there just as the French were repelling an attack on their sap. There was a heavy fire on both sides from mortars cohorns & guns, & the musquetry was loud & frequent sometimes almost like platoon firing. Our own guns were almost silent – So that they have not carried out the entrenching work which they started, we fire at night to prevent the repair of the enemy's works. The fact is our own are so much damaged that we are obliged to cease firing to get our own embrasures fit for the next days work. It was all over by eleven & we came back.

Saturday 14th.

Went down to Balaclava, heavy sea fogs coming over in rain. Saw Sir C. Campbell. He has got a batt[n]. of a reg[t]. of Turks of the rediff or militia. Met Omar Pasha on my way coming to a Council of War at Lord R's. Col Dan Lysons says they expected this morning they were to have attacked the place. He says every thing is ready. There are 200 tents here at head quarters which were to have held the 39th. in case we had stormed the first day after the fire & the huts of that reg^t. had been wanted for hospitals.

There is to [be] a Gen. C^t. M^l. on Monday at 11 on a Scotch soldier P^{te}. Wilson 93rd. for desertion & attempting to go over to the enemy –

The Council lasted till dark so nothing will be done tonight probably. They say that Sir Geo. Brown went away looking well pleased & Gen. Jones looked in better spirits than he has since his pet battery was snuffed out so quickly. Chetwode says that this afternoon our batteries were firing 7 to 1. Estcourt says that Peel told him today that he had twice seen the gunners in the Redan when loading leave the rammer in the gun when it was fired off, which does not look like their usual coolness & sangfroid. Coupling this with the story of the officer gesticulating on the parapet it presents an appearance of discouragement in the men.

Tomorrow being Sunday I should hardly think we should choose that to make an assault. Sir C.C. does not seem to apprehend any attack he thinks all the works of the Russians are for defence & to prevent our making a move across the Tchernaia. He says all the projecting cliffs are having batteries formed on them & all the slopes strengthened with entrenchments. The way down to the Tchernaia by Tchorgoun is also cut off by earthworks. The appearance of this large body of Turks marching in & camping in full sight of them must make them apprehensive of an attack. I wish they would take up the line of hills from Bosquets Telegraph overlooking the Tchernaia to Traktir & fortify them and occupy Kamara, ~~extending~~ removing the camp of the 93rd. & Vynoi's to the low hills taken from the Turks the day of Balaklava. It w^d. make it very difficult then for them to look into our Camp & there w^d. be no fear of Balaklava being taken by a Coup de Main. They c^d. easily & unperceived be reinforced behind the low screen of hills nearest to Balaklava, and be a good offensive position in case of a move.

The Medals for distinguished Service in the Field for the men have arrived.

Sunday. Ap[l]. 15.
Fine weather again.

Vico tells me that the French near the Central Bastion have advanced 80 metres, that they have taken all the rifle pits and that their men now can keep up a fire of rifles from the open embrasures. The plan they propose is to open a battery of 8 guns agst. the Mamélon & overwhelm it, fire & then take possession of it.

Lord R. gave me report of San[y]. Com[rs]. on Balaclava to answer. Wrote one requiring them to send in estimate as they have only now found out that they have not power to procure men & materials for their works as they said they had. He read it & said it would do perfectly.

Sent Mem[m] for Adj[t]. Gen[l]. about the Croatians who are to be tried at Constan[le].

The French were to have blown up a long mine leading to the Flag staff battery which was to be converted into a communication for a lodgment. Lord Raglan & all the world was informed of the time & notice sent to every one not to be alarmed at the noise, after waiting till dark I came home. It eventually exploded partially but not so as to enable the Fr. to get all the use of it they intended, as the Russ[ns]. made a very sharp attack on them between 8 & 9 PM they did nothing but repulse them. The firing was as heavy & continuous as any I ever heard. There was an attack also made on our lines & the French at Inkerman, but on us it was very slight & only 3 men were wounded.

The weather continues mild & very pleasant.

The 10th Hussars landed.

Monday, April 16th.
Went to Balaclava to a General C[t]. M[l]. on a man of 93rd. who was caught deserting to the enemy. He was found guilty & sentenced to 6 years Penal Servitude. The Turks under Omar Pasha seem to have taken up the whole ground of ~~Omar P~~ Espinasse's Division & defend both sides of the road as it comes up to the plateau from Vynoi's camp to head Quarters.

M[c]Murdo shewed me a despatch from L[d]. Panmure asking him to see & report upon the fitness of Sinope for a camp for a large army of reserves. This despatch was founded on a letter from Major McDonald late of 42rd.

He also shewed me a letter from L^d. Ellenborough who said that he thought judging from L^d. Panmure's countenance when he mentioned the subject, that he meant to recall Filder.

Vico says the remaining part of the extension is to be completed tonight & some fighting is expected.

Stoppard says tomorrow at 1 PM there is to be a General assault, I doubt the fact very much. If it is to be on the whole town I think it will fail to do so much, but they may gain a part at a great cost of human life. I believe the Russ^{ns}. will fight to the last.

Today they blew up the magazine in N°. 8 Battery, (the advanced batt^y. in right attack) killing one & wounding 9 men. I walked up to the front at 7 PM, but there was not much going on, not more than usual. Canrobert came to have another consultation – Gen Brown was there.

The French calculate the Russian loss in their attack on their lines on Sunday night at 6 or 700.

My Polish Servant Yan has volunteered into Zamoiskis polish legion & is gone.

Tuesday. Ap^l. 17.

The French did not complete their communication but occupy a part & guard it. They are still 60 yards from the Flag staff battery. They have made an advance of 140 yds towards the Quarantine. It appears that the number of shells per gun are reduced to 30 per diem. Which looks like the beginning of the end of the bombardment. I think it will be agreed to be a failure, and that further active measures will be postponed till there is an investing army. Lord R. said as I had the trouble of writing I might as well have the trouble of keeping the papers of Sanitary Com^n. Saw Sir J McNeil about establishing bakeries. Mr Beatty wrote to me offering to ~~establish~~ build bakeries & L^d. R. ordered it to be submitted to Mr Filder, which I told him I considered signing its death warrant. Sir J McNeil said he had had great difficulty in getting him to use Sinope & Samsoun as places for procuring cattle &c. He made the consul Mr Gruiciardini write a[n] offer for

3 Per Cent profit, to furnish any quantity of cattle &c. Mr Filder having the fear of Sir John & the Court of Enquiry before him, accepted & then came & announced to Sir J. what he had done. Filder is now contracting for bread from Constantinople, but it requires a mallet & chisel to eat it.

The deserter who came in today was employed in the hospital & being beaten by the doctor ran away. He says there are no doctors to attend to the sick & wounded, that as many as possible are sent away to Bagtich Serai.

Beatty is to floor my hut for me.

The explosion of the magazine in N°. 8 Batt^y. did not stop its firing, as there remain two magazines which are suff^t.

Wednesday Ap^l. 18th.

This is the last day of bad weather according to the Tartars. It has every appearance of settled fine weather, and has come in with the new moon. The Tartars have such fixed times for the weather that generally the seasons must be very regular. Lord R. has given an order that all the correspondence with the Sanitary Com^n. shall be conducted by me. When Lord Raglan heard that Gen Forey was going away & had called, he was going to call on him, but thinking that after all the lying calumnies which had been circulated[55] he w^d. prefer a letter, he wrote him a most kind & courteous farewell. Gen Forey was much struck with this & was speaking very warmly about it to Gen Canrobert while Vico was there. Canrobert said Qu'il est un brave homme Milord! Vico repeated this to L^d. Raglan who was much pleased.

Today there came a foolish letter from the San^y. Commiss^rs. ordering some offal to be buried near the French Hospital. Lord R. said write an answer to them and tell them I am not scavenger to the French Army.

The mail has not arrived yet 10 PM – My papers came in just as I had written these words.

The Fr. are said to have been very successful last night in completing their communicatn. & are very near the Flag staff battery. There was very sharp firing of musquetry on the spot and a tremendous explosion took place either in the Quarantine or

Flag Staff battery & after the explosion several shells burst, so no doubt a magazine was blown up. My roof rattled again and I thought the windows would have blown out.

Today some 800 Russians shewed & some came onto the plain & fired off their carbines, but at what object no one c^d. tell. The Fr. soldiers at Bosquet's look out saw two Batt^ns. of infantry in the rear of Canroberts hill. At two o'clock this morning Bosquet sent to Vynoi's who sent on to Sir C Campbell to say that there was movement heard in their front & that the sound of carriages & of the passage [?] of soldiers was heard. The Guards & all the camp had orders to stand to arms at 4 AM, but when daylight came nothing was to be seen.

Rode with Genl Estcourt round the Division, he says they are going to diminish [?] the number of men on working pties and that the Turks are going to help them.

Yesterday a gun went off in the French Engineers Park without any apparent reason, it had been damaged & brought out of the batteries when loaded with shell. It did no harm.

The Fr. were firing today from their advanced battery called the Cavalier.

Thursday Ap^l. 19th.

I was awoken this morning at half past two by heavy firing & got up & dressed & went out. The sentry said it began by the ship coming in & "pitching the shells into them by basket fulls". I could see the shells coming into the town from the sea. The attack to judge by the musquetry was from the Quarantine battery to the Flag staff, and was very heavy. It lasted till three and then ceased. There was one discharge as if a platoon on our r^t. front and then it was quiet. The Turks had fired one gun from Omar Pasha's hill and the French cavalry were getting ready to move. The "Advance" had sounded twice to the French infantry during the sortie.

When I went out to walk before breakfast I found that all the Head Quarter Staff were out on horseback and that the reconnaissance had actually come off. The orders to Col. Parlby of 10th. Hussars were only sent after 10 PM yesterday, and it was kept so quiet that the A.D.C.s knew nothing about it till after dinner I soon got breakfast & started with Blane we saw the Turkish infantry at Kamara & soon reached them. There was a troop of English & of French H^e. artillery. The relics of our Heavy Cavalry Scots Greys & Dragoons and the 10th. Hussars were thrown out in skirmishing order. The Cossacks were on the brown rocky hill above Tchorgoun looking down on us. Hardly a Russian was to be seen on a spur of the hill across the Tchorgoun valley & North of the Tchernaia were four field pieces, but they did not fire. We rode to the different parts & had good views of the country & the Baidar road running through the deep valley leading South. The Turkish infantry occupied a height above Kamara & Omar Pasha went there to have a view. He then came to the front and a battalion of his chasseurs was ordered to advance & clear the Cossacks. To help them the French rocket troop came forward & threw some rockets on to the hill & behind the breastwork driving the Cossacks away. The Chasseurs mounted in very good style but found no enemy and then Lord R. & Omar Pasha & all the staff went up after them. When near the top we heard a smart discharge of musquetry. It appeared that a number of officers had gallopped [*sic*] on ahead into the village for fun & plunder and the Russians fired a volley which made them scamper off. Last time the troops came to this hill they were so late with both shot & shell, this time they were more courteous. There were not 500 Russ^{ns}. to be seen any where. I think they must be intending to make another attack on Eupatoria. We found the work they had made very slight indeed. There are the remains of old earthworks on the hill below Kamara Church & between it & the brown bare hill.

The country to the East & South is wonderfully tangled and intricate. It was very picturesque covered with young wood just becoming green. There was a great variety and abundance of flowers. The single peony a dark blood red, primrose buttercup &c &c.

It was all over at 12.15 and the party on the return. The 10th. marched past Omar Pasha & Lord R. in single file that the horses might be seen. They were splendid thoroughbred Arab horses, each one like a racer, and the men fine soldier like fellows but rather heavy for the style of horse. The horses are valued at 50£ each. It appears that the French were attacked three times last night & lost 100 men killed & wounded. The Valorous & Retribution[56] went in last night & threw about 150 shells into the part of the town where the Russ[n]. reserves are kept. The Retribution was struck twice. One shell bursting between the masts.

The morning early was fine & warm by noon the wind was strong & cold from ENE.

Estcourt says L[d]. Stratford is coming tomorrow. He tells me he never sees Lord R. now, as he transacts all his business with Gen. Simpson.

Friday April 20th
Cold ENE 48° at 8AM

Last night there was an attack made on the pits in advance of the rt attack by the 77th. The leading men crept on all fours out of the trench until they were seen & a volley fired at them when they jumped up & ran in with the bayonet. The Russians bolted & three men were taken prisoners one of them a cadet. One small pit the furthest was so much exposed to the fire of grape that it was abandoned. The others were held & the men worked vigorously until 1 AM. Poor young Lempriere was killed in the first attack & Col Egerton who was commanding, one of the finest men & the best regimental officer in the service picked him up in his arms & carried him out of the pit into the trench but he was dead. Egerton received a contusion in the groin & felt very faint when in the trench & sat down. The faintness went off & he got up right again. At one o'clock the Russ[ns]. came out in great force & fired upon the men in the pit & the working pty they were obliged to abandon the furthest pit as it was quite open to their fire. The Russ[n]. reserves came up to attack support was sent for but so heavy was the fire that 56 men were killed & wounded & poor Egerton was shot through the head & fell dead. The communication was however completed. One of the first men into the pit was the drummer of 77th. He attacked the bugler with his sword & took him prisoner. 7 dead Russ[ns]. were seen lying on the ground at daylight. Two Engineer officers were wounded

By daylight our men were well covered in. The two admirals Lyons & Stewart Capt. Drummond, Talbot & Lord Clarence Paget were at lunch. It was a singularly clear day. I could see the French close to the flagstaff battery apparently. Two men were so close that they appeared to be over a gun which the Russians were firing. The Russ[ns]. are very busy still fortifying the plateau & the ways leading up to it from the Tchernaia. The Russians fired very little today & we not much more. The Fr. however kept up a heavy fire on some points in their front particularly the Central Bastion. I could see the Russ[ns]. quietly at work on the citadel à la Ferguson[57] which they are making in the town round the flagstaff of the Governors house. It will be a formidable work to destroy or storm. The 48th. 860 men & 2nd. Bat[n]. Royals 650 & a draft of 120 convalescents arrived today. The mail came in at 10.30, but Lord R's dispatches had not come in at 11 PM. Dined at Lord R – Mr Calvert Consul at Gallipoli & farmer of the Troad[58] was there.

The wind has dropped & there is heavy firing on rt & at the French attack.

Saturday April 21st.

Gen Simpson called early & gave me papers stating death of D[r]. Gavin of the Sanitary Commission. He was killed by the accidental discharge of a pistol in the hands of his brother M[r]. W[m]. Gavin Veterinary Surgeon of 17th. Lancers, attached to Land Transport Corps. Lord R. wished to know what steps sh[d]. be taken. I went down to Balaclava as Pres[t]. with D[r]. Sutherland San[y]. Com[r]. & D[r]. Anderson P.M.O. Balaclava as members. We received satisfactory evidence & found that it was accidental & no blame c[d]. attach to the brother. Came up & wrote dispatches to Lord Panmure for L[d]. Raglan inclosing copy of finding of Court.

Last night we took & destroyed the only remaining rifle pit in our front. The Russ[ns]. fired heavily on the working party & killed & wounded 17 men.

It appears that the night before when we took the pits the Russians were frightened & left them without fighting. That when they returned in heavy numbers they brought out field pieces &

fired grape at a short range and this was when their men were in advance & must have been hit by the shot.

The firing in front was dull & languid, ours is only continued to keep the Fr. in countenance. They are to continue to sap! We have sent to Malta for another siege train & 500 rounds a gun. L^t. Col. Dickson called. He says that when the magazine in N°. 8 exploded by falling of a 13 inch shell on it, two men were killed & 7 wounded only though there were 7 men at each of 5 guns. All the guns but one were smothered with earth, and before the earth had done falling or the smoke cleared away Capt. Dickson [*sic* – actually Dixon] had fired shell upon the Redan from this gun & continued to do so until he arrived from Camp. Seven men in the trench in front of the battery were wounded by falling earth & wood. Cap^n. Peel offered Col. Dickson 20 men to go and clear the battery but L^t. [blank space – not identified] who had lately joined came out & said all the men must be withdrawn, so Col. D. did not take the sailors but went in himself & got the men to clear the platform of earth. Some of the men had to be dug out of the earth but were not hurt. The one gun continued to fire. At night all was cleared. Col. D. brought to Lord Raglans notice the good conduct of Capt. Dickson. Some days after Lord R. coming out of the trenches & told Col. D. that another shell had fallen on the place where the magazine had stood. After the first explosion the floor of the magazine had remained smooth & hard, the force being upwards leaving a large crater of earth. 18 cwts of powder had blown up.

Sunday

Lord Raglans despatches have not yet been found, though we received our mail in due course. The French blew up a mine last night near the flagstaff battery, and have lodged themselves nearer to the works. There was comparatively little firing today, & hardly any on our side. The Russ^{ns}. are making a new battery behind the redoubt blanche nearest to the Russians. They were openly working while I was looking on. I think they are making a mine under the present advance of the French as I saw a constant stream of men coming out of the ditch in front of the flagstaff battery carrying each a sandbag on his back. Had a conversation with

Lord Raglan about Mr Uptons case,[59] he wishes the court to express an opinion. It is thought very strange that Lord Stratford & the Caradoc have not arrived. Some days ago a guard of honour was sent. There is still a cool northerly wind, but I am glad of it as I fear the hot sun.

While I was walking with Lord R. I noticed that the Turks had struck their tents & Gen Simpson asked if they were going to Eupatoria he said some of them were. If all go it would look very much as if the idea of an assault had been given up and a strong reserve no longer needed.

I should be glad to hear that something towards an investment was to be attempted.

Monday April 23rd.

Only 10,000 Turks have left for Eupatoria. There was a great meeting of Engineers and Artillery men at Gen[l]. Jones at 8 AM. There has been a return of scaling ladders called for – As none have been used the number ought to have been known. Tom Taylors brother called for an attested copy of the finding of the court. He is Sec[y]. to the Com[n]. He did not know that I had anything to do with it, and spoke very highly of the way in which they had always been treated.

Very late council of war at Lord Raglans.

The other night when the single rifle pit had to be taken the night after Egerton was killed, Walker an old subaltern called for volunteers drew his sword & jumped into the rifle pit. They found only two dead bodies, but every one thought it was full of the enemy – it had been full of them all day.

The flag of truce today lasted half an hour the Russians gave us up our dead body & we gave them four, the rest they took in. The day after Egertons death a Russ[n]. was seen lying from the left attack lying behind a small heap of stones from which apparently he had been afraid to run. He could not be seen from the right attack & he had to lie all day without moving hand or foot and round him were six corpses, some close to him. At night he got away. Sacry Gabriel a refugee Pole calling himself a Hungarian has come to me as servant.

Tuesday April 24th.

We were all expecting a reconnaissance at 3 AM. The Highlanders were cooking all night. Vynoi's division had their coffee &c by 3½ AM & were all ready when a counter order came & they turned in. The reason given today is that Gen Canrobert is too much engaged in front. He is too jealous of Bosquet to allow him to lead. There were to have been 10,000 Fr. Inf[y]. all their cavalry & the Highlanders were to have advanced to protect their rt. flank. What they expected to do I don't know.

Rode down & saw Sir C. Campbell he is always very kind to me. He was complaining of the way in which a mob of idlers were allowed to accompany the expedition the other day. He said Omar Pasha who had come out to see the country before him, was unable to get through the group to the front of the hill over Tchorgoun. He said when I go out with my three regts I will allow no one not even Romaine, yes perhaps I may allow Romaine to go.

Went up to Camerons quarters with Sterling to hear Uptons case, by Gen Order dated 21 Ap[l].

Cameron was speaking of the 88th. He said he has been with them in camps & stations now for nearly 30 years & the mutual wish of the regts was that they might be neighbours in fights. The first thing we saw when we came up the hill at Alma was the 88 coming pouring down the hill as hard as they could run.[60]

At Inkerman they did not distinguish themselves, so much as other regts.

There is another council of War tonight.

Lyons Stewart Bruat, Canrobert at Lord Raglans I was at the door when they came Canrobert said he was so fatigued he c[d]. hardly walk up the steps. he had been walking through the Fr. trenches. He said that Batt[y]. N[o]. 40 – N[o]. 40 is ready & the guns will be mounted there tonight. I went to the front & met Adye there who said that every thing was going on well that the French were working at the place as if it was a regularly fortified place & that they are very near & in a few days must be in the flag staff battery. This battery today was only held by musquetry. I saw one man going slowly down the slope into the ditch to the place where I think they have made a mine.

There is no doubt that it was intended to storm the other afternoon. We have now three new batteries nearly completed & the Fr. have new batteries to fire on the Russ[n]. second line. The Governors house battery was firing today on us. But the round tower redan & mamélon were almost silent. The Fr. were busy shelling some new works the Russ[ns]. are putting up behind the nearest of the redoubtes blanches.

The Electric Telegraph is finished from the Monastery[61] to Vienna by Bucharest.

1500 men go down to the trenches of our side every night. At 8 PM a very heavy musketry fire began, no doubt to hinder the French sap, and it has been kept up till now 10.30.

A Russ[n]. prisoner said to Calvert that in the three first days they buried 2000 men, I cant quite believe this.

He said to test [?] the prisoner "We shall take the town" to which the Russ[n]. answered "Then where is God."

Heard again from Denison.

Wednesday Ap[l]. 25

The night was comparatively quiet. The Engineers had a great talk with Lord Raglan. Adm[s]. Lyons & Stewart slept here and no doubt plans were settled for the day of assault as to what part the ships were to take. Gen Neil was there.

Attended Board at Sterlings hut Col. Cannon there and the greater part of the time Sir C. Campbell came & sat there. Between the intervals of the exam[n]. of the witnesses he received his visitors & amused us much by his extreme vivacity & humour.

He told a story of Col. Webber Smith, who was at Waterloo shut out of a square of infantry & pursued around three sides of it by a Fr. Cavalry officer. Smith calling out for somebody to shoot the French man, he only saved himself by the fleetness of his horse & its being very handy in turning. The 23rd. had been sent for in a great hurry to the rt. of Hougoumont to stop the attacks of Fr. cavalry there. They were brought up in great haste through the deep corn & were close on the dragoon regt. before either party was aware of the others approach. The 23rd. fired a volley & formed square instantly the dragoons turned off & three of the officers pursued Smith round the square while the men were loading & when he saw it was time, rode off saying to his dragoons that it was a reg^t. of recruits. But when the reg^t. came to attack the 23rd. soon after they fell like partridges in a stubble field & c^d. make no impression on them.

Rode up with McMurdo, he says three ships have been despatched with huts from England, one of which is arrived but no use can be made of them because there are parts of each hut in each ship!

He received a few days ago harness for 30 mules, & on turning it out of the casks he found it all useless as there were no traces or back bands to any one of them!

A Telegraphic message in numeral cypher was sent to England by Vienna from the Monastery it w^d. go in about 8 hours to Vienna!

Dined with L^d. Raglan. He told me an anecdote of the Duke[62] who on arriving at Elvas occupied a large building, with a long passage and his room at the end. He had just reached his room door when the Commandant came out & spoke to him & said that he had lost all his horses & effects & was beggared. The Duke said that he was unable to do anything for him. The Commandant said then it only remains for me "bruler la cervelle." The Duke made a low grave bow, said Je suis faché & turned into his room. – The Com^t. did not blow out his brains.

I observed that the French were making a sort of small fascine about 2½ to 3 feet long which it w^d. be easy to make a soldier carry in addition to his firelock &c.

Vico says they are making bags stuffed with straw for the same purpose namely to fill up a ditch.

When McMurdo heard our men were to do the same he offered a quantity of wool he has to stuff packsaddles, as it c^d. not be set on fire by a hand grenade as the straw c^d. He had a sudden order for all the gabions in store to be sent up to the rt. attack this evening.

Thursday Ap^l. 26.

Mail came in. Went down to Sir C. Campbell again on Uptons case. Found Sir C. blacking his leather trousers with ink. Lord & Lady

Stratford & Lady G. Paget arrived in the Caradoc. There was heavy musquetry fire as usual in French left attack. They say that the soldiers go down with 2 or 300 rounds & keep up a rolling fire all night, but under cover of this as it were, the Russians make new rifle pits & improve the old ones. This they have done in front of the central bastion, and as often as the French have ventured to take them away the Russians have retaken them at the point of the bayonet. They are certainly steadier at a hand to hand fight than the French. We had a splendid review today of the army under Bosquet amounting to about 30,000 men. They were in fine order, but I fear the enthusiasm has been a good deal worked out of the soldiers who have passed the winter here. The cry of Vive l'Empereur was much louder from the newly arrived regts. The review of each Division ended with a speech from Gen. Canrobert. He told them that 65,000 Frenchmen were coming, that they were here to take Sebastopol, that if they c^d. not get in at the door they must go in at the window that in 15 days they w^d. be in the town &c.

Friday April 27th.
Gen. Airey sent for me to meet Alison & settle about getting 1000 more Croatian labourers I told him that M^r. Calvert c^d. get any number of men at 1^s. a day, and that I thought the wages of the men we now have should be lowered.

Went to review of the division under Pelissier, he has not the appearance of a wholesale roaster of men.[63] He wore the rose coloured riband of Grand Cross of order of Legion of honour. The Miss Cannings were there.

The appearance of the regts. of the Imperial guard.

The grenadiers chasseurs voltiguers & Zouaves were admirable. As they marched by Canrobert said to Lord R. "Voilà des masses de braves, concentrés pour résister à l'ambition d'un homme."[64] As L^d. R. said afterward, as if he thought he c^d. humbug me as he does his own countrymen. The French are still busy making new advanced batteries, but still there is the old difficulty, they must take the bastion du mât because it is mined, and until that is taken & a lodgment effected nothing more can be done on our side, as the Garden batteries w^d. fall then & we c^d. advance –

Thursday. May 1ˢᵗ.

A real May day.

Attended General C^t. M^l. on John Grame of 19ᵗʰ. for shooting his comrade.

Went out to the front of 3ʳᵈ. Div^n. & to Maison d'Eau the Russians have now their ambuscade in front of flank of Flag staff battery. The French yesterday sprang two mines to form entonnoirs & are within 65 yards of the outwork in front of the Central bastion.

An expedition is preparing for Kertsch, they say Gen. Brown is to take the Highland Brigade. It seems a strange & rather unfair arrangement. I suppose Sir C.C. cannot be spared from Balaclava or Gen Brown as 2ⁿᵈ. in Command has a right to the command of a separate expedition. He will make a mess of it – he has not a generals head on his shoulders as Sir C.C. has.

Dined with General Simpson. Lord Stratford returned early this morning from Eupatoria.

Omar Pasha showed him over the fortifications which are said to be very strong. They talk of joining the lake & the $fortificat^{ns}$. the whole length of the 4000 yds. There are 117 guns according to Adm^l. Stewart [see Figure 9].

They report a strong body of cavalry in front but only 7 or 8000 infantry at some distance. Omar Pasha has 4000 cavalry.

There seems to be no doubt that the Conference[65] has broken up without coming to any conclusion except, I suppose, that we asked such terms as we could insist upon only if our enemy was beaten, whereas he is not only not beaten, but not likely to be, as Austria will not make war on Russia.

The ships are to go to Kertsch & establish themselves there they take 2700 English provisions for 14 days, 800 mules, 50 sabres.

At half past nine began a tremendous fire on left of French, the musquetry as heavy as I have ever heard in their front – There is a perpetual stream of shells from either side, everything perfectly quiet on our side. At half past twelve it is still going on.

Figure 9. Plan of fortifications at Eupatoria (from journal dated 1 May 1855).

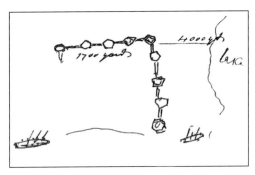

2 May.

At half past one McMurdo came in being still busy about shipping medical stores & arranging with Dr. Hall for their carriage.

L^d. Stratford is still out in the front.

The report is that the French have made an attack on the outwork in front of the Central bastion and hold it.

Cambridge University Library: Add. 9554/4

28

Romaine to C. J. Selwyn

[Holograph. The last sheet is folded and torn. Some words are lost and have been inferred. They are shown in square brackets.]

May 2nd 1855

My dear Selwyn

You don't deserve a line for I have not heard from you so long that I have forgotten the look of yr hand writing –

The news of the final breaking up of the conferences which I suppose has reached Head Q^{rs} by the submarine Electric Telegraph from Vienna seems to have revived our great nation –

Last night at 9.30 the French made a dash at an advanced parallel of the Russ^{ns} in front of the Central Bastion took it, and in it 8 small mortars called cohornes, they bayonetted a great number of the enemy in the trench. They then set to work & joined the work to theirs making a fourth parallel of it.

The Russ^{ns} sent out three battalions to retake it but they were driven back with loss – the most tremendous fire was kept up from

9.30 P.M. till 2. AM – 2^d May – It was bright moonlight like day – The French behaved very pluckily & are in great spirits.

We are now doing a thing which is putting me in a fever – There is an expedition planned & sails tonight for Kertsch (see map) straits of sea of Azof. You will hardly believe they send Sir G. Brown to command, and give him the Highland Brigade taking it away from Sir C. Campbell who has commanded it since he left England – The Highlanders worship him & w^d have fought twice as well under him as under anyone else.

Brown is just such another blunder headed fellow as Gough.[66] If he meets a battery he will put his splendid highland regts at it as a fool w^d try to break a cob-nut with a gold watch –

He commands French & all – They have given him their worst men, the marine infantry chiefly, who as Brown told me this afternoon, always run away – They are the fellows who left the Zouaves in the lurch in the attack on the Volkynia redoubt – They will make this a reason for asking to command our army some time by. He has got a good Engineer officer with him, Gordon, I hope he may be able to give him good advice. If Gordon had commanded in chief at the siege, we sh^d have been in Sebastopol by the end of October last.

Now in the 8th month of the siege we are finding out that our batteries might have been made some 1000 yards nearer than they were – The mail which sh^d have been here on Monday has not yet come (Wednesday 10. P.M.). I am expecting any minute to hear a fresh attack begin. The moon is as bright & clear as a May moon can be. I have a pony ready to gallop off to the Maison d'Eau – I don't think the French will attack as they have plenty to do strengthening their parallel – There is only the usual constant quantity of firing but the air is in that peculiar state that is not uncommon here, every shot echoing agst the houses here & the heavier guns making the ground shake & the roof & windows rattle again. I shall leave off here as the mail won't go till Saturday.

Would you like to have my Diary of last year to read. Mind it will cost you a fortune for postage. Its very dull & very hard to decypher, let me know –

I am keeping a much more copious one this year in a larger book & better written. When it is full I will send it you & I think it will be interesting at all events parts of it, as it is a full chronicle of the most interesting days – The days on which nothing happens I merely make a short entry in the diary. The Army has unanimously given me the credit of the article in the Quarterly (Campaign in the Crimea) and they will not believe my denial & assertion that it is Layards. So I suppose I have most unconsciously gained a literary character.

Saturday May 5th. I was up late last night writing for my masters and [have been?] at it again this [morning early so?] I shan't write any here to yours.

There is no news – The expedition is gone.

Y^{rs} ever

W. G. Romaine

Cambridge University Library: Add. 7633: 5/23

29
Journal for 2 to 15 May 1855

[Holograph]

Wednesday May 2nd.

Therm. 62°

The French have taken 8 cohorns and are lodged in the outwork which they carried with the bayonet. Three Russ^n. batt^{ns}. came down to assault them but were driven back and the French are now busy completing the communication. It was a preconcerted attack of the French they sent down 13 batt^{ns}. but gave no notice to L^d. Raglan, & no doubt w^d. have called it a sortie of the Russ^{ns}. if it had failed.

The French seem to have behaved very well. Vico relates a story of two French soldiers carrying off a Russ^n. officer wounded, one going on his hands having the Russian on his back & the comrade of the Frenchman driving him like a wheelbarrow [see Figure 10] so fashion. The fire was so heavy in front of the trenches that no one c^d. stand up without great danger but they brought him off.

Figure 10. French soldiers bringing in a wounded Russian (from journal dated 2 May 1855).

The warm weather is beginning again.

Mr. Brodin attaché to Lord Stratford was taken prisoner of the French having wandered down beyond the Maison d'Eau.

There is still a heavy cannonade going on, but scarcely heard here, whereas last night every musquet shot c^d. be heard.

There was a good deal of firing on left of French & they were hard at work deepening their parallel & keeping up a musquetry fire on Russ^{ns}. in the Central Bastion. Rode from 3rd. Div^n. to look out in front of 3 mortar battery. They are moving the beds of the mortars to the left of 21 gun battery. Saw seven Russ^n. batts. coming from Bagshash Serai, they did not cross the bay but went into the Camp above the long row of houses, (the lower camp). So I suppose they are only the exchange batts. for those which have been working in the town.

3.30 P.M. While looking out, to right, 2000 Russ^{ns}. rushed out of the Central bastion or thereabouts & went at the works they lost last night. The French met them with a heavy fire of musquetry & then their cannon opened, they were quickly repulsed & then the Russ^n. cannon opened & there was a tremendous cannonade, in a short time nothing c^d. be seen for the smoke. Galloped to the 3rd. Div^n. & down to rear of Chapmans battery. Found smoke very thick & returned when I met Gen Eyres halfway, he s^d. he was Genl. of the day & asked me if there was any attack on us. I s^d. no & he asked me to ride back with him which I did, until he descended the last ravine to go into the battery where I left him, returned to French. When the smoke cleared, the French were plainly seen in their parallel firing away. The French loss last night is said to have been 20 to 30 killed & 200 wounded.

On my return had a talk with Genl. Brown He commands, Gen D'Autemarre is Gen of Div. Gen S^t. Paul [*sic* – St Pol] commands one brigade & Gen [blank space[67]] the other.

Gen Brown said they had given him the worst troops, a number of infantry of the marine who always run away. He says D'Autemarre is a great chasseur.

There is some evil fate about us to appoint a blockhead like Brown when we have a man like Sir C.C. The men w^d. have fought as well again under Sir C^n. I hear they are much disgusted at being commanded by Sir G. & no wonder as it is notorious that he threw his division headlong at the enemy at Alma & never thought of deploying till sent to by Gen Airey & then did not know how his right were placed or how much room they wanted to deploy (ex relatione Col Dan Lysons 23rd.)

Sunday. May 6th.

There was a smart sortie on our lines last night and we lost two officers & 17 men killed & wounded and three men taken prisoner. One of the officers was wounded by jumping off the parapet & falling onto the bayonets of his men in the trench. The other was wounded posting sentries. The enemy appears as usual to have succeeded in getting into the advanced trench.

Most unwelcome news arrived that the expedition has returned without having accomplished or even tried any thing.

There has been blundering & great weakness on the part of Genl. Canrobert. It appears that some time ago the expedition was planned & then he said at the last that he c^d. not spare the men. The idea was given up & it was so signified to Paris. When the plan was again taken in hand at the urgent desire of all the Admirals no notice was sent that it was to sail, until the day before. A Telegraphic message from Paris must have crossed on the way, directing Gen. Canrobert to send all his available ships to Constan^{le}. to bring troops to the Crimea. This order was no doubt given in ignorance of the sailing of the squadron, but he thought it necessary to send a recall. It reached the expedition at the rendezvous when all was arranged for the embarcation.

It turned out too that Gen. C. had not sent all the troops he had engaged to supply, 1500 men & a battery of artillery being left behind & no notice given till they arrived at the rendezvous. Instead of three batt^{ns}. of Zouaves promised. Two regts. of Marine infantry were sent and a batt^n. of Zouaves only numbering 480 men instead of 800.

The [the entry ends abruptly here.]

Monday May 7th.

Calvert who went with the expedition says that the anger & indignation of the French was as great as that of our commanders. Lyons was furious he s^d. C. was a chicken hearted ———.

The Fr. Captain of the Fulton a very fine fellow much liked by every body, came on board & said, Will you take me into your service will you give me a ship, I will have no more to do with the Fr. Marine &c &c. Every one seems to have felt confident of success. Comd^r. Spratt had been off the place, got capital soundings plans drawings, marks of range of enemies [*sic*] guns &c, the hills in the neighbourhood were actually in sight. If they had been successful & captured the guns the Sea of Azof w^d. have now been in our power. Every day now will make it more difficult. There are three strong gun boats in the Sea of Azoff, but we had 9 though not such solid vessels, but frigates drawing only 13 ft if such there are c^d. have entered.

It is a grievous disappointment & will be a grave shame & scandal to both armies. And after all the end is not answered, as the troops were not disembarked this afternoon & so nearly two days have been lost in which time the coup might have been made, if at all.

Went to Balaclava by L^d. R's. request to see M^r. Upton & try to arrange his affair by offering him 500 & a free passage to England for himself & family. I saw him & had a talk, telling him to think it over with his wife, he says he expects employment in his profession as C.E. from Peto Brassey & Co.[68] In the evening received letter, but I thought rather evasive & have written again to put the proposal on a footing so plain that there can be no dispute.

He looks to me like a man predestined to spend his life in dodging about an unwelcome visitor at the offices of great men – a small Baron de Both [?]. I have tried to save him from so melancholy a fate. I told him that if he reached England with a promise of employment and 500 £ in in his pocket, he might consider that he was well out of an unpleasant position. That if he did not get immediate employment it w^d. at all events secure him time to look out for it.

Thursday 10. May.

Slept at Sir C. Campbells, heard heavy musquetry fire in the night. Rained in the night & very heavily till 2 PM today. More of the Sardinians are arrived, but none can now be landed owing to the state of the ground. There seems to be much doubt about the coming of the Emperor.

Saw L^d. R. about C^t. of Enquiry into Capⁿ. Cox [Cocks?] conduct & the posting of the sentries, on report by Genl. Eyre. They acquitted him of all blame – Genl. Eyre chooses to take this as a condemnation of himself & has resigned. This is the 4th. time I think that he has had quarrels since he came out.

It appears that the men behaved very well in the sortie last night agst. our rt. attack. The advanced sentries saw or heard them one of them came in quietly gave the alarm & when they came, they were received with a volley & a cheer & fled. They tried this twice again, each time with smaller numbers & gave it up. I ventured to say to L^d. R. who read out the report – that I thought the sentries who had behaved so well sh^d. have some notice taken of their conduct & Gen. Simpson with whom I dined today says that it will be done tomorrow.

They report that the ground was covered with dead & that they send in a flag of truce to bury them today. We had only 13 men wounded, not one killed.

Friday 11th. May

Last night there was a very serious sortie principally on our right they came out & attacked in line with a reserve. Luckily the sentries were on the alert ran quietly in & gave the alarm & every body was ready & they were received with a volley & a cheer. They were so near that they must have suffered a great loss. They made a second attempt by coming in more to the right but with the same result and a third attempt with only 200 men was also repulsed. Today they sent in a flag to bury their dead we handed over 12 corpses to them. We had 13 wounded and three killed. It appears that after the men ran in some five of the enemy must have crawled up to the parapet on their hands & knees ready to jump on when the rest came up. Their bayonets were seen over the parapet and they were all ready for them when they came on. These five men actually got over the parapet & were all killed but not before one of them had killed an officer of the [blank space – actually the 68th, Captain Richard Lloyd Edwards] regt.

Omar Pasha came as I was with Ld. R. about Gen. Eyre's case & Capn. Cocks of 4th. Regt.

Dine with Genl. Simpson.

Saturday May 12th.

Still wet weather, cold fog & wind from S.E. Another attack last night which was repulsed in the usual way, but some men & an officer of 68th. killed.

There was a long conference from 1 till eight PM. Gen Della Marmora left at 6 & went to Balaclava, but Gen Canrobert stayed till eight.

Sunday. 13

Omar Pasha slept at Lord Raglans. There seems no hope of the Emperor coming. I suppose affairs are too grave in the rest [the entry ceases at this point.]

Tuesday. May. 15

Went down to breakfast with Sir C. Campbell – went to Crimean Army Fund & saw Power & Egerton. Col. Cameron came to Sterling's & we signed report on Mr Uptons case. Came up & found the mail had come in. About 6000 Turks left for Eupatoria. Omar Pasha has departed. Steele is better but looks as if he wd. have an attack of jaundice. Had a walk with him in the vineyard. He says the French are not attempting to advance now. Our armament is very strong, all heavy guns & nearly all new. Steele told me that a short time ago Canrobert wrote to Paris enumerating his forces & said I have 60,000 men and the English 20,000 <u>and they are worth 40,000</u>. A copy of this was sent to Lord Raglan from Paris. I gather from Steele that there will be great difficulty in making up force enough to invest the town & that he is of opinion that if it is invested there will be found 5 months provision, that if we gain a victory in the field, there will be a second army to fight before that time had elapsed & no sufficient reinforcements to come and that we should have another winter in cantonments perhaps in tents – That the French will have to live all their time within 50 yards of the place and we are now within 150 yards. The French say it w^d. perhaps cost 15,000 men to take the place by assault & that it is too hazardous.

When the French were recalled from the Kertsch expedition by Canrobert, Lord Raglan wrote to Genl. Brown to say that if he & Adm^l. Lyons thought they c^d. effect the object of the expedition without the French he had full authority to attempt it, and that he w^d. take all the responsibility of failure.

They had a consultation but the English ships contained many of them, French soldiers, their ships must have been sent back, there were 11,000 Russ^{ns}. and it was decided not to attempt it. The newly arrived French are camping close to the Imperial Guard in our rear here at H^d. Q^{rs}. Thank God the Cholera is diminishing yesterday 2 cases were reported in 3rd. Div^n.

A wounded Russ^n. prisoner who was taken in the sortie the other night said that when they were brought out they were told they were going to attack the French.

Trollope who was commanding in the Trenches the other night when there was a sortie, said our men were coolly firing over the parapet load^g. firing and joking as if it were the best sport in the world.

Cambridge University Library: Add. 9554/4

30
Romaine to C. J. Selwyn

[Holograph]

May 21st. 1855
Head Q^{rs}. Crimea

My dear Selwyn,
Your stingy pen has at last produced an epistle – Now for its answer – We so continually ask for more guns shot & shell but you

cant make & send them as fast as we can shoot them away – The last bombardment used up every shell in the stores at Malta – We are now ready for another start – Thank goodness Canrobert is gone to command his Division & Pelissier reigns in his stead – He is the man who roasted the Arabs in the Cave in the Kabyle.[69]

The first fruits of the change of dynasty is that the Kertch expedition sails tomorrow with 14000 troops, hardly enough I am afraid as 3000 of them are Turks. I fear Brown goes in command so that there is still every chance of a failure.

What can have possessed you people in England with an idea that we were going to abandon the siege – we don't want to do so & we could not if we would without taking the place or receiving permission to embark from the Russkis – Such a notion never entered any body's head out here & was a pure shave got up for your benefit at home. The Russkis have been wonderfully quiet lately –

You people at home are quite insane – you send us out hospital huts three ship loads, you so arrange that when one ship arrives, not a hut can be put up as a part of each hut is [in] each ship so if one had been burnt or lost the whole w^d have been useless.

You send out 30 crates of harness all useless because the traces & back straps have been forgotten.

You make a Major General of Turkish Contingent of the idlest and most inefficient Assistant Q^r Mr Genl [not identified by Romaine, but clearly Colonel Cunynghame] in the army (son in law of Ld Hardinge's) to make a vacancy for young Lt Col Hardinge (son to Ld Hardinge) as Ass^t Q^r Mr Genl of 1st Div^n. They have not reported him as such yet & perhaps in present state of mind of John Bull Ld Raglan will be allowed to keep the present man in viz Lawrence Hardwick[70] who is a capital officer –

The Sanitary Comm^{rs} are turning nasty on our hands. I think we shall have a blow up & a blue book very likely – There is I think no hole in our armour except that they have never been able to obtain the labour &c which they required – But the answer is that it is unattainable. We can hardly get any one to come here. The real fact is that Cholera has begun they are of no use & want to bolt.

The Railway has been wonderfully successful & seems now so much a matter of course that the days of the muddy roads seem as far distant as those before the flood.

I have just been giving a learned opinion on a poor fellow's will, who died in a few hours of Cholera, Captn Norton of 88th. He very nearly had it before the Alma after landing in Crimea. He was in an Araba when the battle began, crawled up to his Reg^t went through the battle & then back to his Araba until he c^d be put on board ship. This time he was taken ill in camp & next morning at 7. dead.

The French ought to attack the Central Bastion tonight it w^d draw off attention from Kertsch & make them concentrate their forces near Sebastopol. The Russ.have heavy forces of cavalry near Kertsch 3 Reg^t Cossack. 3 Dragoons 1 Hussars, [illegible] infantry and artillery a fortified position & they have received warning. You abuse Ld Raglan for doing nothing. If he had 50,000 Engl the place w^d have been ours since long ago, but we are placed thus [see Figure 11] & cant go in and storm the middle if they won't come –

Y^{rs} ever

WGR.

On looking over your letter I find I have forgotten to congratulate you on your new dignity – What a queer name for it Commissary of the University. Do you have to find for them – They evidently don't find food for you, if your salary is only £6 per an. I hope however it gives you the opportunity of letting them now & then hear a view from the outer world.

It is at all events highly complimentary coming from such a man as Ld Synodent.

Figure 11. Disposition of the Allies in the siege lines (from letter dated 21 May 1855).

I have heard today that the bombardment is to recommence on 27th & that it will be followed by the storming of the redoubts of Volkynia Selingkinsk and Kamskatka (or Mamelon vert) the last being the only one which so completely enfilades our advance in front of the Redan as to hinder our progress. The Times has all its places so confused as to sound like nonsense to any one who has studied the siege as I have.

I believe Pelissier will do the work & he c^d not have a better backer than Ld Raglan – He was ready at the end of the second day of the last bombardment plans laid, hand fascines & scaling ladders ready, but Canrobert w^d not face the possible loss of men –

If we are still here come out in the Long Vacation. I will put you up & feed & mount you as long as you like to stay.

Goodbye Y^{rs} ever

W. G. Romaine

May 21st 55.

Cambridge University Library: Add. 7633: 5/26

31

Journal for 24 to 28 May 1855

[Holograph]

Thursday May 24th.

The French made another attack last night about the same hour 9 PM and completely succeeded in taking the whole line of Russian trenches & pits & converting them into part of their attack. I have read the copy of the Official Report sent to Lord Raglan by order of Gen Pelissier, he says it is a most important success & will have a material influence in the operations of the siege. The troops which had been engaged [in] the affair the night before, asked to complete their work last night, which they were allowed to do. The Russians made a comparatively feeble resistance, but the French lost 400 & 9 officers. The Russians fought admirably with the bayonet but they have received a severe lesson. The French say the Russian loss must have quintupled theirs. Today is the Queens birthday and there is a full dress review at which Omar Pasha &

Pelissier assisted. Our cavalry two troops of H. Art^y. 1. of field art^y. the batt^y. of 18. pounders & 32 p^d. howitzers. It was a very fine spectacle & took place on the high ground between Kirani & the Monastery, where there is a splendid view of the hills to the eastward of Balaclava.

The troops will move out tomorrow, but what the object is I do not know.

Pelissier had expressed an opinion before he had the Command that the National honour was tarnished by the construction of the Mamélon & that if he ever had the opportunity it sh^d. be wiped away.

Friday. May 25th.

A very quiet night at Sebastopol compared with the two preceding. At 12. night the French artillery began to move to the right and the troops to the number of 15,000 got under arms & proceeded to the heights overlooking the Tchernaia. There were 15,000 Sardinians who moved to heights overlooking Tchorgounia & the Turks under Omar Pasha occupied a second line on the redoubts famous in the story of 25. Oct. The Chasseurs d'Afrique crossed the Bridge at daybreak at Traktir & some shells were thrown over them & the staff at that time from Russian guns above the redoubts and by them as a tête de point.[71] The Fr. Cavalry went up a very steep place in the hills but found the Russ^n. fire heavy & retired & went round the hill to another place, so outflanking the Russians who had about 5 batt^{ns}. & they retired to NE up the valley of the Chuliu towards Mangup Kaleh.

The Russians fired continually upon the redoubt as soon as the French had possession of it, but the distance was very great from the plateau of Inkerman & most of the shells burst in the air about half way the round shot plunging now & then very near the redoubt. The French continued to shell the Russians as long as any were within reach. There were so few Russians on the Inkerman plateau that I have no doubt the heights might have been taken possession of as easily as the position they took. I could see only 50 men at the flag staff redoubt about 50 at another redoubt at 7 two battalions were marching to our right along the cliff top past the place where it is a steep scarp to the place where there is a not very difficult ascent. The 5 Russ^n. Ba^{tns}. w^d. have been quite cut off from the defence & driven [?] away. Came back, saw L^d. R. he s^d. to Vico while I was there C'est dommage qu'ils n'ont pas communiqué leurs idées.[72] Vico s^d. that he thought Genl. Pelissier did not himself know what was to be done. This was incorrect as Pelissier was out with the troops as well as Canrobert with his division. I told L^d. R. how few troops the Russ^{ns}. had & that it seemed to me that the plateau might have been taken. He said it was proposed & that he believed it might have been done.

Col. Gordon came in some time later L^d. R. having gone out at 9 with Gen. Airey & Simpson &c. He said that the French had retired across the river, leaving Della Marmora in an isolated position above Tchorgounia with his rear on Kamara. That he said he had no one on his left & no one on his right & c^d. not remain so. Omar Pasha was furious at being left behind. He said I never was placed in the second line before. He had 18,000 men with him.

So small a result makes such a movement look very foolish. Della Marmora has no water with^t. going down to the river which now that the French have abandoned their excellent advanced position they cannot depend on.

Whit-Sunday May 27th.

This morning early Derriman came to my house with news of the taking of Kertsch & Yenikali with the loss of only one Highlander killed by accident. The boats being ready to land the gunboats went in & fired a few shells when the Russians blew up the fort & abandoned it. Our troops landed & after some delay, pushed on. Kertsch was abandoned in the same way, when the troops came near it two companies, one Fr. one Eng. were sent in & placed as sentinels all down the street. The Austrian consul & others had come out & demanded protection which was promised. The troops then marched flags flying & drums beating through the town at quick step, not a straggler being allowed. They went through the town & camped. Brownrigg then went back called in all the sentries & left the town.

A steamer with a barge in tow was seen to leave & pursued, the barge was stopped & taken & found to contain archives & much valuable property, money, &c. The expedition pushed on to Yenikali which was also abandoned & 18 gunboats & other vessels entered the Sea of Azof.

A letter was found only three days old from an officer in Sebastopol to a wounded comrade who had gone to Kertsch, he says Sebastopol is a pest house that the men were dying like rotten sheep.

The prisoners taken by the French state that the town was choked the night of the 22nd. with dead & wounded. Claremont says that the French handed over 1500 dead bodies to the Russians during the flag of truce which lasted from 12.30 to 5 PM. The demoralisation seems to be extreme there.

There was a heavy cannonade last night during which the French completed a new parallel opposite one of the redoubts on the right.

There was also a heavy firing against our lines but cause not known, supposed to have been an alarm on their side.

The news was put in General Orders & an order was sent to the Divisions to give three good English cheers. Codrington told me it was done most heartily. The sailors jumped up on the parapet & gave theirs.

Went to the Sacrament. L^d. R. came in after being with Pelissier & arranging the expedition to Anapa. L^t. Col. Dickson R.A. told me he was to have the command of the artillery at that place, but that he hoped to be back in time for Sebastopol. If so they must hope that the Russians will abandon the place without fighting.

Thunderstorm & heavy rain.

Monday May 28

The Turks are going under Omar Pasha along the Baidar or Woronzov Road. I hear that the Russians have fortified a post at the head of the defile leading from Baidar to Bagtschi Serai.

The second division of the Sardinians has arrived.

Lord R. sent for me and shewed me letter from L^d. Panmure N°. 110 May 14, stating that he had heard that Filder had not made the use of the Railway that he might & that he was to be called on for an explanation of Mr Beatty's report[73] to his employers to that effect of the date of Ap^l. 13th. & if it was not satisfactory L^d. R. was to relieve him of his duties.

He asked me to have an enquiry viva voce.

He had shewn the papers to Filder, who called upon me directly afterwards. I recommended instead of an enquiry that Mr F. sh^d. have the papers & Mr Beatty's report & be called upon for a written explanation, which was done.

The mail came in in afternoon.

Steele tells me that in the house it was stated by the D of Newcastle that although he had called for a list of names to be recommended for the "Bath" that no list had been sent. This he says he has written to contradict. He sent a list to the Duke but it appears he never read his private letters.

Rode out with Simpson & dined with him.

Cambridge University Library: Add. 9554/4

32
Romaine to C. J. Selwyn
[Holograph. No date. Context indicates late May/early June 1855]

My dear Selwyn,

I send you half a line though no doubt you will hear the Kertsch news from the Times. They have already taken 160 vessels principally a sort of decked barge or sloop for carrying grain. 7 steamers are destroyed leaving to the Russ^n. marine only an old iron ferry boat in the Sea of Azoff. But now they are committing a horrible blunder I don't care whether the expedition is successful or not.

They are wanting to take Anapa – What does it signify to the issue of the war in the Crimea whether Anapa is taken now or 6 months hence. But there Sir Brown is gone – I was talking my mind about it yesterday & saying before long you will have him writing for 5000 more men as a reinforcement. Oh, said —— that is done already we are sending him 1000 English or rather Scotch &

2000 French. This is all done because two of our Engineers looked at the place from the sea side & s^d. it c^d. be taken in 48 hours.

Now the Russians were 7 months before the place in 1850 & then had to buy the Pasha out.

However we must play the game very badly not to win now – The quantity of stores taken by us or destroyed by the enemy is enormous. Hundreds of thousands of quarters –

There were 100 guns taken at Kertch instead of 50 –

The Russians evidently have been misled as to our game – They are now assembling their forces at the Mackenzie Farm & making great fortifications there. Our plans I hope will be to march from Baidar or Alouchka (see map of s. Coast) on Bagtschi Serai or Simpheropol. Threatening an attack or making the attack & bombardment at the same time. If the march on Baidar is made by the Turks it will so far simplify matters – as they will have a job to themselves & we shall have one fewer Com^r. in Chief –

I am sorry to say the Cholera is here again – Ten Guards died yesterday I hear – 120 sick in the Brigade. They are moved out to a new camp today.

Ever yours

W. G. Romaine

Our batteries & trenches are all ready & at least 700 rounds in them. The day kept perfectly secret.

Cambridge University Library: Add. 7633: 5/50

33
Journal for 2 to 12 June 1855

[Holograph]

Saturday. June 2nd.

Rode down to the French redoubt towards their left attack. It was just as the Imp^l. Guard was going into the trenches and the Russians threw a number of shells. The French have nearly completed the batteries in the advanced ground they took on 22nd. & 23rd. May. The Russians were firing shells from Fort Constantine as well as from Batt^s. near the sea. At the Clocktower the French have a General Hospital which being within range is protected by gabions & in the rear were 50 or 60 stretchers whose discoloured appearance sufficient[ly] shewed the bloody work they had been used in.

Sunday. June 3rd.

There was a reconnaissance this morning at 6 AM. French & Sardinians towards Baidar. No enemies to be seen. The Russ^{ns}. still fire occasionally on the parties of French horses going to water near the bridge by Traktir. Our men are doing the last touches to our batteries preparing to unmask the guns & moving on to the platforms those which had been put aside out of fire.

Monday June 4th.

News came from the Sea of Azof of continued destruction in enormous quantities of corn, capture of shot & shell & boats. The Russ^{ns}. had only a short time ago got on foot in a regular manner supplies from Kertsch at the rate of 1500 araba loads a day. They evidently thought we had no troops to detach as they had not mounted a single gun landwards. Soujuk Kalé 12 miles from Anapa has been blown up & abandoned. 60 guns & 10 mortars taken or destroyed the troops retreated on Anapa, where there are 10,000 men. They hope to send boats into the Putrid Lake or Sea to cut the bridge, if they succeed the Russ^{ns}. will have only the one road by Perekop left & they w^d. be much distressed if they were not starved or compelled to retreat. Their retreat even now unmolested w^d. be an affair of the greatest difficulty especially if they attempted to carry off their sick & wounded. It is almost impossible to move large bodies of troops across a steppe country in summer, as there is a great want of water. They have we hear withdrawn two regts. of Cavalry. I sh^d. think they must be concentrating their forces on Bagshi Serai & Simpheropol, leaving a strong body on the Mackenzie plateau & relieving the garrison of Sebastopol from Bakshi Serai.

Last night we fired a number of Carcases (of A.D. 1811) into the town from the Sea Service Mortars but they had no effect probably not reaching far enough.

Cadogan says the valley of Baidar is a perfect level with hills all round, his beau ideal of a race ground.

Wednesday June 6.

Pelissier came here at 6 AM & brought a box full of finery which he put on in order to have his portrait taken in daguerreotype by Mr Fenton. About 10 he was still at L^d. Raglans and he & Omar Pasha & L^d. R. came out in front where a small table was placed with a map on it and their portraits were all taken in a group.[74]

Pelissier stayed till nearly twelve.

I began the work of rewriting the Articles of War. They are now a mere piece of patch work from the numerous changes and additions which have been made to them, often by unscientific hands.

Heard that the bombardment was to commence at 3 PM and rode to the front. A signal gun was fired by the French, on the Victoria redoubt five minutes before 3, and the firing began though not with a great discharge at once, but it soon became general along our lines and on the French right towards Careening Bay. The Russians were evidently taken by surprise and had but few men in their batteries and apparently not many rounds quite ready. The French over our left did not begin when we did, nor the Russians upon them. The Garden batteries began to fire briskly about 3. and then the French opposite the Bastion du Mât & the Bastion Centrale opened about four batteries and kept it up very warmly till sundown. The smoke hung heavily and obscured every thing after the first half hour drifting slowly to our right & up the ravines. The Mamélon kept up a very active fire & the Inkerman batteries across the Bay also took part. I hear that tomorrow at 2 PM the French are to assault the mamélon, but this does not agree with what Sir Colin was told viz that we were to take the Quarries. The French are to make a battery of 15 guns in the Mamélon, when taken.

I c^d. not see that any impression had been made on the fire of the mamélon at nightfall.

De Bathe told a funny story of the two sailors who were stopped by the sentries in the advance & begged him to mind his own parsnips & let them mind theirs. On being obliged to give an account of themselves, one of them s^d. Why Sir You see this Battery Bedam does all the mischief and Bill's got a bag of nails & I've got a hammer and if so be you let us go we'll spike every —— gun in the —— Bedam.

Chapman R.E. said that today he was going by part of the trench they have been repairing it is very much exposed & has been repeatedly knocked down by the Enemy's fire, there he found three young soldiers playing at cards at 7 AM. He said You're in the only place in the trench, where you stand great danger of being killed, come away. "Yes Sir" s^d. one of them & in the same breath "Play to mine Ben," throwing down his card for his comrade to play to.

One of the 77th. was heard saying to his friends Whats the use of humbugging about batteries & trenches Why don't the General say "The Light Division will parade in the Round Tower tomorrow morning at eleven o'clock. Sure we'd be there fast enough."

Thursday June 7th.

The vertical fire was kept up at night on the Mamélon the Round Tower Redan &c. and the direct fire renewed at daylight. The French left attack quite quiet. The Russians opened this morning apparently with all their strength but it gradually fell off and the superiority of fire on our side decided very soon. At 10.30 AM our No. 9 Batt^y. blew up luckily only one man was killed & one wounded.

By the middle of the day the Mamélon had ceased to fire. The shells were falling into it 4 & 5 a minute. I saw 4 or 5 men standing on the angle of the Mamélon nearest to us walking on the parapet. The Garden batteries kept up their fire all the afternoon.

At 3 PM our batteries were throwing 20 to 1 Russian. The French throwing rockets from their extreme left. This seemed the signal for the French left attack to open fire, it was answered by a severe fire from the Russian batteries which are very numerous from the Central bastion & in rear of it and the Flagstaff battery.

It had been settled that the attack was to be made at half past
5 PM, but I met Gen[l]. Barnard who told me it was postponed till
6.30 PM. Went to the right & saw the heavy French Masses
moving down by the different roads. As our men moved down,
there was a good deal of cheering. The French in preparation for
the attack had got pits ready dug about 30 by 15 ft. they were by
the road side & their troops actually had to march past them.

Directly the attack was known to be about to be made the
officers sent in official letters volunteering. There seems to have
been some blundering about the men to go and men were
separated from their own officers. The men to go were fixed upon
at head quarters with[t]. consulting the A.G. office and therefore
without knowledge of what men were available. At half past six the
troops were in their places and three rockets from the Victoria
Redoubt was the concerted signal. The French troops rushed out
of the trenches in front of the Mamélon crossed the Russian
trenches which had been abandoned and spread in loose order to
the second line of ambuscades. These also were empty and they
got into the Mamélon with the loss of hardly a man. Very few guns
being ready to bear on them. This was all that they were ordered
to do, but elated by their success a body of them rushed through
the Mamélon & soon appeared on their way to the Malakhoff.
They appeared to be only three or four hundred, then a few
stragglers and then some three hundred more & a few stragglers.
They were met by a heavy fire of shells & grape but made their
way to the abattis & began firing, numbers falling they found it
impossible to enter & the head of the flock turned to the left to
seek an entrance, the ditch is 12 to 14 feet deep and the abattis
impossible without axes ladders fascines &c. They endured the
terrible fire for some time & turned. The Russians got up out of
the ditch on to the slope of the parapet inside the abattis & poured
in a heavy fire. The French began to retire, paused in a sort of
hollow with broken ground, & the Russians came out to attack
them from the reverse of the tower and drove them with great loss
into the Mamélon.

The retreat of their men caused a sort of panic to those who
were holding the mamélon and all fell back to the edge maintained

a fire thence for a minute or two & then went down to the first Russ[n]. line of ambuscades. The Russians pursued firing, drove them out and into the trenches from which they had started.

Directly after rockets were thrown again and the guard in support advanced, they too had a very loose formation, but were a formidable heavy body of troops which in its advance covered the whole face of the mamélon took it with great ease driving out the defenders, who retired down the reverse side towards the back of the Malakhoff. Most unwisely they were pursued again by the French who attempted to take the Malakhoff from the rear. In this after a bloody struggle they failed. The Malakhoff which had apparently been silenced, during the attack was one blaze of fire, from its own guns the musquetry fire which sparkled round it and the storm of shells falling into it. During the second attack it fired only from its rear, the flashes of the guns lighting up the clouds of smoke which hung round it. The moment the French held the Mamelon shells began to fall into it.

While this was going on the two redoubts to the right of the French were attacked & taken. The guns across the harbour keeping up a heavy but not very destructive fire. Here a number of prisoners were taken, both men & officers. The third redoubt at the extremity of the Sapoune ridge was not attacked & did not fire.

Many instances of surpassing bravery I saw. On our left of the Mamelon during the hottest of the fire two men got on the parapet with a flag, one of them a French Colonel, he was shot down and a second succeeded him who was also immediately killed and a third but without the flag took the place. In two other places men stood with flags on the parapet cheering on the men below. On the first advance up the Mamélon a French officer rushed out alone & ahead of all crossed the Russian trench & still kept his lead a hundred yards before every one, he reached & entered the mamelon.

Where I was I could command a view of the Quarries which our men were to take under the Redan. They had chosen a place for Lord Raglan in front of the Lime Kilns of 4th. Div[n]. but on going there I found you c[d]. only see the crest of the Mamelon & therefore not the French advance so I went to a spot in front & right of Cathcarts Hill, where both attacks c[d]. be seen.

The smoke from Gordons battery was so thick & constant that I c^d. see nothing of our men. The work was admirably done with only 15 wounded – An officer and several men were taken prisoners one of the rifle pits in advance was blown up and an English officer in it but he was not killed. L^t. Col. Edwards sent out a hundred men as skirmishers & sharpshooters towards the Redan. They crawled to the embrasures & reported that no one was in it. But our troops were not numerous enough to attempt its capture. Col. Edwards said if he had had a thousand men he c^d. have taken it & that the Russians finding the enemy in their rear w^d. have abandoned the Malakhoff during the second French attack.

Friday June 8.

Went up to the Front at 2.30 AM. The French were working away at the Mamelon. A heavy fire from our batt^y. on Round Tower and Redan and our men were plainly seen in the quarries, some few red coats close up to the Redan. They had been attacked four times in the night by the Russians each time driven in and each time driving the enemy out with the bayonet & sometimes unwisely pursuing up to the Redan. The musquetry was still going on when I was there, but soon after ceased, though a gun from the garden battery threw a shell every few minutes amongst our fellows. They had completed the Communications with our parallels & were still at work. It came on to rain & blow & be quite cold. There is one gun in face of Redan which can fire on the Mamélon and three from the Malakhoff & a mortar below in front of the Karabelnaia Suburb, and a battery in front of the Arsenal, which also fires on the Mamélon. Every shell seems to tell on the French there as every explosion is followed by one or two stretchers going to the rear.

The French put their loss at two thousand men. They have taken several hundred prisoners and 60 guns in the three places.

A dispatch came from Adm^l. Lyons from the Sea of Azof giving an acct of the destruction of stores at Marioupol Taganrog & Eisk. At one place they say our men drove off 5000 Russ. soldiers & lost only one man wounded.

155

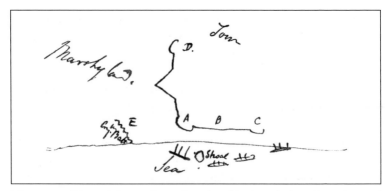

Figure 12. Plan of Anapa from Burghersh's description (from journal dated 8 June 1855).

Today the troops were to land at Anapa, if the wind which though strong is off shore does not prevent it.

Burghersh describes the place thus [see Figure 12].

He says our three deckers can get within 600 yards of sea wall towards A, B, & the heavy steamers towards C, can fire and defilade D that the troops can land at a small place 3 mile North of A, that the batteries will be made at E breach A and take the place.

Gordon R A is gone to Constan[le]. to get guns &c to fortify Enikale.

We send tonight very heavy supports in case of an attack on the Quarry again tonight.

The French repulsed one very sharp attack on the Mamélon.

Calvert says the Russian prisoners were delighted at being taken & being safe & at rest.

I saw no convoys coming into the town on N.

Saturday June 9th.

A quiet night, no attack on the French or us. Blane who has been up to the front reports that a large train of carts came in empty to the North fort and halted, that two vessels one a two decker and one frigate apparently empty have been brought alongside the Arsenal, either to embark stores or to open a retreat for the men if they sh[d]. be beaten.

They brought out a third vessel a two decker near to the Arsenal but a 13 inch shell fell very near it & the small steamer towed her out to mid channel where she anchored.

About 1 PM there was a flag of truce and both sides were busy burying their dead. I rode out to the middle ravine and on to the French advance works where I left my horse & got over the parapets – the dead were lying about here but not in great numbers, some few were lying on the slope of the Mamelon collected by the fatigue men. I then went into the Mamelon. It is a great monument of labour begun & finished & used under a more terrible fire that ever a work was held under before. It was large a large honeycomb with the walls some 12

[This sentence was left unfinished. Perhaps the writer lost his thread when he turned the page.]

[See Figure 13.]

The guns were lying in the work very heavy ship guns on ship carriages. The magazines were admirably made & quite capable of holding a fire of 13 inch shells. The cells made by the gabions & sand bags were of great strength but so deep that there was no escape from a bursting shell & one c^d. quite believe what the Russian officer reported that he had lost 300 men from the time the bombardment began to the time of assault. He said they were quite taken by surprise & had no men in the Mamélon or Malakhoff but the men working the guns. If the French had had their supports ready they c^d. have taken the Malakhoff.

Our loss turns out to have been 600 men & 40 officers. Today we have lost a good many men in the Quarries, one round shot from the Garden Battery killed 8 & wounded 4 men. There were a good many of the Zouaves Indigenes killed in the assault.

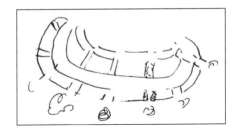

Figure 13. Plan of the Mamélon (from journal dated 9 June 1855).

157

The Russ[n]. officers w[d]. not let us approach the Malakhoff & objected to our officers looking through their glasses. But they worked at the embrasures of the fort & cleared them out & got the guns mounted during the truce.

Sunday. June 10.

Today the attack on the fort of Anapa was to take place. The Russ[n]. ships have been moved out into the bay. They are moving the guns from Fort Paul but whether to use against us here or to take across the bay no one knows. The French were to have their battery in the Mamelon armed tonight, but I doubt it. They say they lose 300 men a day there. Pennefather says he lost 60 men of his division last night in the Quarries & trenches. The Fr. consider that when the battery in the Mamélon is complete the town will be in fact invested as their communicat[ns]. will be obstructed across the harbour.

There have been a number of boxes of powder found in front of the Redan which are made to explode by placing the foot on a tin tack which communicates with a glass tube inside full of nitric acid (!) the glass tube becomes broken by the pressure lets out the acid & the powder is exploded.

There was another consultation today. L[d]. Burghersh who is always sanguine was telling Somerset that in a week he w[d]. have to go to England with despatches. General Niel is all for going on but Pelissier will not. He is obstinate. The French say their artillery general is only fit to dance waltzes & are very angry at the delay in getting the battery open in the Mamélon. The Fr. have lent or rather returned us 1000 shells of the number we lent them.

There is a strong wind blowing from Sebastopol but the sound of the guns is very loud.

The flies in the houses are a great nuisance at night they cluster in swarms every where & give out a curious buzz & murmur every time there is a loud explosion which jars the air. This evening we had apparently silenced all but 3 guns in the Malakhoff one in Garden Batt[y]. one in E flank of Redan two behind the Redan & some behind the Tower. But the Russ[ns] are evidently short of shells & powder. I cannot help thinking the ships are brought out ready for sinking if the assault sh^d. succeed. Those alongside the Arsenal may be intended as a retreat & refuge for the Garrison. It was reported that they were debarking guns for the Malakhoff but I think that is a mistake. The Sardin^n. [illegible] & the Fr. Cavalry made a reconnaissance to Baidar to have another look at the 5 Cossacks!

Monday. June 11th.

The Russians opened a heavy fire on the French left attack about 10.30 PM last night and there was a general musquetry fire for a short time. The French got out some field guns & poured grape into them at a short range, but the guards of the trenches remained under cover & the Russ^{ns} soon retired, but must have suffered severely. The night was very quiet along the rest of the line. The French say that the White redoubt is the best constructed piece of work ever seen. There are bomb proof casemates made of heavy timber from the ships, gabions fascines & sand bags. But the very completeness of the work was the cause of its easy capture for the defenders were all quietly eating their supper inside with only a few sharpshooters in the pits outside when the Fr. column came on. They ran in with the tirailleurs at the gorge and took prisoner all the garrison who were not killed at the first rush.

The quarries are now well connected but we lost 40 men in the 24 hours.

They must have a good many men in the Mamelon still. This afternoon the Fr. are reported to have five guns placed in the Mamélon.

There is some hitch on the Railway about getting up the guns & Dacres has been to me to complain of Beatty –

This afternoon came news of the capture of Anapa that the Russians had abandoned it & ~~embarked~~ carried off their troops. Two of our regts are already off the harbour on their return. The Circassians are said to have been placed in possession.

Genl. Eyre was close to Pelissier when the Fr. troops were repulsed from the Mamelon. He says he never changed countenance but very quietly ordered up the reserve to retake it.

These repeated bits of good news must have a great effect both in Europe & Asia.

The intended attack on the Mamélon was known in Sebastopol at 5 PM but although preparations were made in the interior of the Town they had not time to communicate with the outworks. The informant s^d. the truth of his story c^d. be known by their seeing a great number of persons coming down to look on.

Tuesday. June 12.

Burghersh told me that the destruction of Anapa by the Russians was found out by Mr Hughes who has been employed among the Circassians he was coming in a boat to Kertsch, when passing Anapa he saw it was deserted and on communicating with the Circassians he found that they had taken possession of the town after the Russ^{ns} had set it on fire & were plundering it. Our vessels had seen long strings of Arabas going in & out, but they thought they were engaged in provisioning the place for a siege. Two ships have gone there to destroy the fortifications. Adm^l. Lyons who appears to have wasted time sadly in appearing before Anapa, has stopped, as he says only for a few hours to bring away the guns at Theodosia.

We got two mortars into the advanced battery of rt. attack last night. The Russ^{ns}. are still hard at work at their batteries. Sir C. Campbell visited the redoubt on Fr. right & he says that the officer there told him that but for the surprise they c^d. not have got in as their advance ran in across two planks over the ditch that being once in on the parapet they were able to look down on the defenders No one attempted to defend himself except the Gunners who ran to their pieces & were bayoneted. The Fr. suffered much loss by advancing to the third redoubt at the end of the Sapoune ridge when they were fired at by two batteries of horse artillery which came out in the rear of the Malakhoff. The French then abandoned it & in the night the Russ^{ns}. came & apparently drew the guns off & threw them into the sea.

Their total loss has been variously stated but it seems to be above 3000.

The Fr. battery in the Mamélon is progressing rapidly.

Rode with Genl. Simpson.

Called at camp of V. Battery to see Mr Cockerill & give him the charge &c.

A powder box blew up in front of the Quarries in a place in which our men had been constantly walking for two days, at last someone put his foot on it & it exploded killing 7 & wounding 3 dangerously. Our men consider it as an unmanly warfare. The town is reported to be full of these powder boxes, the position of which is marked out by little flags while the enemy is there. We have dug 30 or 40 out of the ground of our trenches in the Quarries.

Cambridge University Library: Add. 9554/4

34
Romaine to John Harvey

[Holograph]   Head Quarters
                                                      June 13th. 1855

My dear Harvey,

Here we are in the full tide of success and with every prospect of a speedy possession of Sebastopol – One can no longer hope to send news to England by post as you get the results of the last move every morning by Electric Telegraph. The abandonment of Anapa by the Russians was a great coup for us as it would have be [*sic*] a great misfortune if ten thousand good troops & the ships had been kept away for the siege of a place entirely unconnected with the operation here in the Crimea and which might have been as advantageously captured 6 months hence.

There has been a slight delay in the return of part of the Expedition as Adm^l Lyons who is not a bit too rapid in his movements has chosen to try & get the guns at Kaffa.

We have had news from an excellent source that Michel Gortschakoff has written to the Emperor to say that he has 50,000 sick & wounded at Sebastopol and that the men w^d prefer to go out of the place if they were even to be killed for it, to remaining in it any longer – They have typhus of a most deadly kind. They are short of provisions too – In fact his dispatch was a request for orders to leave the place. The delay which is now taking place is not wholly against us, though the enemy are labouring hard to erect & repair batteries, as such a state of things as he describes always gets worse from day to day. The French are putting up 60 guns & mortars in the Mamélon against the Malakhoff and its flanks, and we are getting some strong advanced batteries against the Redan and its supporting batteries. When all these batteries are ready which will be in two or three days we shall command the communication across the bay now carried on by the enemy in boats and the South side may then be considered as invested.

I have got a drum for your hall at the Bury[75] captured in the attack on the Malakhoff tower. I hope I shall have better luck in getting it home than I had with the other. It is not so smart a one nearly but it has seen plenty of severe service & was with the Russ[n] troops in the Mamélon when they were driven out by the French.

It will not be hard to drive the Russ[ns] out of the Crimea when we have the South side as they have not stores for a long siege there and they are encumbered with such a mass of sick & wounded.

We ought to take every man prisoner & capture all their artillery & then leave the Crimea to the Turks keeping a small garrison at Yenikale & a strong force of gunboats. The Russ[ns] then being restricted to one road viz by Perekop, the other being easily destroyed, they w[d] not venture to send a formidable army across the steppes to attack a place 500 miles from any of their great depots.

All that we have done now, we might have done in April if the French had had a general at their head as brave in command as he is at the head of his Division & under orders. We have fired hardly at all the last few days & committed a blunder in keeping up the fire 48 hours after the Mamélon was taken when there was no determination to go on with the assault immediately.

The Sardinians have had a terrible bout with the Cholera & it has not yet left them. All our newly arrived regiments have suffered more or less, but they are right again, and every body is in good heart & spirits. The men a little impatient at not being allowed to go in at them. As the 77th man was overheard to say "What's the use of humbugging about batteries & trenches, why don't the General say the Light Division will parade in the Round Tower tomorrow morning at eleven – sure we'd be there" – and I suppose some of them would.

I put off your letter till this morning in case any great event sh^d occur, but nothing has happened & the next move is not known – there have been the tallest kind of tales once or twice a day, You will get the result of them long before this reaches you.

My best remembrances to Mrs Harvey and to the Lady of the Green and her household.

I wish you c^d come out & take a share of my house, it is charming as it has four stone walls & does not get so hot as the huts. In a few minutes it will be chock full of red coats engaged in trying an unfortunate Doctor.

Goodbye & believe me ever

Y^{rs} very truly

W. G. Romaine

Cambridge University Library: Add. 7633: 5/27

35
Journal for 13 to 17 June 1855

[Holograph]

Wednesday June 13th.

There was some firing for a few minutes on the French last night but nothing of any consequence. A despatch has been received which states that Michel Gortschakoff has written to the Emperor of Russia, "that food is scarce in Sebastopol that they have 50,000 sick & wounded, that the men wd. prefer to go out of the town & be killed to remain in it & live." He is evidently asking permission to withdraw. The disease appears to be typhus.

A deserter or prisoner told us that nearly all the marine artillery are dead and that they have to rely on the field artillery for their gunners. The French are to have four batteries in the mamelon, 62 guns, they have already 11 mortars & several guns there.

There has been a conference this evening and there is to be another tomorrow morning to decide on the course of operations. The question seems to be whether there is to be a general attack on the town or a partial one on the Malakhoff & Redan.

Sunday June 17.

Got up at 1.30 and called Marsh & Kirkland & Blane & before 3 we were in front of Cathcart's hill, it was a very warm & close morning calm but clear. When daylight came the coast far to the North c^d. be seen – The two camps & the ships both inside the harbour & off Kamiesch. One of the gun boats came in fired a shell & sheered off but otherwise there were no signs of hostilities.

At a quarter to 4 a gun from the French extreme left near the sea was fired and soon after a gun from the new Fr. Batt. in the Mamélon which threw a shell into the Malakoff then gun after gun in the different batteries took it on this side of Dockyard harbour, each jet of smoke arose separately & well defined for a short time, marking the position of the battery to which it belonged. Then the Fr. Batt. of Left attack fired, the smoke gradually swept down to seaward with the lightest possible air, the different volumes of smoke collected & formed a dense curtain dragging itself lazily along the ground & shutting out the town from view. The contrast between peace with the larks singing and the cocks crowing & the tranquil looking sea & land as day broke & the crash and roar of this unequalled bombardment half an hour after was striking & not easily to be forgotten.

Rode across to Bosquet's observatory to see what the Turks & Sardinians were doing.

The Sardinians went out to the left, in front of Tchorgoun & found only a few squadrons of cavalry before them with a couple of guns which after firing a few random shot retired across the hills.

The Turks formed 3 batt^s. & 2 squadrons which after some skirmishing also retired & the Turks piled arms & camped sending out their men unarmed for water, in front of their advanced pickets although the Cossacks were peering [?] about.

The officers are busy writing orders for tomorrow.

The bombardment is going on in the usual way, a certain amount of damage done to the enemy's works & their guns gradually silenced. The garden battery however even at sunset kept on five guns on our trenches at the Quarries in front of the Redan.

Dined with Neville & Keith, DeBathe, Astley, Hepburn & Gordon – Caulfield came in in the evening. He evidently had a presentiment he s^d. he felt sure he sh^d. be hit hard as his party had an awful bad place to go at in the Cemeteries at ~~Picket~~ Dock Yard Ravine. He s^d. his reg^t had to parade at 1 AM & that he w^d. not lose 3 hours of his life by going to bed. Neville too seemed rather to expect a misfortune to himself.

Cambridge University Library: Add. 9554/4

Part 4

Failure and Success

Fourth bombardment and unsuccessful June assault

The fourth bombardment opened on 17 June 1855. The next day (the anniversary of Waterloo), as the staff watched from forward viewpoints, the allies assaulted the main Russian works, the British attacking the Redan, and the French the White Tower on the Malakhov. The British attack, ill-planned and not well executed, failed with high casualties, including several senior officers. The plan had been to co-ordinate the two nations' assaults, with the French going in first against the Malakhov and the British attacking the Redan when a signal was given that the Malakhov had fallen. The French had courted confusion by altering, at a late stage, the time of their assault and this had been compounded when General Mayran, commanding the right-hand French division, mistook a random rocket for the signal to attack and went forward some twenty minutes early. Nevertheless the French had some early success against the Tower, but were also eventually driven back. Unfortunately, while French troops could be seen on the Tower, Sir John Campbell, leading the left flank column, saw them and thinking that the Malakhov was taken pressed forward, spurning advice that the French were already withdrawing. It was a mistake that was to cost him his life. It was not the only error made. The British trenches were in rocky ground and had not been pushed forward nearly as far as the French had been able to dig theirs. Where they had some thirty yards to go across open ground to reach their objective, the British had nearer three hundred. Further, the British approach trenches were narrow and quickly became congested with returning wounded so that reserves could not get forward.

There were many examples of outstanding bravery by officers and men, but sadly there were also instances when ill-trained recruits, recently arrived, refused to leave the trenches. The army, after months of overwork, malnutrition, exposure and disease, was not the one which had landed at Kalamita Bay.

Illness now struck down several of the senior officers and staff, but Romaine's duties continued as he managed to negotiate to prevent a strike by the railway workers, dealt with the court martial of a young assistant surgeon, and advised on the legal position of men in the newly formed Army Works Corps. He also continued to lobby the authorities at home over his pay, and discreetly pressed for the CB that he coveted.

Shortly after the failed assault Lord Raglan had become ill and he now deteriorated suddenly and died, some said from a broken heart. However, as Romaine had reported, more conventional sickness was prevalent among headquarters staff. General Simpson, who had been sent out by the government to be Raglan's Chief-of-Staff, was now, as the senior officer on the spot, pressed reluctantly into command. Romaine doubted if he was strong enough for the job and feared for the combination of Simpson with General Barnard as his Chief-of-Staff. From an early stage in his attachment to headquarters, Romaine had favoured Sir Colin Campbell as the best general to be Commander-in-Chief, and he was disappointed when he heard from a correspondent in England that Campbell would not get the job. Romaine assessed the other generals and placed Codrington – of whom later – in fourth place.

The pressure of work on the soldiers did not ease, and British casualties from death and wounds ran at around thirty to fifty per day.

Battle of Chernaya and fifth bombardment

In August another attempt by the Russians to break the siege was defeated by the French and Sardinians at the Battle of Chernaya, in which only a handful of British troops were involved.

British administration improved as a new road was built alongside the railway from Balaklava to the camps

The fifth bombardment followed, but once again was inconclusive as the Russians continued to rebuild their damaged defences and replace unserviceable guns from reserves. The siege and the bombardments were nevertheless taking a steady toll on them. Food was short, aggravated now by the Allied successes at Kertch and in the Sea of Azov. Their medical resources were unable to cope with mounting numbers of wounded and sick. They began to construct a floating bridge across the harbour from Fort Nicholas on the south side to Fort Michael on the north but continued an aggressive defence with regular sorties at night. On several occasions British troops disgraced themselves by running away from such an attack.

The September assault

On 8 September 1855 the allies launched another assault upon the Russian fortifications and Romaine records a detailed timetable of what he saw. The French had pushed their trenches to within a few yards of the White Tower and Little Redan, and sprang out of them and forward to the objectives at noon, the time when the Russians changed shift at the Tower, foolishly withdrawing the old guard before the new guard marched in. The Tower fell to the French and they held it despite determined counter-attacks, but their assault at the Little Redan failed as did their attacks elsewhere.

Meanwhile the British attacked the Redan. They were driven back ignominiously, many men conspicuously failing to do their duty. Gloom descended over the British staff that night as the unwelcome details of their defeat became known.

The fall of Sevastopol

Astonishingly, the following morning revealed that during the night a few men of Sir Colin Campbell's Highland Division, who had been warned to be ready to assault the following day, had entered the Redan, having found it unmanned. The Russians had vacated Sevastopol, moving across the floating bridge to the north side, leaving many sick and wounded behind.

Sevastopol had fallen, but the manner of its fall offered little cause for the British to rejoice, and there was much heart-searching over the reasons for yet another failure of an assault on the Redan. At home, too, elation at the news of the fall swiftly evaporated when accounts of the assault began to arrive. Simpson found himself the target of the same sort of criticism that had been levelled at Raglan and Airey and had lain behind his own appointment. He was an unwilling holder of the command, reluctant to take the authority and with no experience of anything remotely like the situation he now faced. Romaine sums him up as 'a man who is not a soldier at heart'.

Why the assault failed

The fall of Sevastopol left the British army deflated. The French assault on the White Tower at the Malakhov had been successful, and that by the British on the Redan had failed – again. There were several reasons for this, some unavoidable and some stemming from culpable errors, including the foolish repetition of mistakes which had been made in June.

The French had sapped forward until they were within a few yards of the Malakhov, but the ground before the Redan was mostly hard rock, and digging trenches in it was impossible. Consequently, British troops had to cross several hundred yards of open ground under the fire of case-shot from Russian guns.

The White Tower was a closed fort, and so once occupied could be defended by the takers against those they had expelled. The Redan, however, was open-backed, and attackers entering it were vulnerable to fire from defenders in positions behind it. These disadvantages were compounded by poor planning and execution.

The choice of generals and troops was ill-advised. The 2nd and Light Divisions were chosen to lead the assault, under the command of Codrington and Markham. These troops had borne the brunt of the campaign and had therefore suffered most from casualties. There were many young soldiers, conditioned by months of trench duty to crouch in a safe corner when under fire, who were reluctant to 'go over the top' despite the valiant efforts of their company officers and NCOs. Their generals contributed nothing to the action. Neither Codrington (on whom Romaine's judgement is savage) nor Markham was an inspirational leader.

The approach trenches were far too narrow. This hampered the initial deployment so that the troops were not all forward when the signal to leave the trenches came. It also made it all but impossible to bring reserves forward against the streams of wounded who were trying to get back down the same narrow passages.

The British had also attacked somewhat prematurely. Although the agreed signal had been given by the French as they entered the Malakhov, fighting continued there and they were unable to dominate the Russians in the Redan as had been planned.

Despite these shortcomings, the Russians had felt compelled to retire. In the early days of September the bombardment, in which the British artillery was pre-eminent, had made the town uninhabitable. The Russians had acknowledged this by their preparation some weeks earlier of the floating bridge as an escape route. Their choice was stark: stay and be steadily pounded to death; or evacuate, perhaps to fight again from the north or the interior. Nevertheless, despite these facts, there was disappointment in the army, and at home, that at the end the French assault had been successful and the British had failed.

Over the next few days the staff had their first views of the inside of Sevastopol, and Romaine was as interested as any.

36

Journal for 18 to 28 June 1855
[Holograph]

Monday. June 18th.

Started at 2 AM with Lord Raglans staff to the front. They went down to the 3rd. parallel of rt. attack and I went to the front of the ~~Light~~ 3rd. Divn picking up Chetwode on my way who had lost the escort. The morning was exceedingly close & sultry and the smoke hung very heavily near the ground. During the night there had been firing from the mortars which obscured the view a good deal. At 3.10 the musquetry began in front of Malakoff and speedily became a great battle.

At 3.16 a rocket was fired from the Victoria Redoubt perpendicularly with many falling stars. Two more being fired from parallel in front of Mamélon.

This heavy fire lasted with occasional alternations of greater & less intensity till nearly 5. At one time through the smoke I fancied I saw the French struggling vehemently to get over the parapet. Numbers of the Engrs being seen thus exposed encouraging their men When the firing ceased, one of the two three deckers in the harbour fired some broadsides, with what effect I cd. not tell.

At 5.30 the guns of the French left attack opened, which was but very slightly answered by the Russians whose fire was almost entirely directed upon us.

The smoke had become so thick that nothing cd. be seen in front of the Redan & very seldom for more than a minute at a time any thing in the Malakhoff. I saw what I took to be Fr. soldiers climbing over the parapet & numbers of Russian soldiers standing in clusters on the parapets firing down upon the French below. The Russns. hoisted a long blue pennant on a high pole on our left of Malakoff in one of the newer parts of the rear of the work. The Fr. artillery wagons came down at a great pace & went back unhurt.

5.45. The French have evidently been repulsed unless they have made a lodgment in the suburb of Karabelnaia.

A Russian ship or floating battery has been firing broadsides & keeping up a tremendous fire on the Batteries blanches.

6.15. French batts. began again in rear of Malakoff it has not lasted very long.

A Russian three decker has been firing broadsides on the French.

French batterie blanche nearest to Malakhoff firing again. Heavy fire from Barrack battery.

8. Dr. Hall reports death of Sir J. Campbell & repulse of our men from Redan & that our troops in left attack in Dockyard ravine have taken houses below Redan.

Attack subsided on Malakoff & Redan & only cannonade kept up. When our batteries opened on Redan the place was lined with men. There are constant vollies of musquetry followed by dropping shots from the dockyard ravine & men seen in the trenches under the Garden batteries firing. The Garden batteries firing exclusively on Gen Eyre's men in Dockyard creek.

A sergeant who came up reports that the attack was to be renewed by French & us, but after waiting a long while saw the troops begin to defile to the rear & come to camp.

The new Cacolets were used & performed admirably.

Heard of death of Sir J. Campbell, Col Yea & Col Shadforth 57th. Col Cobbe wounded Lord Ward [*sic* – surely a slip of the pen for 'Lord West'?] wounded. Poor Caulfield who sat by me last night & told me he felt he sh^d. be hit hard has been shot through the thigh – while I was at Keith's hut his servant came in to ask for a bottle of Champagne for his master who he s^d. was sinking rapidly & was asking for champagne. His thigh had been amputated high up.

Lord R. went to No. 9 Battery the most exposed place in the 3rd. parallel & remained there peeping out of a hole made by a shot in the parapet just in front of the storm of grape fired from the Redan at our storming party.

The French say that they twice had possession of the Malakoff but had no supports & were driven out. They estimate their loss at

5000 – Peel led the party of sailors who carried the scaling ladders, the engineer who had to conduct one party of them lost his way or did not know the right place & they say they found no soldiers near them when they had got up with the ladders, the other party led by Graham of the Engineers were taken to the right place & put several ladders agst. the parapet but also found themselves without soldiers. Out of 120 – 64 were killed & wounded & 7 officers. Peel was wounded & came with his coat & shirt torn, head up & a little excited to Lord R. & said "Well my Lord we've failed but I've done my best." He is a noble chivalrous fellow.

Our attack was made when it was supposed that the French had taken the Malakoff & having failed was not renewed because the Fr. did not attack again when repulsed.

While some of us were sitting outside Lord R.'s door in the afternoon a private soldier of 89th. came up & being asked by Steele what he wanted s[d]. "to see Lord Raglan." What for? – Well Sir I'm sent by my comrades to say that we want to be allowed to go & take the Redan or the Round Tower tomorrow morn[g]. at half past three, we only want one regt. to support, we don't care which. The poor fellow while speaking was nearly overcome by his emotion, his hands working, while standing at attention. Steele went in to see Lord R. & Airey came out & asked him "what's your story my man" – Our regt. Sir wants to go & take the Redan or the Malakoff at half past three tomorrow, and to have one more regt. to support us. We're sure we can take either of them, and as things went a little backward today, we wanted to tell Lord R. that every man in the reg[t]. wants to go at the place & they've sent me to tell him. Airey s[d]. How long have you been a soldier "Half past three if you please Sir" So full was his head of his errand that he did not until asked a second time comprehend the question. He then s[d]. ten years. Airey s[d]. You know my man these things are done by arrangement but tell y[r] comrades that Lord R. is very much gratified by this offer and when the thing has to be done again he will remember their noble offer & feel sure they will do their duty.

While Steele was absent the poor fellow was so much excited that he c[d]. hardly suppress his sobs & walked on one side. Vico called to him "Soldier Tell to your comrades that the French officer makes his compliments to them."

Comte de Revel s^d. the sang froid of Genl. Jones was very remarkable he was making a report to Lord R. when he was struck on the forehead by a bit of grape, he quietly put aside those who wanted to come to his assistance & went on with his report to Lord R. at the word he had left off at.

Our men were very savage at not being allowed to go in again – They s^d. there's plenty of them to go in & take the place.

Tuesday June 19.

Last night McMurdo sent report to me to say that the navvies had been quarrelling with their officers & the Railway drivers had struck work & that if they did not resume work "he sh^d. be stumped" & asked me to be down there this morning at 7. So I rode down to his camp on the Highlanders hill & we went into Balaclava, where the men were to meet their officers. M^r. Beatty has been gone ten days, M^r. Camidge who is sick in a hut on the hill lacks energy M^r. Parker the next cannot manage them at all & Mac says he can get no work done. I had a curious task we moved to the Railway station & asked what their complaints were – Several very cantankerous fellows opened upon me with a string of grievances – After a while I got them to hear me & I answered their complaints one after another, some unjust which I got them to abandon, others fair which I promised to get set right by Lord Raglan and me as the officers refused what I thought just from fear of responsibility I took upon myself the responsibility & the officers promised to carry out.

I promised the men to see them again & they all agreed to go to work. After breakfast came back & saw L^d. Raglan he approved what I had done & directed me to draw up a memorandum for him to sign. I drew up one for Filder and one to clear Mc of the responsibility I had undertaken both of which he signed.

Wrote Mem. for Adj^t. Genl. of a case of Desertion at Halifax in 1848 L^d. Bate Rif. Brig. Man found here in disguise.

Case for Gen Simpson about some suttlers in Bazaar who threaten Col. Harding with actions for shutting up their shop.

Wrote opinion for Col. Shewell 8 Hussars on Rg^l. C^t. M^l.

Long enquiry into case of spies, Greeks & Armenians conducted through an interpreter & Calvert.

Wrote to Charles about Mortge [?] of Governs [?] for 12,000, got Bank transfers signed by Kirkland & Lindsay & Gen Simpson & sent them off.

Sent Gen C^t. M^l. to J.A.G. case of Ass^t. Surgeon Cockerill Ord. Med. Dep^t.

Dined with Lord Raglan. He s^d. that Pelissier changed the hour of attack after all was arranged against his own conviction at the instance of the Gen^{ls}. of Divis^n. That Moran [*sic* – Mayran intended] began 20 min. before the time mistaking a rocket for the signal – That Genl. Brunet did not advance knowing it was an error & D'Autemarre did not advance until his signal was made when it was too late. Polignac says that two regts got into the Malakoff & the flag of one reg^t. was flying for 20 mins. & was riddled with balls.

One batt^n. which went in 750 strong brought out only 60 men voltigeurs, another only one officer & some 35 men.

Pelissier had agreed to make a second attack, but countermanded it & sent to say that all his monde was killed & hors de combat.

If their supports had come up they must have succeeded.

Col. Dickson R.A. says that nearly all the men who went as spiking party were killed & wounded – But the men who remain unhurt & their two officers have already put in their claim to go again they say they have a right before any body else. Col. Cole 17th. says that after their repulse on the Redan, some one s^d. that one of their Capt^{ns}. was left out wounded. 5 men instantly volunteered to go out & bring him in, & in the face of the terrific storm of grape they went coolly out over the parapet of the trench found him & brought him in & all escaped unhurt. He called them out when the Reg^t. paraded & spoke to them & to two of them he gave medals for distinguished service in the field.

Lord R. said "I quoted two proverbs to Pelissier one French & one English 'Reculer pour mieux sauter' and 'Delays are dangerous' Retards sont dangereux" – It appears that the French are to sap up to the Malakoff & we to the Redan –

Gen Eyre had lost at 10 today when Burghersh returned to Lord R to report – 83 officers & 600 men. He retired his men with all the wounded after dark last night. We do not hold the cemetery but by our heavy musquetry fire prevent the enemy from holding it.

Genl. Brunet was an officer who had a dislike to the English & during the truce in front of the Malakoff & Mamelon abused us to the Russians. [blank space] who was near was told of this & Gen Brunet received a lecture from Pelissier.

The Second Corps Bosquet's is not well affected to the English beginning with Bosquet himself –

Lord Raglan speaking to me of the fire from the Redan when he was in N°.9. said "We never used to treat grape with any respect before this" –

The fire was so incessant into the place where he was that they made him move He s^d. there was a hole in the parapet made by a shot & he found it impossible to keep looking over with his lorgnettes. Young Jervoise stood up while the rest of the staff were sitting down & quietly told what was going on.

There was a flag of truce, but no one could get leave to enter the trenches – The only people who got in except those on duty were people who had got down out of sight before the line of sentries was formed. The bodies had turned quite black & were scorched [?] so as not to be distinguishable.

Genl. Sir J. Campbell was buried this afternoon the mail was going out & L^d Rs despatches not finished & he c^d. not go –

Sir John was found close to the abattis, the enemy had taken his cap & boots, Yea was found. There was an officer also lying near the abattis.

Prince Edward of Saxe Weimar is staying with Lord Raglan. After dinner all the party turned out & had tea in front of the door.

Capt. Drummond says that during the attack on the Malakoff the boats of the harbour were all full of soldiers escaping to the North side – that after eleven the tide set the other way & the top of fort Constan^{ne}. became crowded with soldiers, the guns manned & soldiers peeping out of the embrasures.

Thursday the 21st. June.

Conference again. I fear it is decided to send for more guns from England and that we are in for another winter in the Crimea, and then months at least more of open trenches. Pelissier, Omar Pasha & Della Marmora were here.

Wrote to L^d. Raglan a letter on legal position of the Army Works Corps coming out.

Col. Warre 57th. called. After Gen Sir J. Campbell was killed & Col Shadforth of 57 he had the command of the left attack. He says he c^d. not get more than 250 men of the 300 to go out of the trenches of these 105 were killed & wounded. He says his officers even the boys only three days out from England, kept their senses & did as they were ordered.

But he says there was a terrible want of arrangement. It took him two hours to march his party to the advanced trench they were constantly halted by the ladder party being in their way or the men with wool bags and the party relieved returning.

Long before any one was ready or the ladders were to be found, Sir J. Campbell thought the French were in possession of the Malakoff & ordered the advance. Warre had seen the Imperial Guard repulsed & getting under cover from a terrible fire & went to him & s^d. it is a mistake I can see the French column retiring. But Sir J was too much excited to listen, jumped on the parapet & s^d. "Who'll be first in the Redan," ran out was wounded went out to within 20 yds of the Abattis when he fell dead. Shadforth was killed within a few yards of our trench & Warre was in command. He says he stood for a minute or two & got the men out & reached the abattis and the Russians ran from the parapet but the grape continued his men fell no one came on & he was forced to return, he c^d. have taken the flanking battery but saw a body of Russians below which he thought was sent to outflank him, though they were in fact retreating from Gen Eyre's attack below, and being but few he felt he c^d. not hold the battery if he took it. Lord West who commanded the 21. tried hard to get his men out but they w^d. not go. Warre says the fire from the guns was so badly sustained at last that the Russians were seen cramming stones into their guns, chains & nails & that they were so badly rammed home that they did not reach the trench but fell dead on the ground and he is certain that if the attack had been supported it must have succeeded. He thinks also the Redan might have been taken by an attack to the left where only 2. guns c^d. have borne on them. He says only 50 of the 100 men who volunteered to carry wool bags came to the advanced trench and only one wool bag was thrown into the ditch.

When the Black Sea fog was seen hovering over Balaclava last night making our clothes damp, D^r. Hall said, now we shall have a return of the Cholera.

Estcourt is ill with it. Gen Brown is ill Gen Codrington is gone on board ship, Gen Pennefather is going home. Vico is ill Burghersh is ill. Pakenham fell ill this morning after his ride.

Thursday June 28th.
After dinner here 3.30 PM at Head Q^rs. Lord Raglan was suddenly taken much worse than he had been. He had felt much better in the morning & great hopes were entertained of his recovery. A telegraphic message was sent for Lord Burghersh in case he sh^d. be with L^d. G. Paget

The prince rode full speed to the Monastery & Curzon to the 4th. Div^n. Somerset & Burghersh & Ed^d. Somerset all came & were admitted to see him. Rev^d. M^r. Wright was sent for to administer the Sacrament but he was no longer conscious or if so, had not physical power to receive it & he read the Commendatory prayer & he died with a calm smile on his countenance. Poor Steele was overwhelmed with grief and no wonder for he was a father to him. He died at 8.15 PM as near as possible.

Cambridge University Library: Add. 9554/4

37
Romaine to Lord Mulgrave

[Holograph]   Head Quarters
                                                July 5th. 1855
My dear Mulgrave,
I wrote you a long letter by last post but it was concluded in a

hurry – I asked Steele how it was that the War Office could have no record of Lord Raglans letters about me – he says they were written to the War Department & not to the War Office. I am very much obliged to you for having taken the trouble to enquire about my affair, but I do not expect them to do any thing. If I were coming out now instead of having been out here all the time I should be paid as other civilians who have been sent out in responsible situations namely very liberally. I cannot even find out whether as holding Her Majesty's Commiss^n I sh^d be entitled to half pay if I remained to the end of the war or whether I should be liable to be "rubbed out" as our friends the Red Indians used to say –

I have lost a good friend in Lord Raglan one for whom it was a real pleasure to work –

I cannot believe that General Simpson can stand the work long – it is evidently too much for him and he is oppressed by it and if he were to have the least touch of illness, his only chance of life would be to go on board ship at once. I am sorry to say Codrington does not recover as quickly as one could wish. He landed at Kazatch when Lord Raglans body was put on board ship but he was looking thin and weak. I hope you liked my translation of Pelissiers General Order announcing Ld Raglans death. The one made by the official was so French, and so angular and read so badly that I ventured to change it when General Simpson gave it to me to write some sentences in acknowledging it in our General Orders – After they were written & approved came in the Sardinian Gen Order & then it was necessary to acknowledge both & my exquisite phrases were backed. The French are going to put up some mortars of 21 inch diameter for the Russian ships. Our advanced battery to fire on Redan & rear of Malakoff is ready for the guns. There is a fine row of 20. 32 lbrs waiting to go in when the French are ready. A paper of Instructions for Officers in the trenches is being printed. It won't be many days before we have another try at the Malakoff. If that falls the rest goes like a pack of cards. That is supposing the French able to live in it and establish a battery. I expect they will blow it up if the French establish themselves there. There is no doubt they have wires to enable them to fire their mines by galvanic batteries. It is late good night.

Y^{rs} ever truly

W. G. Romaine

Cambridge University Library: Add. 7633: 5/28

38
Romaine to Lord Mulgrave

[Holograph]   Head Quarters
                                                 July 10th. 1855

My dear Mulgrave,

You are in the way of seeing members of the Government, so I want to tell you one or two things that have caused some annoyance out here. One is to see officers who have been spending months in England, some who have been absent from the Crimea all the winter, coming out again with the medal on their coats while the men who have been here enduring everything out here have not even the small satisfaction of wearing the bit of riband at their button holes as they go down to the weary trenches – A certain number are killed & wounded every day in these trenches both guards & working parties. It w^d be a great thing for many of these poor fellows when invalided to England to carry their medal with them – Why is it they can be found for people at home & not for the soldier out here.

Another grievance is a speech of Mister Peel in the House about bestowing the Order of the Bath. He thought if the order were given for every battle it w^d be exhausted. Those who remember the way it was given right & left for the China campaign and those who know what the battles and what the service out here have been and all are most intensely disgusted with the speech of red tapist. I have not heard such indignant language on any occasion from men high in the Service –

It will not be easy in a short time to find an officer who has been through the whole affair – The number of men is already very small.

Never was such a melancholy break up as our Head Quarters, Steele has been obliged to go on board ship. Calvert the head of the Secret Service is lying dead of cholera & Col. Vico the French Commissioner cannot live out the day. Pakenham & Curzon are the only two left of the original party except General Airey & myself.

There is not much fear of the "Bath" being exhausted by bestowing it on officers out here. Death scratches out the names faster than officials at home can put them in –

There is one warning that I have no doubt has been given which is that if we have to hold the siege during the winter there must be another 25000 men to diminish the work in the trenches and every one must be hutted, or there will be the same loss in the winter –

The last winter was unusually wet, but it was unusually mild. The Duke of Newcastle took as his authority on the climate of the Crimea a book of Dr. Lee who spent a few months of autumn here – My authority is poor Calvert who lived at Kertch 13 years & was in constant correspondence with people in Sebastopol. He said there was only a difference of two degrees of "Reaumur" between the two places – Sebastopol being two degrees warmer.

Our left attack has begun a warm fire on the Redan to damage the battery which impedes our works – I was up there at 3.30 AM today – I am afraid I shall lose my pet horse which I gave Anderson 75 guineas for. He has been terribly bitten and it has turned to an ulcer, and as something very like the Indian bursotty is about I do not expect to ride him again –

The weather has become very hot again but the health of the army is very satisfactory. Not a case of cholera at Balaclava! Yet I do not consider any mans life worth a months purchase – Out of the circle of my acquaintance I know no one except Gen Dacres & myself who have not had a grave attack of disease within the 15 or 16 months since we left England –

I wrote a long letter to Lady Normanby by last mail about her friend Lord Raglan and the gossip of the camp in general.

Gen Simpson has had a slight touch of gout in the ancle [*sic*], who is to command if he gets laid up? Gen England? I hope not – He is too indolent to look after his Division & does not appear to me to care for any thing but getting home in some way which will not draw the "press" down upon him. I wish he had the gout very bad & was obliged to go – The idea of his commanding is like a night mare on the army. Right or wrong the officers who have served in India with him have a bad opinion of him – Gen Simpson is gradually withering up into the thinnest & driest of mortals – He is a capital office man & easy to do business with – clear head & strong will & narrow intellect, with a hearty detestation of the French the Russians the siege the Crimea the War and every thing outside of the Horse Guards & Pall Mall.

We shall use up Admiral Fremantle in a very few weeks at Balaclava. It is a fine way to clear the half pay lists to send us old men. The air is poisonous to new comers, it reeks with odours of death & corruption. The Sardinians have lost six per cent of their whole force in one month. The Land Transport Corps 76 men out of 700 – All the new regiments have suffered severely – I should think [the] Roebuck vote of censure[76] must have fallen through – So they have just begun to abuse Lord Raglan as his death sickness began. Goodbye. Ever y^{rs} faithfully

W. G. Romaine

Cambridge University Library: Add. 7633: 5/29

39
Romaine to Lord Mulgrave

[Holograph]   Head Quarters
                                            July 12th. 1855

My dear Mulgrave,

We have just got the news of the new appointment – Gen Barnard to be Chief of the Staff – I don't think that you yet appreciate the difficulty of the task before us – Here at the head of the army are now two men who know nothing of war capital officials no doubt, well bred gentlemen and all that – But they have not to command a district in England, but to take Sebastopol and beat the most determined & vigorous enemy we have ever met in the field – They are in a position so strong that they expected a determined attack and have thrown us back another month if not longer – Another experiment is to be tried – the Russians have been reinforced – the French army is dwindling – ours suffering a heavy daily loss in the trenches & by disease. Not a single inch of the original Russian position has yet been won in nine months. We cannot have success and we shall not have success under these conditions before winter sets in again upon us – And if we take the field how are men like Simpson & Barnard to conduct a campaign – To beat the Russians we must have soldiers to command the army. I declare I have never looked so despondently on our prospects –

My idea of a fighting army would be

    Sir C. Campbell – Gen in Chief

    Gen Markham Chief of the Staff

    Gen Airey Quart^r Mr Genl

    Col Pakenham Dep Adjt Genl

Men like Gen Eyre, Brig Gen or rather Col Cameron 42nd. Gen Codrington – Col Percy Herbert. Col McMurdo and men of that stamp commanding Divisions. Men whose heart is in the concern.

Today Friday 13th. There are all sorts of rumours, that Airey goes home – I am sorry for it as he knew his work well and attends to nothing else. That Lord Rokeby has sent his papers in, I wish he w^d go home & have a campaign in Pall Mall, which he is used to & would do well. That Barnard is suspended. I hope it is true for a man less fitted for the rough work to be done here could hardly be found. Besides he has never commanded a regiment of the line & how should he know any thing of their discipline, the feelings the interests of the 40 or 50 battalions which he has to govern. I hope we may be spared the calamity of the army falling under Gen Bentinck or General England. The last rumour is that the Duke of Cambridge is coming out to command. But that I am sure is not true – I hope the great men at home remember that in all human probability Gen Simpson cannot hold the command through the winter even if we do not move from here –

The huts for the winter ought to be arriving as it is a slow operation with hard worked men putting them up even in fine weather.

The huts of last winter will want a cover of canvas & paint to make them water tight, cotton sailcloth from America would do capitally.

Saturday. It seems certain that Airey will go and I don't wonder at it – Now there is here Col McMurdo who was Quarter Master General in a very arduous war in Scinde and did his work well –

I doubt if the French are prepared to pass another winter in the trenches and they have certainly prepared for themselves the means of embarking at Kamiesch by making large forts to protect that operation. Unless a large army is sent to operate on the communications of the Russians, large enough to fight a relieving army, we shall certainly not obtain the evacuation of the Crimea this winter.

Our men, now only get two nights in bed out of three and when large working parties are called for, not so many – Therefore we can spare none for an advance as long as the trenches are held – I doubt if the French could spare ten thousand men away from the siege – so there remain only Turks & Sardinians – The taking of the Inkerman heights is out of the question, it is a position far stronger naturally & now by art made as strong as the position of the Russians in front of Sebastopol – It is a lofty plateau with high cliffs of limestone rock, in most places naturally nearly perpendicular, where it slopes it has either been scarped or the heights defended by intrenchments and batteries of earthworks. This position is of many miles extent and is almost destitute of water – The Russians must keep comparatively small bodies of men to defend the weaker points and all their heavy reserves are apparently camped near the Belbek. I believe an army would have great difficulty in living on the plateau in a position to attack the defences on the North side. A blockading army would therefore have to take up a position either on the main North road near Eupatoria or have to march on Simpheropol from Kaffa or an advance might be made from Kaffa and an attack threatened from Eupatoria, to be pushed or not according to the degree of success of the force coming from Kaffa – But this force must not be taken from the French & English here – We can fall back on our old position in front of Balaclava & spare you all the Turks & Sardinians which now occupy the Tchernaia & Kamara & Vernoubki. But the rest of the forces must come from France & England –

Some such plan will have to be adopted this year or next I feel convinced – We have a General out here who has handled with success larger armies than we have here and this man is now having the Guards Brigade taken from him and is to command a Highland division of 4 regts making 1600 men! I hope we shant be taught by disaster that the command of an army in the field should be given to the best general no matter what his age or want of connection –

I hate to think of the effect in England of a great disaster here – However I have written you enough of my gloomy thoughts – Goodbye – Yours ever
W. G. Romaine

Cambridge University Library: Add. 7633: 5/30

40
Romaine to Lord Mulgrave

[Holograph]   Head Quarters
                                               July 31st. 1855
My dear Mulgrave,
You will have seen by my letter to Lady Mulgrave by last post the uncertain position in which I stand out here. Gen Simpson has written to Lord Panmure quoting the previous letter of Lord Raglan, to back my claim. I ask either to be treated as a lawyer & paid as such or if considered as forming part of the army to be allowed to receive such honours as a civilian may gain – Every body at Head Q^rs considers my claim as a just one and I hope it will succeed – I feel I am useful out here and in a position that I am equal to and I have the entire confidence of the Chiefs of the Army – But I cannot help feeling that even a refusal with an immediate return to England would be so agreeable that I sh^d bear a rebuff with rather more than equanimity & that I w^d. return home having seen what I wanted to see at a very small cost.

You may remember I told you Genl Simpson could not retain the command long, it w^d knock him up. He is far from well. Saturday & Sunday he had diarrhoea yesterday he was a little better, today he is not at all well, & is losing his appetite – Gen

England is going home crippled with rheumatism. So if Simpson is ill Gen Bentinck w^d command!!! Eheu! The next to him luckily is Sir C. Campbell an iron man and a good general – I hope to God it will come to him before long – Gen Markham is getting a little strength & is able to take a ride in the afternoon – He stayed with me some days after his arrival, but he was hardly the shadow of the man who was shooting the ovis Ammon[77] in the Himalaya with me in 1851 – We hear that Sir W. Molesworth is Minister for Colonies – I hope it is true, it is the right man in the right place –

I wish it was decided where we are to pass the winter, whether in our present position or in a position round Balaclava – I am pretty sure the French mean to camp their Army within the fortified lines at Kamiesch. They bring no huts on to their present position, whereas we are going on carrying up huts &c as if it was settled we were to remain where we are in all events, whether we take the South side or fail – Now we cannot hold our present camp if the French withdraw to Kamiesch. We ought to be able to begin by September to devote our time & labour to preparing for winter – Tomorrow is 1st Aug^t.

If the French return to Kamiesch for the winter and the South side is not taken it will be equivalent to a total defeat & must be followed by an evacuation of this part of the Crimea – as of course it w^d be folly to begin the siege again next year having all the outworks to take and approaches to make to a place stronger than it is now –

The world w^d bear a different aspect if we took the South side & destroyed all the shipping – Austria w^d speak out as she w^d see hopes of our armies being let out of prison & all to appear in line with hers in Gallicia, or Bessarabia.

Our men are in good health but lose from 30 to 50 by death & wounds every 24 hours – The lists of casualties published by authority so often in the papers give the Russians plenty of encouragement to go on throwing their missiles into our advanced works – I think they should only be published once a month or so, or the number & names of those killed sh^d be given & not the number of wounded.

I saw sometime ago that the most wonderful reason was given in the House for not giving us a Money order office with our post office. "That possibly the camp might move and then the Post Office saw difficulties in carrying it out" – ! And for such a reason it could not be done when the camp was stationary for ten months & might be stationary for ten more! As if it w^d not be sufficient to notify when the camp did move that no money orders would be issued. Numbers of men w^d avail themselves of the money order office & send money to their families which is now spent in drink – It would be an immense convenience to officers in buying & paying for things in England &c and would really sensibly diminish the amount of cash required to be sent out – as all the money would of course be paid into the Commissariat chest office – But it w^d give a little trouble to the Post Office no doubt – but they have a large staff in the East to do their work and are well paid.

It is just post time goodbye

Remember me to My Lady & all the little ones

Ever y^rs faithfully

W. G. Romaine

Cambridge University Library: Add. 7633: 5/31, 53

41
Romaine to Lord Mulgrave

[Holograph]   Head Quarters
Augt 1st.

My dear Mulgrave,

Although the mail only went yesterday & I wrote to you then, I can't help preparing [?] a line for you in consequence of a report we have at Head Quarters – They say that Gen Airey is to go to the Ionian Islands & Col Gordon is to be Quarter Master General – It will be a great misfortune to the Army if Airey goes but a positive calamity if Gordon succeeds him – He is horribly unpopular though I don't think that alone of much consequence, but of all the slow dull narrow minded red tapists he is perhaps the worst. As I heard a man say just now – if they are going to feed the army during the winter on "returned requisitions" Gordon is just the man to keep their bellies full. A "returned requisition" being a "refused request" for something. He was positively hated in his office – It is but fair to say that a more conscientious zealous hardworking & painstaking puzzle headed slow coach never refused an application since there was a Quarter Master General to an army.

Poor Simpson is failing fast I think and I begin to see land, for they say Bentinck wants to go home, & they w^d hardly let him command even if he remained I should hope.

Sir G. Maclean[78] has reported himself and is in orders today. He is a hardy looking man & has an excellent character as a man of business.

Augt 4th. Yesterday I received your letter of 21. July – I am very much obliged for your exertions in my behalf – you will have seen by my letter of last post what Gen Simpson did for me, and I hope my future will be decided one way or the other before long – I must thank you for your interesting letter full of the political news of the time, a letter from you shows me better what has been going on than all the articles in the Times. I think nothing strengthens the Government with thinking men so much as one of those scurrilous speeches of Disraeli on a great question – It shows such an utter lack of statesmanlike views in the great gun of the opposition.

We have had a sudden change of weather to heavy rains, but now it is fine & hot again and the ground dries very fast – During the first night of the wet 7 men of the 72nd died of cholera & 3 Guardsmen, young men just come out, all of them. The next night the first Div^n lost only 3 by cholera and I hope it was only a casual visit of the disease. Yesterday & all night the Russians kept up a very heavy fire of shot & shell, they are evidently at least as well supplied with ammunition as we are –

Saturday Augt. 4th. You ask about the Land Transport Corps. They have been very unlucky in officers, some dead several sick & several sent away for misconduct. In an hours time I am going to try one of them by General C^t M^l for defalcations in his accounts.

Gen Simpson has come to the rescue of Mac Murdo and will give him some officers. MacMurdo has had fever very badly but is better again. He is terribly overworked owing to his staff failing him. He works day & night & will kill himself before long, but he won't rest.

Gen Simpson is better I think or was yesterday. He is a fine old gentleman, but should be at home. I dreamed last night I was going home. The last man who has retained his health the whole time since leaving England, is gone home sick – Gen Sir R^d Dacre. To be sure he had got all he could. Now it is my turn to be ill, but please God I shall do all I can to keep well –

I like work, but I like justice also, and I have felt unfairly treated & have consequently been disgusted & determined to come home. However either alternative will make me quite happy. To be well treated & stop or snubbed & go home.

Gen Airey, Steele, Harding and I had a rubber of whist last night, absolutely the only piece of amusement or distraction since landing at Scutari in April 1854 – Work seven days a week. Goodbye. I must clear decks for action.

Kindest remembrances to my Lady & her flock.

Ever yours faithfully

W. G. Romaine

Cambridge University Library: Add. 7633: 5/32

42
Romaine to C. J. Selwyn

[Holograph]   Head Quarters
                                               Augt 10th. 1855

My dear Selwyn,

There is not much chance of this letter finding you in England for some time – I hope it may cross you en route for Balaklava – If not, and the ties of home still bind you, I want to tell you that one part of my request has at length been complied with and an enlightened Whig Government has raised my pay to 800 £ per annum paid quarterly – and I decidedly think I have a chance of a Civil C.B. – it is but a chance – Airey however thinks it is a good one – Ld Panmure in a telegraphic message said "Mr Romaine's name was not brought before me until now" – The increase of pay obliges me to stay with the army.

I do not think our General can last long he has had Diarrhoea on him for several days & cannot shake it off.

The last rumour is that it has been decided not to assault but to get out more troops & send them all to Eupatoria – I would long ago have sent Omar Pasha & all the French & English Cavalry to be under his orders & act with his infantry & cut off supplies –

In the mean time the French have made good approaches against the Malakoff with trenches capable of holding a large force close to that work. But it is a place of enormous strength with casemates to hold a large garrison.

I hear Kinglake is coming out again if he is well enough I hope it is true – Layard too is said to be on his way, it will be difficult to receive him as he was before, but if he comes to me I shall take him in, as I hope never to forget a turn done to me in my many travels, and I have always taken his part whenever it was possible & been heartily abused for it –

You see I was right in making a row about my being improperly paid and I think it has the further advantage that if I go home & they do anything for me, the thing done would bear some proportion to what I had had here & if I had put up with ill treatment here they would have thought that I liked it perhaps & was very 'umble and would have trodden on me a little more. Luckily I felt strong enough to rebel and they think the better of me for it I am sure. –

Our mail was late and I have a number of letters to write so good bye – I hope you are coming out.

Y^{rs} ever

W. G. Romaine

Cambridge University Library: Add. 7633: 5/33

43
Romaine to Lord Mulgrave

[Holograph]   Headquarters
                                                    Augt 10th. 1855

My dear Mulgrave,

You will I know be glad to hear that the striving of my friends here and your exertions at home have been successful and that a despatch arrived today to the effect that I am to receive 800 a year from July 1st. –

Last night a telegraphic message was received from Ld Panmure stating that my claim to a C.B. had not been brought before him until Gen Simpson ment^d. it – Gen Airey says this is a favourable answer, that if he had intended to refuse it, he would not have answered in this way –

I hope I may get it, I think I have some claim to it as I have been under fire as much as some of those who have received it and besides carrying on my own department without reproach I have had all the correspondence of the Railway & Sanitary Commissioners from the beginning, when neither one concern nor the other was popular and both have gone on smoothly & been successful – When every body has been abused, the one who has brought no trouble may be rewarded without doing any injustice and as I stand alone, there is no jealousy or envy excited – I declare I feel much more pleased at the recognition of my services than by the receipt of a larger income – I shall work with a lighter heart & a better will –

I mean to give up my Chambers in the Temple as it is not worth while to risk the loss of £120 a year. There is one rather large picture which if my Father does not give house room I have directed may be sent to you as I am sure you will take care of it for me as it will not disgrace any room in the house.

<u>Friday Evening</u>. I have just read your and Lady Mulgrave's most kind letters, it does me good to feel one has such friends.

I laughed immensely at Lord Panmures laconic note to you – I had forgotten the letter & should not have known what the subject was, but for the words Mister Peel – I remember I was very angry when I wrote that – If I am to write to you freely you must exercise a good discretion as to showing a letter to the great ones –

If I tell you all I think at the moment of writing, it may not be worded for inspection and you may get me into a scrape – It will be better perhaps if at any time there is anything worth hinting at Head Quarters that you sh^d. give an "Extract" as our good Rulers do for the Honourable the House of Commons. But I trust that to you – I don't mind risking something on a worthy occasion and I think if I were Minister I sh^d like to see what is thought and said by a looker on at the game.

I would have given something to have seen Lord Palmerston reading my letter if he did – for he hates bad writing and small, and mine must have been detestable, it always is when I write in a hurry –

I have had a capital letter from Kains the Chairman of Com^{ee}. at Chatham. I sent them 10£ for their registration expenses & he gives a good account of the state of affairs –

What a charming notice of Lord Raglan's death there was in the Times copied from a Russian paper –

Lord Rokeby has dug his first parallel which reaches to Therapia, I think his second parallel (flying sap) will take Malta and that he will then effect a lodgment at Dover and get into the Round Tower (at Windsor).[79]

Gen Bentinck is longing to go away I wish he w^d be a little sick and a good deal frightened & go – Then we should have a fighting army Sir C. Campbell (for Simpson cant last) Codrington Markham Eyre I sh^d hope Cameron w^d get one Div^n. & such men as Dan Lysons Trollope & others – If we had a campaign in the field we should feel the want of a cavalry officer very much – Scarlett & Paget are nought. Our best artillery man is gone home, Col Dickson, he had either to lose a good place & home for his family or go to England – It is a great pity. In spite of his being so praised by Layard on all occasions, there is no one to be compared to him to command the artillery for this siege – The men worshipped him as a fire eater for he always stood with his eye glass during a heavy fire looking on without ducking which is a virtue in their eyes, and the officers knew him as a cool pragmatical man in action – Dacres has got a K.C.B. and a cold in the head & is gone to Therapia and I hear is croaking κοαξ

κοαξ[80] like a bull frog – The last rumour is that it has been decided that there is to be no assault but that all the troops now on their way are to go to Eupatoria. I should long ago have sent Omar Pasha & his Turks or as many as could be spared & given him the command of the English & French cavalry & horse artillery – The horses and appointments of these arms are splendid. Some of the cavalry can't ride, but are learning.

McMurdo tells me that he can move the army any day that he is called on. He and Beatty the Railway engineer get on capitally, and I have drawn up conditions under which the latter would I think gladly remain as long as the railway is wanted, and I think they are such as might easily be arranged – A man so thoroughly up to his business and so accommodating should not be allowed to go away – He is entitled to be in England by November –

It is very good of you to think of getting the back pay for me. I thought they would have given it from January when Lord Raglan wrote, but if I get the C.B. I don't care about the money.

The Duke of Newcastle is I hear gone to Kertsch for a day or so.

I wish Barnard could get the Governorship of Barateria, he is the mildest old woman that ever put on a uniform – You should hear Simpson say with his broad Scotch brogue "Its just one of Barnard's mares nests".

We are taking a lesson in the art of looting or plundering – Some of the Land Transport wagons were sent to Baidar to bring away wine from a Villa there and the report of the officer was

	"Sir,
<u>Margin</u> –	I have the honour to report that there was not
1 Sofa	wine enough to load all the wagons & that I
2. Tables	loaded the rest with the articles detailed in the
12. Chairs	margin
– Beds	There were two side saddles but I only
&c &c	brought away the best.
	I have &c
	Yr. obed^t servant
	Dugald Dalgetty"

Our invasion will be the making of the wine growers in the Crimea when peace comes – There is a sort of dry but sparkling champagne which is excellent and a very good sort of Burgundy – The grapes are as fine as those of the Delta of Egypt –

Tell my Lady I owe her a letter and many thanks, some of which I hope to send by next post.

I am very glad you have settled the letting of the Alum works. You will enjoy your holidays and rest at Mulgrave after your hard work & it is to be hoped you will not have an election –

If we only get on tolerably here I think the Ministry will be safe for the next Session – I hope the hutting is forward – Soyer called on me today. He is going to camp up with the Divisions and enlighten the minds of the soldiers as to the capabilities of salt pork –

There is a terrible system of plunder of officers parcels still goes on as well as of Government property on board the transports. When will they adopt the economical plan of a super cargo with every ship – whose sole duty should be to have charge of the cargo and see it safely delivered to the consignees –

I have written little Laura a long letter – I direct this by Lady Mulgraves advice to the Castle where I hope it will find you all well.

Goodbye, ever yours faithfully

W. G. Romaine

Cambridge University Library: Add. 7633: 5/34

44
Romaine to Lord Mulgrave

[Holograph]   Head Quarters
Augt 13th. 1855

My dear Mulgrave,

I told you in my last letter that Ld Panmure had directed Gen Simpson to communicate to me his despatch authorizing him to increase my pay to 800£ per annum. The General did this in the very handsome letter which follows & the receipt of which gave me the greatest pleasure.

"Sir, I beg to transmit to you the copy of a despatch I have lately received from Lord Panmure, and in congratulating you, as I do most sincerely, on the information contained therein, I have great pleasure in bearing my warmest testimony to the zeal & ability you have at all times, shown in the discharge of your duties; and in thanking you for the many occasions on which you have undertaken at my request duties not belonging to your department, and have cheerfully carried them out to my perfect satisfaction"

> I have the honour to be, Sir,
> Y^r most obedient humble servant
> James Simpson
> General Commanding

The General has been ill several days, and the day before yesterday had ordered his carriage to take him on board ship for a change of air when news came in by deserters that the Russians had received large reinforcements – two divisions and meant to attack us at daylight today – All the world was ready at 3. AM, reserves of infantry & artillery & all the cavalry artillery &c in the Balaclava Valley – But there was no sign of a move – Nor did I ever for a moment believe that the Russians meant to do so absurd a thing as attack our trenches in daylight – They must despair of a defence they have so ably protracted before they do so foolish & hopeless a thing –

I wish they had ventured to attack when we were all ready. They also made not the slightest sign of a move along the course of the Tchernaia & line of the Baidar road.

Tuesday Morning – Mail is in. There is no news.

I am sorry to say McMurdo & Col Napier of Land Transport Corps are both very ill – the first with ~~fever and the~~ dysentery, following diarrhoea & the second with fever & McMurdo says he must go home. Mac Murdo has overworked himself & now will take no rest, he says his reputation is at stake and he must stay by his work as long as he can hold a pen – I don't know any one who could replace him – The concern is now immense & complicated.

Best remembrances to all your household
Yours ever faithfully
W. G. Romaine

45
Journal for 16 to 17 August 1855

[Holograph]

Augt. 16th.

Last night a despatch was sent from both French and Sardinians that they were expecting an attack in the morning. At sunrise this morning the Russians were seen advancing against the Sardinian position North of Tchernaia they held it for some time until the artillery of the enemy became too much for them when they retired across the river to their main position.

Their batteries have been strengthened by some 18 pounder guns of ours which were of great value in the contest –

The Russian tirailleurs descended the slopes and exchanged fire with the Sardis – The Sardinians abandoned an isolated conical hill on which they had a small redoubt but never gave way on their principal line – The tide of battle gradually turned from there to the plain in front of the bridge & [brow ?] of Traktir. The Russians brought a great number of guns on the hills above the tete du pont which they held in the winter from which they fired into the French position – Their guns advanced in great numbers along the Mackenzie road towards the bridge and westward along the course of the Tchernaia, i.e. down stream. Their guns were backed by huge masses of infantry in the plain on the ridges above and in the valley of the Chuliou, above Tchorgoun.

Large bodies of cavalry supported their troops and were ready to take advantage of any success. In the plain alone the Russians brought into action about 40 pieces.

By 6.30 the firing was heavy from Sardins, on brown hill from French ridge W. of Tchorgoun & from Russn. batts. opposite –

At 7.15. There was a steady fusillade near the village of Tchorgoun and outposts of French appeared to be attacked.

At 7.30. Balls & shells from Russian batteries which had approached the stream of the Tchernaia fell fast on the French ridge – The French battery nearest to Bosquets observatory on the ridge below opened fire – The Rgts. c^d. be seen behind French ridge began to ascend. A Russian caisson explodes.

At 7.45. The Russian guns are everywhere attempting to cross the Tchernaia, in face of a heavy fire. The Russian infantry supports the guns. The French in the Aqueduct keep up a good fire on the Russ[ns]. Two French caissons explode. The Russian tirailleurs ascend the ridge in front of Tchorgoun in retreat fired upon by the Sardinians. The report of the 18 pounders may be distinctly heard –

The Russian guns made a very determined attempt to cross the river, one got in & was extricated with great difficulty & I think the fear of losing some, spoilt their attempt. They remained firing between the trees & bushes & lost a good many horses there. Some of the infantry crossed but advanced very little way beyond the guns. A battalion of Russ. infantry came very far down the stream looking for a place to cross they were in no order were fired upon by the French tirailleurs in the aqueduct and fell back in disorder towards the slopes of the Gringalet battery.

A heavy mass of infantry & cavalry was formed in columns along the Mackenzie road back to where the road turns to ascend the plateau –

The ridge which runs back from Tchernaia was also covered with troops of all arms.

8. The Russians were retreating on all points – The artillery retired from the river & formed in front of a low range of hills N. of Tchernaia, protected by line of lancers. Their guns also formed line E of Mackenzie road protecting line of infantry retreat.

By 8.25. The firing in front of Tchorgoun had altogether ceased the fighting in front of the bridge was over and a Russian battalion of infantry which had been left behind in the bed of the Tchernaia had to run a la [illegible] across the plain towards the slopes of the Gringalet battery pursued by shot & shell from the French batteries.

By 8.35. All firing had ceased – Red flag struck – During the whole of the action the Russian heavy guns on the Mackenzie heights fired shot & shell on the French drawn up in order of battle.

Our cavalry & reserve artillery were drawn up on the Turkish redoubts, but did not come into action they had been placed under Della Marmora's orders.

Rode to Sir C. Campbell & had breakfast.

Found Col. Ross of 93rd. had just reported to him that 30,000 Russ^n. infantry were in column of attack & c^d. be in Balaclava in two hours! The Highlanders were in the trenches –

Rode home & found mail had arrived, with letter from Mulgrave say^g that it was not the intention of Gov^t. to put Sir C.C. in command in case of Gen Simpson going home.

In afternoon rode with Steele to Traktir bridge where the recent fighting had been. The Russians had brought wooden platform bridges to cross the aqueduct. They had driven the French outposts across the bridge and then had mounted the ridge on either side, their dead were lying on the crest of the ridges on both sides.

Here the 2nd. Zouaves had been surrounded by Russ^{ns}. and while cutting their way back had been rescued by a bayonet charge of the 62nd. line. The wounded were lying thickly strewed along the whole face of the ridge, in great numbers along the course of the aqueduct & in the river. Here some 300 prisoners were taken unwounded & I met them going up under an escort of cavalry. The French cacolets were bringing in wounded Russians. Many of them had just come from a 3 months march from Warsaw & looked thin & pale & worn. They had all four days black bread with them. The Russians fired some shots at the bridge while this was going on but I suppose seeing that their own men were being carried off they ceased. They very nearly killed D^r. Hall and one of their shot struck a wounded Russian & cut him in two.

The Artillery of the Imperial Guard began to arrive and strong reinforcements.

Pelissier had at one time intended to pursue the Russians who were jammed up in the gorge at N. end of valley.

A Russian officer who was prisoner, asked whether any attack had been made from the town they had been told that 40,000 men w^d. make a sortie at the same time.

Della Marmora has had an A.D.C. wounded. Some Turkish battalions were sent down as a reinforcement after the battle, and a number of the Imperial Guard.

I told Gen Airey that the French had asked why our cacolets did not assist and he ordered 50 to go down.

Augt. 17.
At daylight the English batteries opened on the Redan & Malakoff and the Karabelnaia & the Barrack & Garden batteries, the first gun from the Redan was fired in 7 minutes. Our advanced batteries in left attack particularly 7 & 8 met with a heavy fire from Garden batteries.

The Russians threw shells & shot over our heads into camp.

At 4.25.

The Careening Bay batt. opened & Malakoff began firing. Our signal for opening was three shells from Greenhill –

At 5 min to 6.

The Mamelon began to fire & it was returned by Malakoff directly –

The fire continued heavily all day at 4 PM when I went up by [?] Maison d'Eau the Redan & Malakoff did not return a shot in a quarter of an hour.

The garden batteries & Karabelnaia fired at intervals.

The French fired a few guns from the left attack and the mortars in rear of the Mamelon –

At 6 PM an explosion took place in rear of the Mamelon followed by the bursting from 40, or 50 shells.

A General Wredo was found dead on the field of battle with the plan of attack & Gortschakoff's orders, & the numbers of the 10 columns –

They were to have marched straight on Balaclava and a sortie was to have been made at Careening bay, the Central Bastion & Quarantine, none upon us apparently.

One of the prisoners asked how many guns we had in the battle & being told 150 said we heard you had only 56, & Martimpré [*sic* – actually Martimprey] said, that was exactly the number we had horsed.

Cambridge University Library: Add. 9554/4

46
Romaine to Lord Mulgrave

[Holograph]   Head Quarters
                                               Augt. 18th 1855

My dear Mulgrave,

I have only a few minutes to write as the General C^t M^l will assemble in my hut directly but I cannot let your letter of Aug 1st go without an answer.

You will have received my thanks for your exertions in my behalf and I really feel very deeply your active remembrance of the absent.

But there is something more important in your letter – With regard to Simpson's successor I have not heard anything that grieved me so much since Lord Raglans death as that Campbell is not thought fit to succeed in case of his going away –

I am confident they are mistaken in his character. He is the only man except perhaps Eyre, who among the Generals possesses the quick eye the firm hand and the sagacious & patient intellect to imagine and work out a campaign in all its details –

So far from being likely to quarrel with the French, there is no officer here possessed with so high an opinion of their character as soldiers or who has lived so much and so intimately with them during the campaign as Sir Colin.

He and General Vinoy, a first rate soldier like himself and a general who must some day command the French Army have been living on the most brotherly terms through the whole winter spring and summer, being associated in the defence of Balaclava –

It is charming to see the way in which Sir Colin is greeted by all the officers of that French Division when he goes down to visit them in the trenches –

No General in Chief out here is likely to be on bad terms with the French as it does not require a ghost to come from the grave to tell him that whether right or wrong he would be recalled –

The present Com^r of the Forces is probably the most unfit man for his position that could be found. What he may have been I cannot tell, but now he is utterly indifferent about all the great questions that arise. He never writes a despatch and hardly ever expresses an opinion upon them when written. I should have thought him imbecile, but he is shrewd and clear enough on any little matter of detail, such as a technical point in a Court Martial. He has never lived in an atmosphere where great interests and great questions were discussed and settled. He hates a conference with the French Generals because they speak too fast and he cannot understand them and he is ashamed of his bald disjointed sentences in their language – He has consequently no voice at a council, and he is actually obliged to have in Steele to be present at secret conferences that he may write the despatch afterwards – When a man like this is at the head, the chief of the staff should be a man of some grasp of mind instead of being a cypher – He is not fit to be churchwarden of a country village – Markham I know well having spent six months with him in the Himalayas shooting &c. A better second in command under a first rate General, no one could wish to have –

If Eyre had entire control over his temper he would be a great man and I daresay will be, in spite of it. Codrington I consider as inferior to either of the three and Bentinck I don't count.

You may make any use you think proper of what I have written as it is the unbiassed result of anxious thought – You won't show my letter to any one, I know, for mere gossip –

I have no time to write of what is passing here –

Good bye.

Kind remembrance to My Lady & the children

Ever yours faithfully

W. G. Romaine

Cambridge University Library: Add. 7633: 5/36

47
Journal for 18 to 22 August 1855

[Holograph]

Augt. 18th.

Had a General C^t. M^l. on Soldier of 12th. Lancers for deserting with intent to go over to enemy.

The firing continued all night. This morning I hear that we have lost a good many men & officers artillery, & navy & many casualties in 2nd. Divis.

This afternoon it was stated that the Russ^{ns}. were in great numbers in Karabelnaia, if so their loss must have been heavy as our shells were falling all over the Russ^{n}. position. The Redan & Malakoff proper were silent, but on proper left of Malakoff & Little Redan they kept up fire on Mamelon [three illegible words] great vivacity. In the Evening a French 11 gun battery rt. of left attack opened on Barrack battery.

At 10 PM a sortie apparently took place as there was heavy musquetry fire for 20 minutes, and a storm of shells from French & us.

Augt. 22nd.

The Russians are working very hard at their bridge from North side to Fort Nicholas – Opinions seem divided as to whether it is intended to facilitate an attack, the defence only or to provide an escape in case of a reverse.

Dined with Genl. Eyre & met Duke of Newcastle, & Keppel &c. Keppel thinks the bridge a mistake and that it can only be made for some temporary purpose as the first westerly gale will break it up. It is made of rafts of timber joined on one to the other and he thinks kept in their places by the chains which reach across the harbour buoyed up by spars.

The Duke told us that during the sitting of Parl^{t}. when he was minister he used to get home to his dinner at 11 PM, sometimes so knocked up that he c^{d}. not write to Her Majesty and that he was sure to have a letter from Windsor the next morning. She used to expect to hear all he had said done & written He said no one c^{d}. have a better mistress to serve, that when he left she wrote him two letters which he sh^{d}. always preserve. The Queen wrote a letter to Adm^{l}. Lyons on the death of his son which gratified the Adm^{l}. very much.

He spoke very highly of Bright, but s^{d}. that he was not a gentleman and that he was disagreeable in society, that at dinner he w^{d}. set to and attack some one in a violent way so as to be unpleasant to the company. He says that his style & manner in the house is improving – that at first he was too combative. But that now he is learning his audience, and that Palmerston has had the same lesson to learn – That he used though constantly in office to come down only from 6 to 7, be away at the questioning time and then after dinner come back about 11 and stay till the house rose.

Keppel s^d. he took the Duke to the advanced trenches and a shell burst over them and a bit stuck into a gabion close to him, he asked very quietly whether the fragment c^d. be got out for him & he carried it away hot as it was. The Duke was unlucky enough to go to Eupatoria the very time of the battle of the Tchernaia.

Cambridge University Library: Add. 9554/4

48
Romaine to Lord Mulgrave

[Holograph]   Head Quarters
                                               Aug. 31. 1855

My dear Mulgrave,

I sent a line to Lady Mulgrave by last post, begging pardon for having been naughty and promising never to do so no more –

And now you are snugly housed and reposing at Mulgrave after a fierce session, how pleasant the woods must be after Westminster and "Siggs on Pheasants" after "Cobden on Peace & War" –

We are longing for the details of the Sveaborg affair – I hope it is thoroughly done.[81]

We are carrying on a hot war of trenches and batteries – The French had a terrible explosion two nights ago, & suffered a loss of 40 killed & 100 or more wounded. Their batteries were not damaged. Our nightly losses by the enemy mount up to nearly 60 or 70 which is a heavy drain, calling for steady supplies of men from home and they arrive pretty regularly to fill up gaps in the ranks.

I have been right in my prophecy hitherto and the Russians have not ventured on a second attack on the Tchernaia –

Their attempt was a foolhardy one & sure to fail, even against inferior troops – Now the position is impregnable.

Our last consignment of guns & mortars is fast getting into the trenches and the fire if it opens throughout the line will be unendurable by the enemy unless their troops are in casemates. If they are kept in casemates, a well devised & sudden attack ought to succeed before they could be in force to repel it.

I think the next attack on the Malakoff must succeed. I think we shall join in it instead of attacking the Redan in the first instance.

I think the French left attack will also be pushed they are very close and have prepared a place d'armes capable of holding a large body of troops close to the enemy.

I have had a good explanation of the saying reported about Simpsons fitness for command. Sir C. Napier used to say that he knew no man fitter for the place of second in command than Genl Simpson as he obeyed orders to the letter – That I can quite understand – I am not sure that it will be any harm his being Com^r in Chief as long as we are in front of Sebastopol as he must play second fiddle to the French – But it would be a bad day for us if we had to take the field. I hope he will get positive orders not to abandon the trenches unless the French do, if winter finds us still outside the town – He has openly talked of retiring to the heights of Balaclava for the winter, but I think it is only talk & no preparations for such a position have been made, on the contrary, hutting materials are carried up to the front & erected.

Markham is back again I am happy to say. McMurdo has been staying with me some days to recruit and is better – Col Napier the second in the Land Transport Corps was very nearly dying, but is now I hope well and at home.

The new Railway Wagons are arrived & a few more men. The road is being made and if McMurdo had another thousand drivers, we should be almost safe for the winter even if the Railway failed – I have no fears for the Railway myself, the Times persists in saying that the rain stopped the traffic for ten days – One line of rails was repaired & worked in less than 24 hours and the other in 48 – There will be men set apart as in all lines, called "repairers" whose business it is to go up & down the portion of line entrusted to them and put every thing in order as soon as a defect begins to show itself.

The French have done wonders the last three nights and are within 35 yards of the salient of the Malakoff and so perfectly sheltered as to be able to work in the day time, they may assault that part any day –

We had an ill managed affair in our right attack the night before last – The working party was surprised & ran in on the covering party which was also alarmed & before the supports could come to their assistance the Russians from the Redan had upset the gabions & spoiled all the work they had done – One officer was killed and 2 wounded in the affair.

The Russians are very busy removing goods of some kind & timbers from the South side but for all that I think they will fight stoutly before they finally quit, in fact I think they will stand a second assault – I wish the French would take our trenches and release our whole army for field operations, to land at Eupatoria & march straight on Sympheropol. We should make prisoners of every mothers son of the garrison – We have transport enough to move & feed us – Only we should want a General – Colin Campbell would be the man for such a soldier like expedition as this would be.

I am afraid there are ten thousand good & valid reasons against such a move –

We have delightfully cool weather and I hope we may keep it yet two months.

Gen Jones is recovering & able to sit up in bed – Gen Airey is much better but will not I fear be a strong man until he has had a run home – We should miss him very much if he went away.

Good bye my dear Mulgrave good sport & plenty – today is Septr 1st. I have heard several shots so I suppose those poaching Russians have tried to trespass on our manor – I am going up to the covert side as soon as post is gone.

My best remembrances to My Lady and her flock –

Y^{rs} ever

W. G. Romaine

Cambridge University Library: Add. 7633: 5/37

49
Journal for 6 to 9 September 1855

[Holograph]

Thursday. Septr. 6th.

Up before daylight. Omar Pasha had come to the conference on being told that the Allies expected positively to be attacked this day. I rode to Cathcarts hill not at all believing that we sh^d. be attacked on the Tchernaia. The enemy's loss was so great on 16th. Augt. and the place is now so strong that he will not venture again to attack there. I waited till sunrise when the French left attack opened in magnificent order from left to right, every gun was seen as it fired and the place where every shot fell in the Russian works, and for a long time the wind blew so exactly along the line of trenches that the batteries of the different parallels and the guns in them could be plainly distinguished. The Russian guns in Bastions du Mat & Centrale opened almost immediately & a heavy mortar battery in rear of B^n. du Mât and the firing was general & very heavy. It ceased nearly about 5.15 but was again resumed. Towards evening the Russ^n. guns on upper & lower Garden battery fired on our advanced batt^y. of left attack. We did not fire more than has been usual lately. While I was sitting near French observatoire, the Russ^{ns}. fired up one shell fell quite close, burst & threw me a piece of a pound or more near to my feet. The embrasures of B^n. du Mât nearly destroyed. Only two guns in Western Angle firing towards evening – B^n. Central still active.

About 8.30. a frigate in harbour caught fire & burned till nearly midnight. It was very bright light, no explosion took place. Airey says that Omar Pasha was very angry & went back to Constan^{le}. in spite of the supposed nearness of a general engagement! His enemies will remind him that he has never yet taken an active part in a General action & that he sh^d. not have run away now. He wants to withdraw his men to Asia. He was reminded that last year the snow fell on 5th. Sept. – but he s^d that between the falls of snow the weather was fit for campaigning.

Saturday. Septr. 8th.

This was the day fixed for the assault on the Malakoff, Redan & Central Bastion, and yesterday 12. noon was settled to be the hour. It was a very stormy morning following a night of blowing weather from N. West. The fleet was to have helped on left attack but so much sea was running that they could not be made of any use.

We & the French were getting so low in ammunition that the day could not be postponed and the firing had begun three days ago. After the bombardment began a supply of 20,000 shells arrived, and the Terrible [?][82] was known to be on her way out.

The line had been so much kept in our front that this morning at 10 fewer spectators than usual were visible at all the lookout places – This might have been accounted for by the Russians by the disagreeable nature of the day. It was a wintry searching wind bringing clouds of dust in one's face. The waves washing over Russian bridge in the harbour – men & carts passing – There was a regular fire kept up from French left attack and from our batteries, but French right attack was silent.

At 11.55. The French mortars in Mamelon opened and their advanced trenches were seen to be rapidly filling with men – The fire which had been burning in the town since morning, did not seem to increase or spread much, but gave up a good cloud of smoke. The Russians in the early morning had vainly endeavoured to put it out.

The Redan fired very few shells since 10 AM – now & then a shot at Mamelon or our 8 gun battery.

Not much movement across the bridge and no sign of unusual alarm in the town or on the North side, working parties & carts going in & out of the town.

At 12.15. The action commenced by the French whose sap was close to the salient of Malakhoff running in without firing a shot, it was admirably done, at the curtain & little Redan the Musquetry fire began instantly and down to the end of the Russian line on the Careening Bay.

The rush of the French into the Malakhoff was evidently a surprise and no defence was made –[83]

At 12.35. The sound of the musquetry was very heavy and smoke very dense, the Russian reserves opposite the French evidently coming into action.

The Redan began firing from its left flank

12.42. The Russians in the Redan firing over the parapet and many of them exposing themselves to almost certain death by standing on the top of the parapet, firing, numbers were seen to fall but their places were immediately taken by others. Our guns still firing into the Redan.

The French have run down & occupy the flank of the Malakhoff & are firing musquetry towards the Redan –

The sound of musquetry at Malakoff & little Redan ceasing.

1.P.M. The Guards Div^n. formed in front of our look out place, a round shot bowling through the ranks now & then and knocking over an unwary man or so.

The fire at the Malakhoff has again become very heavy.

The guns on French left attack still firing.

The Russians still firing over parapet of the Redan.

1.30. Very strong battle going on in rear of Malakoff.

French still pressing in a large party at work at the salient, & head of their Sap.

The Redan firing shells very vigorously but very much at random.

The Parapet still lined with Russians but our attack has evidently succeeded as the parapet of the Salient of the Redan is covered with Red Coats.

1.50. A severe fight is evidently going on inside the Redan.

2.03. The Russians on the top of the parapet of the Redan are throwing stones at our men who are repulsed from the Salient – They had clustered thick on this side of the ditch and on the parapet, but then seemed to stand unable to advance. The Russians firing musquetry at them from the whole length of the parapet on either flank – They run back to trenches.

2.30. Long strings of wounded seen coming up in rear of Gordons battery & by Woronzov road, walking & on stretchers.

2.42. Small explosion in Malakhoff, no noise.

French left attack silent.

3.16. Explosion in front of Mamelon.

3.43. Russian steamer came up to Sapoune ridge moving slowly & firing at French.

French batteries of left attack open.

4.5. Guns open at last from 21 gun battery on the Redan.

4.10. The Steamer [?] in front of St. Paul Fort on fire.

4.30. French fire on left attack ceased again.

4.48. Immense explosion of Gunpowder in or near little Redan.

5.30. Firing much fainter.

5.40. Russian soldiers & carts crossing bridge to North side, probably reserves retiring.

Our reserves sent to Camp.

Sunday – September 9th.

Kelly called me very early to say that there was a very heavy cloud of smoke from Sebastopol. I had heard about ten explosions in the night and guessed what was going on in the town, but was not prepared to find that the Redan had been occupied since 1.30.AM by Sir C. Campbell & the Highlanders. They had sent out parties to look for wounded in the dark and they had not been fired on after 11.30. PM, but it was some time before the officer asked leave to go into the work & see. They found some of our wounded well taken care of by the Russians put in the blindages & water near them.

When I got down to the Redan the dead were still lying on the parapet where they fell – The sight inside was a very remarkable one – English & Russian dead lying side by side, guns overthrown, magazines open & powder in every form lying about, the men were every minute finding wounded prisoners in the holes & corners of the place. Many of the guns on the flanks were quite uninjured I found one loaded & primed & the fuse in it, which I took out –

They had stores as well as barracks in the work and one man had amused himself by making a sort of guitar there were shoemakers & tailors workshops. The work was quite open to the rear – The guns & gunners were singularly well protected both from musquetry & cannon shot. Markham was in command

Figure 14. Plan of gun traverses in the Redan (from journal dated 9 September 1855).

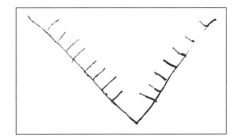

outside & I met General Simpson there & Keppel with whom I went as far as the Salient Brig Gen Straubenzee there joined me. Gen Airey was inside. There was no shelter for the defenders when once an enemy was inside – except the gun traverses thus [see Figure 14] and no soldiers should have been stopped when once they had gained admission.

Cambridge University Library: Add. 9554/4

Part 5

After the Fall

Romaine reflected the general feeling that the victory was largely thanks to the French, and correctly observed that our troops had 'all the fight taken out of them'. He comments unfavourably on the British leadership generally – again comparing Simpson unfavourably with Sir Colin Campbell – and in particular on the command of the assault, noting that Codrington did not show the necessary leadership when it was needed. Others did not escape censure and Bentinck's failure to go into the trenches while commanding them was criticised.

With the Duke of Newcastle, the former Secretary for War and the Colonies who had lost office with the fall of Aberdeen's government and was now in the Crimea as a tourist, he inspected the battered fortifications and ruins which had held out so long. The neglect by the Russians of their wounded and dead appalled him, as did the behaviour of the French troops who looted so mercilessly.

He wondered what the Russians would now do, for with the only declared objective of the expedition having been achieved, the army was now uncertain what was expected of it. There were thoughts of next year's campaign and where they might go. It was debated whether to destroy the Sevastopol docks or preserve them for allied use. He speculated on whether or not the whole Crimea should be occupied.

Firing, generally desultory but sometimes heavy, still came from the Russians on the north side of the harbour. Meanwhile there was determined work on the roads and conditions improved beyond recognition. There were huts to accommodate the men and a steady supply of rations, stores and comforts.

It was decided to destroy the docks. An expedition to Kinburn was mounted.

After the failure of the September assault General Simpson had resigned in protest at the implied criticism of him by the Secretary at

War. His resignation had been immediately accepted, but he had remained in post because the government could not agree on who should replace him. He was now replaced not by Sir Colin Campbell, Romaine's choice, but by Codrington. To his surprise, Romaine soon found the latter easy to work with and was won over by the way he respected and treated Sir Colin.

Romaine discovered that his private letters to Mulgrave had been shown by him to Lord Palmerston and Lord Panmure and feared (correctly as it turned out) that in consequence of his frankness he would not get the CB (that is, he would not be appointed as a Commander of the Order of the Bath) which he felt he had deserved and which he longed for.

He dismissed a mention in a newspaper of a Channel Tunnel as being 'as absurd as the Suez Canal'... He continued to give frank assessments of the generals and staff, including Mr Filder, 'the evil genius of the army', and thought Airey had been unfairly treated.

Finally, his thoughts returned to his candidacy to represent Chatham in the House of Commons and to the meetings he planned with all his friends at home. His long and hard stint at the Headquarters of the Army of the East was over.

Romaine to Lord Mulgrave

[Holograph]   Head Quarters
                                              Septr 11th. 1855

My dear Mulgrave,

Sebastopol has fallen! thanks to the French! and to a skilful surprise by which they entered & carried the Malakoff before the Russians were in force to expel them. Being in, such was the strength of the place that it was out of the power of any number of Russians to turn them out. I am almost doubtful whether to tell you my opinion of the contemptible position we occupy out here, I am perfectly ashamed of the share we have had in the result – Against all the best opinion we again tried to storm the Redan, and to do it with troops who had had all the fight taken out of them –

I told you some time ago that there was but one man who could make an attack on that place successfully. How has it turned out, we have sustained a most disgraceful defeat, and but for the surprise on the Malakoff the Allied Armies would have had such a disastrous repulse as would have prevented any further attempt till next year – Had Sir C. Campbell and his 2000 Highlanders been sent at the Redan they would have marched into it in a body and driven out the defenders like rats – Our soldiers of the storming party made their rush out as well as the miserable nature of our works for such an operation would permit, they crossed the ditch and got on to the parapet and then with few exceptions the men stuck, others remained stupefied on our side of the ditch to be shot down by the cross fire of the Russians from the two flanks – the men having possession of the salient could not by any efforts of the officers be induced to advance and drive at the Russians, though it was then only a hand to hand struggle on clear ground with no artillery capable of firing on them – The officers boys as many of them were behaved nobly – the men of the rifles as on all occasions did their part of the duty in an admirable manner. The

foremost men in the Redan were men of the 90th Reg^t – Windham
after getting in, three times sent an officer to beg for support, but
the men c^d not be made to move. At last unwisely as I think,
Windham went himself to try & get assistance – While he was
away our men were driven out, and I shall never forget the bitter
moment when I saw our men running back to the trenches from a
work they had gained, pursued by volleys of stones from the
Russians on the parapet – This I saw and was told a few minutes
afterwards by one of the officers who had been inside that they
accompanied their missiles with all sorts of shouts and
gesticulations and waving of caps as if begging them to come back.

The French were similarly repulsed from the two other points
of their attack the little Redan and the Central Bastion and
Pelissier has kindly seized on this fact to hide part of our
disgrace –

The siege and the long course of dodging behind bad trenches
has completely demoralized our men – Then, many in all
regiments are mere boys who have never been disciplined to obey
orders, and upon whom neither the words nor the example of their
officers had any effect.

The smoke of the burning town and the explosions of its forts
may hide & cover some of our disgrace and some of it I hope never
will be known –

Our general was in the left attack during the assault made on
the right and when we were repulsed, there was no one even to
order the batteries to resume firing till past four o'clock, and the
parapet continued to be crowded with Russian marksmen who
picked off our men who were crowded in the advanced trenches
– our engineers are children, and their works only fit to hide rats –
I went through the Russian & French works of defence and attack, I
hope our engineers have done so to [*sic*] & taken a lesson –

Well, now the siege is over and we are left with a number of
great questions to be immediately decided and the decisions acted
on – These decisions must be taken with the French, but our
General don't talk French, or only such as he is ashamed to utter
before Pelissier & his staff – so he keeps aloof and takes no part.
The Russian General sends in to beg a truce of 24 hours. The

French refuse without even communicating with Simpson & he only hears of it by accident.

No decision has ever yet been come to with regard to ulterior operations, if the Russians run away & leave the Crimea which I think they are doing as fast as they can, we shall be all right – If they don't, we have taken no step to make them, to follow or harrass [*sic*] their retreat to make prisoners or capture their material – We are stupefied at our success – Gen Simpson has a private letter to write which serves his turn when he wants to act the busy & occupied man and he lets every question be decided by others and is satisfied to put his signature to a dispatch and let things take exactly the course which those about him choose & luckily they are men of sense – But it makes me sick at heart & angry to see the fortunes of England and her army left to such an imbecile. He is an honourable old Gentleman but he has never been used to lead & direct in great affairs and is too old now to learn – A shrewder man to manage the affairs of the United Service Club I suppose you could not find, but for any thing beyond a Committee man of a club – God help us we might as well have Mrs Gamp.

General Barnard luckily has nothing of any great consequence to do, and as he acts always by the advice of others in what falls to him he will not make any great mistake! Luckily Airey & Steele are men capable of guiding affairs and Simpson is quite willing to allow them to rule as long as it does not appear to the world that he is in leading strings – Leicester Curzon the Assistant Military Sec^y has gone with the despatches – He must have seen much of what was going on at Head Quarters – He is a noble fellow, make his acquaintance if you come across him –

I have written you a letter not of news & gossip but of what I have thought & felt about affairs here, if it will do any good I am quite prepared to abide by any risk or loss in letting the truth be known – If as is very likely, it is impossible for the present to make any change why then put my letter behind the fire and forget it. Don't show it to any one for mere gossip, but I know I can trust to your discretion. We had a terrible storm last night and the mail which should have been here yesterday has not arrived.

French troops are on the march to Baidar, so I hope active measures are being taken to pursue the enemy by the French at all events –

As for our doing any thing it is then "happy go lucky" we are fallen to be a mere French contingent and so shall remain while we have a cypher at our head –

I hope all this destruction of Russian property and wasting of their territory with fire & sword may bring them to their senses – But we never should have allowed 50 or 60,000 men to escape from the Crimea, that we may meet them again in Bessarabia, or that they may be employed to menace Austria with continued inaction –

The heavy rain which began last night & is now going on will delay the Russian retreat very much – They are still holding by their rear guard to the North side but in my belief the main army is already far away to the North by the Sympheropol road –

Let me hear from you and my Lady whenever you can find leisure to write even though there may be no great news to communicate.

I expect rather a heavy winter but thank God there are no trenches.

Good bye my dear Mulgrave
Ever yours faithfully
W. G. Romaine

Cambridge University Library: Add. 7633: 5/38

51
Journal for 12 September 1855
[Holograph]

Wednesday Septr. 12th.
News came in that all the steamers were burnt except two which were sunk this morning. When Lord Panmure heard of the fall of the place, he telegraphed "Send an officer home with the despatches." Keppel came up to Head Q^rs. to say that he thought the North side was abandoned and that he wished to be allowed to

row across. We rode with Barnard & Duke of Newcastle through the Redan to the Dockyard, the Russians were firing across from one gun in a half burnt & stranded steamer and from a 3 gun battery on a yellow cliff top Eastward of Fort Catherine – The French returned the fire but Keppels guns in front of the Great Barracks on the terrace did not fire.

We rode down to look at the docks, some French officers were there to settle the ground each army was to occupy – We foolishly I think gave up all the habitable part of the Karabelnaia, but kept the Great Barracks & buildings near the dry docks, enough room to lodge our whole army if put in repair – We then went down to the large row of Hospital buildings and saw such a sight as I should think civilized Europe never saw, the whole range of large buildings had been filled with wounded, they had been left by the Russians when they vacated the place & we did not know of their being there till the flag of truce was sent back for 24 hours suspension of arms. When Boutinieff [?] of the Vladimir came over, it was arranged that they sh^d. take away their wounded, but they left a vast number of dead. – These were today all unburied dying as they had died in their agonies some on the beds & others on the floor – hundreds – one vault was full of dead – and dead of most horrible wounds, utterly untended, & undressed, with no food no water no medicine & no attendance. Men lying dead with legs shot off just as they were brought in from the fight, all livid and putrid, in every ghastly form & attitude as the death agony had seized them –

Wretches were going round feeling their clothes & pockets for money & plunder of any kind – M^r. Goodall the artist told me that he saw a Zouave the day before quickly seize a horribly wounded man & pull off his boots without the least regard to his screams of pain. And he saw another drunken French soldier fall forward with both hands on to a poor wretch dreadfully mutilated & only able to screech with pain, from the brutal touch of this drunken savage. The blackest page of war was here to be seen. Today no living man had been rescued & sent up to camp. There were no traces of any care having been bestowed, no vessels for water, no signs of a doctors presence except a mass of bloody bandages in a corner. In peace I think these buildings must be store houses. Windham reckoned the dead at from 500 to 600 others at 800 – It was no easy matter to know what to do with them – The French say the small houses in the suburb are full of dead – I proposed that a large vessel lying near the place sh^d. be filled with them the hatches then battened down some air holes cut in the decks & that then under a flag of truce it should be towed some miles to sea & scuttled. This is if possible to be done. But if left to Barnard it certainly will not –

They are talking of destroying the Docks, & the French proposed it sh^d. be done at once "avant que la politique l'en mêle". I strongly recommended that the question sh^d. be left open for a time till we saw what turn things took, we might have to stay here for years & want them. The D. of N. was of this opinion

The creepy way in which we do things is very provoking. Fort Paul is said to be one of the places on which Gen Jones is thinking of putting a battery – Four days have gone by – The Russians are certainly clearing out, the tents have diminished in numbers & hardly any troops are to be seen on the North side, a few wagons come down for a load at one or other of the forts or at the pile of bread & go off & a few more are to be seen at some of the batteries, but nothing has been done to hurry them –

The storms have blown over and the afternoon was fine & the sea blue & smooth, yesterday it was green & white & the vessels were pitching heavily to the Westw^d swell.

Immense quantities of naval material is left behind, chains anchors guns spars – There were large stores of cloth but we have allowed the French to pillage the whole – Hundreds of helmets with the double eagle & S^t. George were in another store.

The mail of Monday only arrived this evening.

Cambridge University Library: Add. 9554/4

52
Romaine to John Harvey

[Holograph]   Head Quarters
                                                  Near Sebastopol
                                                  Septr 13th. 1855

My dear Harvey,

At the time your wicked reproach was written about my owing you a letter I think there must have been one of mine lying on your table at Ickwell.

I have never heard of your receiving a Russian drum taken in the assault of the Mamelon – My brother received it and said he would send it to you when he had shown it at home – He is now abroad for a tour, but I will write to know the reason why he has not sent it to you –

It was only today Keppel was telling me that probably he w^d soon be going home & could take a box as big as a Midshipman's chest for me. You know he gave up the St Jean d'Acre to command the Naval Brigade – I asked him if he was not delighted at our lucky success he s^d "Yes there was only one drawback that Sebastopol was taken & there was nothing to do" –!

I passed today hundreds of helmets which had been taken out of a Russ^n store in the barracks but the ornaments had been stripped off – I was offered swords for sale &c but I had not had your letter which only reached me this evening. I won't forget you now – but really the things were so common & so plentiful and there was such a firm order against plunder & the provost sergeants had such strong orders to stop every body & take away their plunder, that as judge! I did not like to be seen riding with "loot" –

A few days ago some French Imprl Guard came to the door of my hut & s^d "Monsr est-ce que vous voulez acheter un Christ?" and they produced a picture on three panels taken to pieces, really very well painted & I think a copy of a Guido. I have got a small medallion which I will send by post to Mrs Harvey it is a poor thing but curious perhaps as a relic – The guns left by the Russians [illegible] will come not to less than 3000 – I cant make up my mind whether they mean to evacuate the North side or leave a garrison to defend it to protect their retreat of their main body their material & wounded – There are certainly very few soldiers left, fewer than yesterday by some thousands. But they were hard at work making new batteries opposite the town.

I saw Keppel yesterday and he will look out for you as well as myself, but there has been such a craze for sending home things that he says in his own Naval Brigade the Mil^a. officers came & outbid his own & took away every thing at absurd prices –

I am obliged to finish this abruptly as I am called away & may not return in time for post going out

Kind remembrances to Mrs Harvey Mr Tennant & the ladies of his household

Y^{rs} ever

W. G. Romaine

Cambridge University Library: Add. 7633: 5/39

53
Journal for 13 September 1855

[Holograph]

Thursday. Septr. 13.

Gen Barnard was unable to go with the Duke of N. and myself as there was first a conference of Admirals & others and he had to be present at a conference of Generals at 3. At 12.30. the Duke came and we started to visit the Bastion du Mât – We had some difficulty in getting into it through the French trenches, having to find our way into the palisaded ditch. In this ditch that the defenders might not be taken by surprise were bomb proof lodgments for men. The ditch was very wide but not very deep – In one place, on the proper left flank of Bastⁿ. du Mât, they had made trous de loup of earth & stones, which w^d. have stopped & destroyed the formation of a column – The gabions were burning in several places & some dead still lying about. The ground was covered with bullets shot & broken shell, & disabled guns. There were very large casemated cells, which formed traverses as well – they were capable of holding a large garrison. The works were so thick with gabions & fascines & earth as to be indestructible by shot or shell.

219

The French were in considerable numbers in the town & the sentries challenged passers by for their permission to be there.

We rode on to the pillared church & then to the governors house which is very handsome with carved or sculptured architrave. Then we went to the loopholed wall, by the Central bastion, to the works over the quarantine side, past a place where there had been a fresh explosion, outside the wall – Then to sea batteries near Fort Alexander which has been partially blown up, to the next fort which is undamaged. Then round the head of the creek, passing on way covered batteries of guns of different sizes to Fort S^t. Nicholas – on a piece of beach W of the Fort were ranged the dead they had found in this part of the town. It was a repetition of the horrid sight of the hospitals of yesterday, but they were more decomposed. Then we went to the monument in the pretty garden in rear of Fort S^t. Nicholas & past the Cathedral where there is a very handsome Bell to the head of the Creek by the Creek battery where the Duke was nearly blown up to the Hospitals to see whether the dead had been buried. The Land Transport wagons had been at work since 4. AM. & had nearly finished. The officers of Windhams staff said they had found 100 more corpses in another cellar, in addition to the 200 they found yesterday most of which were officers & many in shells ready for burial, but in a very advanced stage of decomposition –

The French began firing & the Russians answering from across the water just as we got into the Karabelnaia suburb. Here & near the end of the enemys bridge at S^t. Nicholas was a great number of brass guns & carriages –

The French pitched one shell into the centre of a battalion drawn up under arms, about 150 of the men ran for it, the rest remained very steady.

We then rode under the Malakoff & by the Mamelon to camp.

Cambridge University Library: Add. 9554/4

54
Romaine to Lord Mulgrave

[Holograph. No address or date. Context indicates mid-September 1855]

<u>Private</u>

My dear Mulgrave,

If you have not destroyed my last letters will you mind putting them into some corner of a drawer I think I sh^d. like some day to see what I thought about passing events – Do you remember what I wrote to you when the attack on the Redan of 18 June was repulsed –

That there was only one man who could successfully carry out so tremendous a struggle – Well how does it turn out – our army sustains such a defeat, in presence of the French and with no attempt to retrieve our character as must leave a blot for many a day.

Who was the man upon whom all eyes were turned in the moment of disaster – Not upon Codrington who had remained from 12 at noon till dark in the trenches & had not moved out when his men stuck fast on the parapet for want of a leader – but on Sir C. Campbell whom it is intended to remove from the Army, by an honourable exile –

I said that if the army was trusted to another than Colin Campbell we should meet with disaster. We have – And we have since remained totally inactive.

The Russians have been allowed to finish their batteries on the North side & last night we began to make our first – I now tell you that this Army takes the field under a man who is not a soldier at heart, the men instinctively know it – and we shall again suffer some signal disgrace & disaster –

I hope sincerely we may have no more combined & allied operations under several commands – and that it may be possible to apportion to each army its task – You will hear a hundred commentaries on our failure on 8th. Sepr. Depend upon it that if we had had a General either to command the army or the assaulting column we must have succeeded –

Why the General who led the storming party had only been appointed to them about a fortnight, could he have the sort of influence that makes men blindly follow through desperate danger –

I firmly believe that if Codrington had put himself at the head of his staff and called on the men to follow him that they would have gone in a mass – for Codrington is well known & much liked by both officers & men of his division.

You will all be much disappointed at the inaction of the large naval & military forces here – I see you are calculating on pursuit & flight & a triumphant ejection of the Russians from the Crimea – at least if I may judge from the leaders in the Times –

We cannot suffer for want of anything this winter. A good many men will get shelter by bringing planks &c from the ruins of the town – plenty of huts have arrived and every one is busy in making himself comfortable – The weather is dry with cold winds – not the warm genial autumn of last year, but camp is healthy.

The Russians remain in great force on the Mackenzie heights & the line protecting Baktschi Serai. We hear rumours of negotiations & glimpses of a possible peace by spring – I am not sanguine myself. I want too heartily to get away to allow myself the indulgence of hope, but it should be long deferred. I fully mean however as long as health lasts to stay at my post – My office at home seem anxious that I should.

I shall expect a long letter in answer to mine of last week.

I say again – Why not give us a Post office order office for transmission of money. We cant now be "likely to move" for some months.

Kind remembrances to my Lady and the little ones.

Ever y^rs. Faithfully

W. G. Romaine

Bentinck sent in his resignation & it was refused. Why keep such a man as that in command of troops. He hates the whole thing and never once went into the trenches during the siege! A General in command of a division engaged in the siege!! What can we expect but defeat and disaster.

Cambridge University Library: Add. 7633: 5/51

222

55
Romaine to C. J. Selwyn

[Holograph]

Head Quarters
Near Sebastopol
Septr 22nd 55

My dear Selwyn,

There is nothing going on here but what the papers will have told you – We have I think finished the campaign for this year. There is an absurd demonstration going on just now –

The fleet came off Balaclava last night & pretended to take on troops & then will proceed off Eupatoria & pretend to land them – The hope is that the Russians may blow up the North Forts & evacuate – They will at all events see that we are anxious to get possession of the harbour –

There is firing still going on across the bay and the French are making a work to batter Fort Constantine. We have to a certain extent taken possession of the town & dockyards as the Russians are too busy evacuating their store houses which are within range, to trouble us much except when we fire upon them.

I wrote to tell you of my success in obtaining my demand of increased pay – My view of the case was and really is, that I am more likely to be well-treated, the bigger man I can make myself out to be. If Lord Panmure is not offended by an opinion I gave against him the other day concerning his pet Army Works Corps I shall get a C.B. – In June I wrote to Lord Raglan to say that the Corps w^d not be under the Mutiny Act & Art^s. of War – He wrote back to say he did not agree with my law – so he neglected my advice to have it done by Act of Parl^t – They came out & of course I refused to recommend a court martial to try a man – The question was then referred to the Judge Adv. Genl who backed up every thing I had advanced. Now the Corps is half disorganized from want of proper control & discipline.

I should have written in answer to Roupell directly I got his letter & I actually began one, but I considered that he must be on the wing somewhere & never finished it. I wish he had come the place is healthy enough now when ordinary care is taken.

We are now busy making ourselves comfortable for the winter and I am trying to make my roof water tight, and to get some roof for my horses which last winter had to stand in snow & rain.

We shall not have a very interesting season to pass, there being little in the shape of amusement, but thank God there are no trenches – We have taken some 7000 guns of all sorts & sizes & 200,000 rounds of shot & shell & many magazines of powder – It is hard to tell whether the Russians will evacuate the Crimea or not. I think as a military operation they should, as a political one it may be doubtful. It cannot be told yet, as even if they were going to evacuate they w^d hold on by their rear guard to gain time to move wounded &c –

Goodbye – I shall write next mail

Y^{rs} ever

W. G. Romaine

Cambridge University Library: Add. 7633: 5/40

56
Romaine to Lord Mulgrave

[Holograph]

Head Quarters
Near Sebastopol
Septr 25th 1855

My dear Mulgrave,

There is a small affair out here which I was afraid at one time would have caused trouble. Genl Jones received orders from home to take over the Railway, & workshops upon which it depends for the repair of its wagons and machinery, when the Railway officers & men of Peto Brassey & Betts left the Crimea. At that time McMurdo with the assistance of Mr Beatty the Engineer had been engaging men as well as he could and selecting men from his own corps to carry on the workshops when Peto's men should leave – Genl Jones in accordance with his orders began to make preparations to take over the workshops stores &c, but has never been able and they still remain in McMurdo's hands – Luckily all three of the men concerned are sensible though peppery and there has been no hitch –

Just now Mr Beatty is in a fidget – He has a super-civilian dread of being under the "orders" of an officer of the Army but has no objection to be under his "directions" – Then when Beatty's men left he was to be under Genl Jones directions to whom the Railway was given in charge, since then, he has been attached to the strength of the Land Transport Corps, to act under McMurdo, as engineer of the line which is under Genl Jones orders. This is a little à travers. Beatty has written home to Lord Panmure, but he has not told the whole of his mind as he was afraid of his letter coming back to General Jones after a time and causing a quarrel. Beatty is very anxious that the Railway should be attached to the Land Transport Corps as part of the permanent means of transport of the army – the necessary workshops would go with it necessarily, as they could not be responsible for the traffic unless they had the means of repairing their machinery & wagons in their own hands – This is all out of my line but it so happens that I have heard the version of the tale of all the three parties and am able to act the humble part of the drop of oil between the three great wheels.

I do not think General Jones can stay out here much longer determined as he is not to give in, and go home. But he has been & is suffering terribly from sciatica and is ten years older than when he came out. This place & work ages every one in a most unpleasant manner – I believe it is the "all work & no play" & that it will make us all "dull boys" –

We hear that the Russians are busy in making a tram road into the Crimea – If it could be carried out it would alter the odds, but two hundred miles of railway laid in a desert is an undertaking rather for peaceful times than for a country the seat of war – General Pelissier has sent 2,000 cavalry to Eupatoria. He has I am sorry to say given General D'Allonville, dragoons & hussars, I suppose he did not like to part with his 2000 Chasseurs d'Afrique, otherwise they would have been the very troops for the work D'Allonville has to perform – as they can go their 50 or 60 miles for two or three days running & would have kept the enemy in perpetual alarm – I cant help thinking that we ought to have cleared the Crimea this autumn. We had a defeated enemy before us with a very long line to defend, which our ships gave us the power of turning in three or four ways and the enemy was encumbered with vast hospitals and trains of wounded.

I have heard nothing lately of any ill words passing between French & English officers or men and I hope it was only a passing swagger, which our men would certainly not have spared the French, if we had been the successful parties on the day of the assault.

We are all very anxious to see what the good folks in England think of us and our doings and what effect our success will have in the rest of Europe –

I do not expect peace to be the result – I believe Russia will be as arrogant in language as ever – Russia can not be treated as a European people might – You must deal with them as orientals, thrash them well first and then be as civil as you please – Every act of forbearance is treated by them as a sign of fear – and rightly – We don't burn Helsingfors because we are afraid Russia won't make peace, we don't bombard Odessa nominally because there is British property there, but in fact because we are afraid that Russia won't make peace – We don't blow up the dockyards at Sebastopol because we are afraid Russia won't make peace – I say burn Helsingfors, & Odessa & blow up the dockyards here, burn & destroy every village & town in the Empire that you can – and Russia will make peace, not as long as we only kill a number of her half drilled serfs & stop her trade – In spite of the triumphant leader of the Times about the Asian campaign I fear horribly to hear of bad news there – Omar Pasha can be of no use this autumn, he was too late –

There, I have given you a full dose of politics home & foreign – I am quite delighted at seeing our men enjoying themselves a little – and I am never tired of saying when any thing goes wrong, never mind thank God there are no trenches –

Markham is going home on Saturday – He has been getting feebler for a long time and quite unfit for any work and as he must go, I did all I could to get him off as early as possible – He goes in a steamer direct to England and I have no doubt the voyage will set him up and we shall have him out for next years campaign.

The Russians are making immense works on the North side and I think will try & maintain themselves there especially if there are to be negotiations. They evidently expect we shall batter down Forts Constantine & Catherine, as they are preparing great earthwork batteries to replace them.

I think we ought to knock them down they have too defiant and insulting an air with their stony faces undamaged by war.

I have not the least fear for the comforts of the army this winter, we have every thing well in hand. I only wish we had had more huts on the ground when the siege work stopped as the men could have been employed at once in putting them up.

The enemy have been rather threatening an attack on the side of Inkerman at the head of the harbour & we have strengthened ourselves there – I think it was rather fear of our attacking that made them concentrate there – A successful attack by them would not improve their position as they could not hold any ground they might gain.

If the war is to go on I am not sure that the most damaging course for Russia to adopt is not to hold on to the North side in what I think is for her not only a difficult but strategically speaking a false position – to maintain which she is obliged to drain the southern & most productive portion of her territory of men and animals and means of transport –

If it detains the whole French & English army here in the Crimea it is worth the Emperors while to maintain the North side at the risk of losing an army, and the certainty of impoverishing his Southern provinces –

I was delighted to hear of your sport on the moor edges. I am glad to find that your hard work in London made you return to the country with greater zest. Oh for a lunch in the heather with the sun over my head & the dogs & guns about me. Tell me all about your sport and about every body & every thing at Mulgrave – It carries me away for a time from this weary desert. How does the school get on –

Gerry Gordon of the Fus. Gds now A.D.C. to Gen Simpson had a tumble from his horse & was a little hurt & very lonely in his tent so I took him in for a day or two till he got well again & I turned him out. He is a very good boy & very much of a gentleman –

My dear Lady Mulgrave,

I have sent such a long dull letter about business & politics to Mulgrave that I fear you won't care to read it so I must add a postscript for your own reading – I hope the flower garden and my favourite walk there have been as sunny & beautiful as ever – Please send me an envelope full of verbena leaves, our clothes are washed badly and don't at all smell as if they had been put in a drawer with lavender –

I have become acquainted with His Grace of Newcastle and had some rides with him – He expects preliminaries of peace to be signed by Christmas & peace definitely settled by March. I don't.

I have given orders to clear my effects out of my cosy rooms in the Temple and shall look out for a flat in Victoria Street or a very small house somewhere near the clubs. A friend of mine has offered me a part of his house which is much larger than he can use, but he don't smoke and I could not make his smart drawing room smell, so I shall establish myself somewhere on my own hook, if I return to England –

Give my love to all the children – Pray send a line whenever you can spare time & push Mulgrave into the arm chair in front of the big inkstand & blotting book & make him begin a letter –

Do you remember the light grey socks that M^{rs} —— on the moor edge made for me – I have never had such good ones – I wish she w^d make a dozen pair & send them and the bill to C.A. Govett Esqr. 10. Lincolns Inn Fields to be forwarded to me when occasion served.

Goodbye God bless you all, Y^{rs} ever faithfully

W. G. Romaine

Cambridge University Library: Add. 7633: 5/41

57
Romaine to C. J. Selwyn

[Holograph]
Private

Head Quarters Crimea
Oct 8th. 1855

My dear Selwyn,

I received your letters of 20th & 23rd Sept this morning & I see you expected a letter from me written just after the event – I thought I had sent you one –

Octr 12th. This letter should have gone by last mail – I want to tell you why it is that perhaps I have not sent you as many letters with long accounts of affairs here as I otherwise should – I found that the letters I wrote to Lord Mulgrave were shown by him very often both to L[d] Palmerston & L[d] Panmure and that the latter had expressed a wish to see all my letters & that I sh[d] not know that he read them – Well, it is exceedingly difficult to sit down & write the same story twice over & I think you have been a little cheated thereby – But as I have spoken in the plainest language I think I have done good by letting the truth be known, as I understood it about divers people & things –

I was a good prophet as long ago as the 20th June – I told them that they did not appreciate the difficulties of the attack on the Redan – and that if the storm of that place was entrusted to any one but Sir Colin Campbell & his troops – it w[d] fail again –

I see now that the whole story about the 8. Sept[r]. has come out – All that Russell says in his letter is singularly accurate and is a very good account of our part of the action – I expect by next mail or the one after to hear that you are all in a rage at our having let 3 weeks go by in entire quiet, looking at one another & hoping the Russians w[d] run out of the Crimea – They have not gone but they have left very few men now on the north shore, but they have established & are still strengthening a vast system of redoubts & batteries. Yesterday they diminished their number of tents very considerably, and they are carrying away their store of bread – They have been forced to detach largely no doubt in consequence of the French reconnaissance on their left towards Baktschi Serai – They hold the most wonderful natural position in the world it is a long line of steep cliff – the edge of the plateau – only accessible in many miles at a few points easily defended by guns in position, at all but those few points it is impossible for guns to ascend the plateau as there is a deep scarp – The position is cut in a few places by deep narrow gorges the course of torrents, but which cannot be turned nor forced –

We do not want Sebastopol for our army & the fleet now have plenty of room for the ships that need be kept here during the winter when they return from their expedition – I hope they may do something at Kinbourn to make up for our inactivity – We are <u>now</u> embarking cavalry for Eupatoria I believe, instead of a month ago. But what can be expected from an old imbecile who has as much idea of a great operation of war as of managing a ballon [*sic*, meaning probably a (dancing) ball] – Markham is gone home sick & knocked up for some time – if ever he is restored to do hard work again it will be only after a long rest – Codrington the Court Pet failed signally on the 8th Sept[r]. He had just a grand opportunity when his soldiers stuck on the parapet to have shewn his knowledge of human nature his courage & generalship, by advancing with all his staff and calling on his troops to follow him – Who are we to look to next Spring. Windham behaved very bravely but I think committed a grave error in leaving his troops in the Redan where they c[d] hardly maintain themselves to go himself for supports – It was while he was absent that they were expelled –

I see the Times & the British public won't accept the bitter truth that the British soldier can ever behave badly – It was as much as the officers c[d] do to prevent the men in the trenches who had not been at the Redan – from running to the rear & two officers I c[d]. name actually drew their swords & threatened men who were running to the rear.

If the Ministry expect the Guards out here to maintain their old reputation in next years campaign, they must send out the home battalions & recall them – They are not the troops that fought at Inkerman – there are not ten men in a company of those heroes left – The official people are evidently afraid of giving the command to Sir Colin Campbell for fear of his temper, he has too much of Sir C. Napier in him. But he is a firm handy soldier though an old man and I sh^d like to see him in command when we take the field –

I have given notice to quit my chambers – So if I come home I shall ask for a bed at N°. 45 perhaps until I find out a nest for myself – Do you see how determined the Times is that I should write the despatches home, the 26th Sepr leading article is the third time I think they have suggested that course, which is quite impracticable unless I had access to all the reports that come in from the different Generals – Lord Raglan used to laugh at this idea of the Times Editor – They proposed once that I sh^d send daily telegraphic messages to be published – I wrote a despatch the other day in answer to a telegraphic message about the destruction of the docks forts &c – The Generals here want them destroyed Ld Panmure answers that their policy was not to destroy them – and I was asked to give the reasons why it w^d be advisable to destroy them – So I wrote a despatch which was thought too political & diplomatic for the General to send – But Airey said he thought it so important that it sh^d be preserved & I think he s^d he sh^d send it to some of the big wigs at home –

I had suggested amongst other things – That Sebastopol & the Crimea could only be held with perfect safety to all nations, by Austria. That she c^d enjoy it entirely without requiring a right of way through the Dardanelles which w^d be necessary for England and France – a principle which neither one c^d concede to the other – That their joint occupation c^d not be permanent – That if Turkey held it, in a few years by force or treaty Russia w^d wrest it from her – That in the hands of Austria it w^d become the grand depot of the merchandize & commerce of Germany with the Black Sea & Asia – That if Russia were forced to give up the portion of Bessarabia which borders on the Danube, Austria w^d have a free highway to the Crimea & c^d hold it against all the forces of Russia – I think it w^d be a dangerous & costly gift for Austria to accept, but w^d from fear of Russia ensure her faithful alliance to the Western Powers –

We are having perfect weather now, I hope it may last – We have some 6500 men at work on the roads – If the siege had not come to an end when it did we sh^d have had no better road than last winter – The Army Works navvies melted away to 5, or 600, not more than enough to ballast & put & keep in good repair the railway – and there were 15 miles of new road on a clay soil to make and all the stores to fetch!

Octr. 13. We send a Division of Infantry to Eupatoria & so do the French today or as soon after as may be – But they are not to be an army to fight a pitched battle but to harrass – Which is infra dig – If cavalry only were sent well & good –

I have marked this letter private as there are one or two things in it which I do not want talked about. The Russians are firing so heavily from the North side that I think they must mean evacuation as there is nothing to fire at, no troops being sent in or large working parties. They must want to get rid of their ammunition before going. If they do evacuate it will be a real triumph as they had evidently intended to remain in order to find employment for our armies & keep them from fresh expeditions –

Goodbye Y^rs Ever

W. G. Romaine

Cambridge University Library: Add. 7633: 5/42

58
Journal for 16 October 1855

[Holograph]

Octr. 16th. Tuesday.

No news arrived of the expedition to Kinborsum – Hot strong wind – There was a fire burning last night bearing about E.N.E. of our camp. The Engineers think it is a considerable distance off at the place where the Russ^ns. had the head quarters of their cavalry & where probably large stores of forage & grain were collected.

This afternoon Steele brought me a despatch of L^d. Panmure's N^o. [space left] dated [space left] Sepr. calling on Genl. Simpson to answer certain questions as to the failure of our attack on the Redan – He had left it as usual to Steele to answer it and on his saying that he could not well do it as the attack had been conducted wholly contrary to his opinion – Well s^d. Simpson then I must send it to Col Chapman to answer there are a number of engineering questions in it & I dare say he can do it! Steele then offered to do his best – The reports of all the General Officers were sent and a rough sketch of Steele's answer – Steele said that at the council when all the question of the assault was discussed, Simpson sat at the edge of the table with his head nodding over it asleep! & that he never felt so much ashamed in his life – But that when the subject of having a body of volunteers for this service was ment^d. he refused to allow it. The Marines had volunteered as a storming party as they had had no trench work. They were a magnificent body of soldiers, possessed of great courage & burning to distinguish themselves. But he rejected them on the ground that they did not know the trenches!

Certainly from the reports of the Generals & officers in command no one w^d. gather that a word c^d. be said agst. the conduct of the soldiers, until Col Windhams second report, made after the despatch from L^d. Panmure had been sent. It only incidentally appears that he left the Redan & went back to bring supports & that while he was absent the men left or were driven out of the Redan.

I told Steele that I was a bad one [?] to come to, to held [*sic*, intending 'help'] the General in writing such a despatch as I held a very strong opinion agst. him on the subject – That the despatch w^d. be called for in the House & every word weighed & judged & that in fact it w^d. form the authentic account of the assault, as viewed by the general & his friends. He said the same reason applied to him, but that he c^d. not leave the General without help & wished me to assist him to say all that c^d. be said in favour of the Generals view of the affair –

Steele says there are about 90,000 of the enemy encamped somewhere on the Belbeck, that out of 14 Divisions of the Russian army 12 are in the Crimea & that except the corps specialists there is very little reserve of old soldiers –

If this is the case & they have their army concentrated there fires must be intended as a blind to tempt the allies to attack the plateau & that they have only left a few men to man the forts & batteries with the same idea.

59
Romaine to Lord Mulgrave

[Holograph]   Head Quarters
Decr 4th. [1855]

My dear Mulgrave,

When I received your letter dated Novr. 4th. from Scarbro', how
from my hut I pitied you in that hateful caravanserai – The boards
of my door have spread so that a couple of crown pieces w^d. go
between & there are several knotholes in the wood & it doesn't fit
any where very well, but I felt sure there c^d. not be any such
terrible draughts as in that forlorn room looking on the sea. Where
we shivered through a winter canvass of the good borough – What
did Lady Mulgrave do? Get into fur cloak & muff or did you get
warmer rooms – We have had winter upon us now some ten days,
rain wind frost & snow & today wind rain & fog. But the men are
well fed & clad –

So my friend Sir Colin Campbell is coming back, to take
command under Sir W^m. Codrington The good Queen has put the
comether [sic] on him I'm sure for he c^d. not refuse her and he c^d.
& w^d. any body else.

He is a real noble hearted man. He w^d. have restored the
fearfully relaxed discipline of the army, both of officers & men.

Luckily for the experiment Codrington is not only a perfect
gentleman but as a soldier he appreciates Sir Colin & will not be
above asking his advice, and I am sure that if Sir Colin does come out
will be with a sincere determination to aid Sir William in every way.

There is no news here – the docks &c are to be blown up this
week & as no doubt the Russians will open a tremendous fire,
there will [be] a row as of old times –

You may judge what an operation the destruction of the docks
alone has been when I tell you that it has required 140 mines to be
made either in the masonry of the docks or in the rock – If the
French blow up Nicholas & Alexander at the same time it will be
worth seeing – though one is almost blasé with explosions of one
kind or another.

The question of the dog has settled itself. He was stolen, came
back & was again stolen. I do not think he w^d. have been any use

but as a keepers watch dog, & as he had a marked objection to irregulars such as Croats and navvies I think he w^d. have learnt to look on poachers as his natural enemies –

All my friends are gone but one & he goes next Saturday –

I hate half doing a thing I have undertaken & so have made up my mind if health holds good to stick to the army through the next campaign.

I expect my letters to you which Lord Panmure has seen have quite cut off all chance of the C.B. I should have valued it very much if given with the first batch as I felt I had earned it –

I should have liked to have been at the bombardment of Overdale, I am sure it was successful & followed by an evacuation both of the North & South sides, what list of killed and wounded it is better not to count. Siggs generally knows most about that –

How did matters look at the end of the canvass at Scarboro?

Will there be a dissolution or will Government be able to get in another session – I think there will be a dissolution in the middle of it – The war will lose its popularity with the working classes if prices are to go on rising as they have lately –

The mail has come in (Friday) but I have not read the papers and do not have any news except the possibility of a dissolution – I cannot consider that at all likely unless Government met with some defeat upon a War question – otherwise certainly L^d. Palmerston will avoid dissolving in the 4th. Session of the Parliament – I have settled with you as regards Chatham and leave it in your hands. In case my brother Mr C.A. Govett of 10 Lincolns Inn Fields should be written to by Mr Buchanan I have told him to communicate with you & abide by your advice. I have done this because I told Mr Buchanan a long while ago that if I ever put up in my absence, he must go to him for money –

I think it very probable that the course to be taken by the Emperor Alexander will be very much influenced by the tone of our Houses of Parliament when the war is discussed.

The blowing up of the Docks &c here has been retarded by the rains the Sappers & Miners having been flooded. We have had a story going about camp of troubles with the army in Poland of an important character but such a piece of information if true must have got into the Vienna papers & so to the Times –

How I should like to drop in upon the family ranged before the fire waiting for dinner, which we will suppose to have been announced some time & only waiting for my Lady to come down stairs – What a deal of talk & what a good dinner we sh^d. have – I shall have two or three years nonsense to talk off on my return – I am getting stupid and talk sense always which makes me horribly dull – When M^{rs} McMurdo & her children came out I had some hope – But the Colonel fell ill & nearly died and we had to nurse him & the moment he was strong enough he was sent home – If they had remained I could have gone there & refreshed myself by chattering an hour or two every day which would have done me all the good in the world. Here it is all work & no play – The mill going seven days a week.

I am afraid Codrington works too hard, his labour is never ending, he is an excellent man to do business with, very conscientious & wanting a reason for everything. It is impossible not to like & esteem him – The noble way in which he wrote home about Sir Colin Campbell, won my heart at once –

My kindest regards to Lady Mulgrave & little Laura & the rest.

A merry Xmas to you and all the Castle holds from

Y^{rs}. very faithfully,

W. G. Romaine

Cambridge University Library: Add. 7633: 5/52

60
Romaine to John Harvey

[Holograph]   Head Quarters
                                   Crimea Decr 5th. 1855

My dear Harvey,

What a funny thing that you should send me a T.G.[84] – under your protection but without a letter – my most especial & favourite aversion at Cambridge – a man who wore white kidgloves drank very weak claret & water and sang to the foggy moon on a guitar – & who looked down on us as savages who drank beer & rowed in eight oars till our hands were positively hard, as without the pale of the exquisite salvation –

Natheless the elegant Wilshere made himself very agreeable – which was more than I did to him – though he has written me one or two most thankful letters and now I hear there is a screen arrived in Balaclava sent by him to be put up in my hut to protect me from the draught! To be sure the planks of the door don't touch by a little & there are a few knot holes & the N.E. Wind does blow in sometimes so that the toes being warm at the stove the heel is quite t'other – viz frng – But then the rats eat out the mortar from under the eaves so that it is equally airy above – but it is very nearly water tight which is the great thing. I am so glad the drum arrived safe and that it served to rouse the martial ardour of the Biggleswadians – what a word! It sounds like a name from Knickerbockers history of New York – Are you really going to live under the dominion of Consultore Mazza & El Roy Bomba.[85] I hope your house in Naples has fire places or you will be wretched. I can't get away – When I thought myself ill treated by that noodle Lord Panmure, I asked Gen Simpson permission to go home to set myself right, meaning that if it was not done I sh^d. stay at home – But he s^d that it w^d be extremely inconvenient that he had no one to put in my place & he thought my business c^d be arranged by his writing – So it was and I thought it a great triumph to have screwed 8oo a year out of the Gov^t. who lavish thousands a year on all sorts of ignorant adventurers, & pinch their own hard working servants – Luckily I was so far independent and so well established here that threatening to go, procured me what a feeling of justice never would – I have never asked to go since, & I don't think my request then was considered a real asking for leave –

I like to go the whole hog and see the thing through, and I think a patient hanging on will pay in the long run, when every one is trying to get away to avoid the winter – I would have given a great deal to have spent the winter at home – all my friends are gone – I am especially glad to find that my great friend Sir Colin Campbell is coming back. He is a real noble simple hearted soldier – I am on terms of the greatest intimacy with him and I am prouder of his confidence than of any thing that has happened to me out here.

My poor friend Markham with whom I shot in the Himalaya went home only to die – I hurried him off in the hope that sea air & England might restore him. But he never rallied.

I can appreciate the pang with which you parted with Ickwell for so long a time but anything is better than a long hardly borne expence going on & perpetually galling. It was the right and manful thing to do – If you settle down in London I hope it will not be so near Harrow as Bloomfield Crescent four of [*sic*, meaning 'or'] five miles of pavement are an insuperable bar to anything but the most solemn visits –

I sh^d like you to be settled in town when war is over & to have the McMurdos there & the Mulgraves & then with my club [?] if I was settled there too I sh^d think myself the luckiest person in the world –

I hate promiscuous society, balls & big dinners & such with people I don't care about, but I like to know a few people well & have the entrée at all reasonable houses.

You must know McMurdo if he settles in town when you are there – I think he will be Director General of Land Transport with his office in London as all the Heads of Departments are – He is a fine enthusiastic soldier Sir Charles Napiers Quarter Master General in Scinde and his son in law. M^{rs} McMurdo has been out nursing him in a fearful illness in which he hovered between life & death for some time – first in the crisis his head had to be shaved & a large blister put on coming far down the back of his neck & curiously enough no one c^d be found to perform the operation & every minute was of consequence so I had to turn barber & a great feat of shaving it was for he c^d not be turned & I had to work almost in the dark, but I did it without cutting him once & the blister saved his life. He had severe oppression on the brain, so severe that his pulse intermitted i.e. stopped –& went on –& halted –& then on again – It has always been my fate to have to doctor my friends. M^{rs} McMurdo is a regular Napier strong friend or enemy, the very features of the poor old General softened – they have been married ten years & have eight children – The three eldest came out here with M^{rs} McMurdo! They are all gone – if he had kept well I sh^d have enjoyed the winter as their camp was only three miles & a half off & I used to walk down to save leaving a horse to the care of rascally grooms, and we were to have had great dinners on the moonlight nights, the travelling on the dark nights being bad & not very safe – If you come to Malta & don't come on to Sebastopol I shall say you are not the man I took you for – I can feed you like a prince especially if my cargoes arrive safely and I can mount you on any good number of good ponies per diem that you like to ride –

My hut will hold two – The Wilshere screen is come & put up & really gives a snug air to the room so I will write & tell him.

I'm so glad Mrs Harvey liked the Ruski trinket –

My dear Mrs Harvey, If you reach Malta mind you let Harvey come & see Sebastopol, it is something to see & talk of for the rest of ones life & without having seen it all the descriptions & histories are unintelligible –

How are the Miss Tennants and your father – I don't the least know where this will find you but direct according to orders to Bloomfield Cres^t. near Bath – Great Western R^y – I hope this letter won't cost a fortune in foreign postage – Pray let me hear that your southern sojourn has improved your health. I believe Valencia to be one of the warmest places on the north side of the Mediterranean. Cairo is the real place to go to, it is never cold there. Here we have winter now.

Yours ever very sincerely
W. G. Romaine

Cambridge University Library: Add. 7633: 5/43

61
Romaine to Lord Mulgrave

[Holograph]   Head Quarters Crimea
                                                     Decr 24th. 1855

My dear Mulgrave,
Your last letter gave me great pleasure it is dated Novr 22nd and gave a capital account of your reception at the North Pole – I beg pardon I sh^d say Scarboro – What was the return of frost bites in

your party. It is out of the power of the poor people to give you a warm reception in November –

It did me good only to hear the names of places where I had passed such pleasant hours, Sunny Banks, Overdale Hinebeat [?] &c and to hear such a capital account of Siggs' flocks and herds – Tell Siggs I will bring him home a grape shot out of the famous Redan, when I come.

Dan Lysons is all right and in command of a Brigade I am happy to say – I gave him your message a month or six weeks ago – I have not seen him since your last letter, when I saw him & mentioned your remembrance of him on a former occasion he seemed much pleased & desired me to give you all kinds of pleasant messages – He is an excellent officer –

I received a letter to day from Chatham saying that some of my friends had met and that they wanted to know whether in case of a Genl. Election, I intended to return to England on leave, to stand for the Borough.

I have told them that I consider myself pledged to stand if they call on me, and that I leave it for them to decide – If they think I can win I am ready to come & can have leave of absence – If they can get a man more likely to win, they are [at] liberty to accept him. I said that if elected I sh^d resign my post here to attend to my duties in Parliament. I tell you every thing I do about Chatham in case you sh^d be spoken to by any of my supporters there.

I cannot think we shall have a General Election unless Ministers sustain a fair defeat on the Question of War or Peace.

The French have blown up a portion of the docks, but there is much work to do before the whole of them are destroyed –

What is the meaning of the Times article of Decr 7th abusing Pelissier – are they preparing to abuse the supposed terms of Peace recommended by Austria & France and shewing their anger by abusing the conduct of the war first. What an interesting time this is – I wish I was behind the scenes at home – I mean to be some day –

My fit of seediness some time ago arose from living too low, abstinence from meats &c – I recovered without a grain of medicine by a steady course of mutton chops for breakfast and a little wine for the stomach's sake at dinner –

We have had a day or two of severe cold, strong northerly wind and therm^r at 3° above zero – many men were frostbitten, some even in their huts. The French must have suffered a good deal as they are not clothed & covered like our men.

So I see you meet again in Parl^t on 31st. Jan. I think by that time it sh^d be seen whether these peace rumours have any foundation – I have no fear that they will cause new preparations for the ensuing campaign to slacken –

Russia is too strong to knock under yet – We shall have at least another year of it and I sh^d prefer to stay here & see it out to anything except a seat in the House which "I wish I may get". If I have a chance I won't lose it for want of working for it. Let me hear of your victories over the woodcocks &c. they interest me very much – and if you ever have any reliable political news send me a line – You have no idea how any political gossip is appreciated by us out here – But here in camp, you see, are the very men whose lives & fortunes depend on the turn things take at home – To you in England it is a question of 10 per cent Income Tax – out in the front of the enemy, it is a question of wounds & death – & promotion & honours & rewards – at least for the "Upper Ten" – one of the "Lower Million" has no chance unless he can make himself wanted – or feared – I doubt which pays best in politics – the former is the pleasanter and I should hope the easier line to take – Being a working man it will be my line, I have had some idle time in my life & thoroughly enjoyed it – Give my kind regards to my lady, I think of her every time I open my despatch box for her dried flower garden perfumes all my letters (at least as long as they don't get among the "weeds" which flourish in my hut). What fun it will be when we meet & talk over old times.

Ever my dear Mulgrave yours
very truly
W. G. Romaine

62
Romaine to Lord Mulgrave

[Holograph]   Head Quarters Crimea
                                                Jany 26th. 1856

My dear Mulgrave,

It is some time since I heard from you – but I want to tell you that by last mail I heard from Chatham – My Committee met & read a letter I had sent to them and they mean to call a public meeting & read it and then print it in the Maidstone Gazette.

It was a short letter stating that I left my coming forward to them in case of an election for the Borough – that two years had elapsed & it was for them to decide whether they still wished for me.

They sent me an answer that they had since my departure considered themselves pledged to me, and that they sh^d continue to do all in their power to forward my interests –

They appear sanguine as to the result – they say the Conservative party have lost several of their best men – that Sir Fred Smiths name is never mentioned & that probably Vernon has had enough of Parliament –

I trouble you with all this as you have been so kind as to represent me with my friends at Chatham –

Mr Geo Buchanan who writes to me says that the [portion of letter scored out] registration returns look very well – so mind & don't have an election till I get home –

We are all in a state of excitement. The French have received positive news of the Russians having accepted all the four propositions of Austria without reserve – Lord Stratford has taken no more notice of the affair than if he lived at Nova Zenith.

However the news came in such a way to Constan^{le} that I do not doubt of the truth of it – Arthur Hardinge wrote to say that it was considered settled at Constan^{le} & that Lord S de R had called to congratulate the Sultan.

I shall expect a final bulletin of your campaign in the Mulgrave coverts –

We are all wonderfully comfortable this winter & never cease contrasting it with last – the health of the army is wonderful –

something less of sickness than in the best English quarters – 2 per cent less than the Guards in London.

Layard will have a crow to pick with you about Kars depend on it – But if you have got us such a peace as the one announced every one must be satisfied –

If we had had another years War, we should have taken Georgia from them & compelled them to abjure all Transcaucasia for the future –

We hear of serious troubles in the interior of Russia, if the reports are true, it is sufficient to account for the change in Russia's view of the War –

Austria will gain most by the war and have done least – Though I suppose she must have spoken out at last – It is almost a pity the war had not lasted another year without Austria's help that we might have given Lombardy to Sardinia – as it is I think the Sardinians are sorry that peace has come so soon. If the peace negotiations go on smoothly I sh^d expect to be in England by July – I shall be heartily glad to come home, but it seems too good news to be true –

Mind and propose to the Emperor of Russia to buy all the horses, mules, carts & wagons for the benefit of his impoverished subjects and Her Majesty's poor officers, who have lately had to fill up the places of used up pack horses & saddles &c –

This will of course find you in Town settled with my Lady – to whom give my kind regards & remembrances, and believe me to be

Y^{rs} very faithfully

W. G. Romaine

Romaine with the Headquarters staff in early 1856 after General Codrington had become Commander-in-Chief. Romaine is second from the left, leaning on the stair rail. Codrington is sitting on the steps, in front of the officer in the pill-box cap. (Reproduced by kind permission of the Imperial War Museum, London.)

63
Romaine to C. J. Selwyn

[Holograph]   Head Quarters
Feb 23rd 56

My dear Selwyn,

I have not much news to tell you as there is nothing going on here.

I was very much disappointed in not finding my name in the list of C.B. lately made.

I had been assured I was to have it – I have written a stiffish letter to Gen Codrington and he has approved it & forwards it today with his favourable recommen^{n}.

I have also written to the Judge Adv General & sent him a copy of my letter to Gen Cod^{n}.

What effect it may have I don't know but it will draw out Ld Panmures reason for disappointing me after having in fact promised to give it.

It may be only forgetfulness – but I think it is that I have had to expose his blundering in the Army Works Corps & Medical Staff Corps – The giving the honour to the other non combatant branches of the Service & not to me, was really a censure –

Mind that my bed at N° 45 is aired by the end of July and that there is a bottle of Champagne in ice.

Are you retained in all the causes in all the Courts – I never see a Times without y^{r} name – I was in hopes that you w^{d} have stood for Cambridge instead of Walpole horrid Tory as you are –

I have lately had some correspondence with the Chathamites and stand very well with them.

Do you see that in the marvellous scheme of a tunnel across the channel to Dover & Calais, the materials are to be found in the chalk dug out & made into impervious stone by Hutchinsons Patent! The scheme is as absurd as the Suez Canal –

My friend Colin Campbell is out here, the Queen treated him with marked distinction and I think they have found out they made a blunder in listening to the abuse of him which came from the Guards & their friends to the Court.

I hear that the Manners & Customs of London have changed much in two years – that the strangest coats & clothes are worn and that our old fashioned garments will attract as much attention as a clean shaved face.

Sir R^d Airey was expected out by last mail but we hear now that he has stayed at home to fight his own battle –

Why is the Times so vicious against him & why does it protect "poor Mr Filder" the evil genius of the Army –

Y^{rs} ever

W. G. Romaine

Cambridge University Library: Add. 7633: 5/46

64
Romaine to Lord Mulgrave

[Holograph]
Head Quarters
March 11.1856

My dear Mulgrave,

The mail is just come in and the home mail is going out in a few minutes but I must send you a line to thank you for your persevering advocacy of my claim for a CB – I hold to it very much as it will be all I shall have to show for my two years of discomfort & exile –

You will have received a letter from me by last mail giving an account of my letter to Codrington and his forwarding it for Lord Panmure's favourable consideration.

The Times correspondent out here is I see (Times Feb. 22nd) abusing me gently in my turn for the leniency of the punishments – The best answer is the unexampled good behaviour of such a mass of men –

There are now in this command, of all sorts 65,000 men – and in two years we have only had one execution – The serg^t who murdered a man at Kazatch ought to have been hung but the very intelligent & straightforward Court Martial would not agree with my view of the law and so I have been blamed for their stupidity. But luckily for me the Office is perfectly satisfied with my performance of my duty & as I feel I have done it, I don't care three —— for the press – I am very sorry for Airey – He is most unjustly persecuted, but I have not a shadow of a doubt that he will have a good answer to nearly every bit of the accusation agst him

Yrs in great haste

W. G. Romaine

Cambridge University Library: Add. 7633: 5/47

65
Romaine to Lord Mulgrave

[Holograph]   Head Quarters
                                                          March 23rd 56

My dear Mulgrave,

I am exceedingly obliged to you for your friendly hint about the possibility of an early dissolution after the Peace.

I asked Gen Codrington, a long while ago when I wrote to my friends at Chatham, whether in such a case I could have leave to go home & he said that as I had never been absent a day from Head Quarters, he should have no difficulty in giving me leave. So I shall be able to start at once on getting a message –

You must remember that the Telegraph reaches at present only to Constan^le 86 & that then a message must wait for a steamer to the Crimea & a passenger home must wait for a steamer to Constan^le. So it might be three weeks from the date of the message before I should be in England.

But I have sent positive instructions that I mean to stand present or absent have told them where to go for money & am quite ready for a fight and I believe the party is better organized than the enemy.

Getting into the House is the only thing I care much about, and when I have set my heart on a thing I generally manage it somehow and if [I] can have a fair start and a fortnight in the Borough I think I shall succeed. If I got in I should think it right to give up my appointment with the Army if the war went on. If peace comes I suppose my appointment will cease –

I do not at all expect a dissolution this session but of course you are nearer the scene & can judge better.

I think in my last letter I told you of what I had done concerning the CB. I hope Codringtons letter enclosing mine will be sufficient recommendation.

We have had royal Salutes and Te Deums in the camp today for the birth of the French Prince not a "King of Rome" this time.

I am going to breakfast with Marshal Pelissier tomorrow I have become acquainted with him through Ld George Foley, the Commissioner at French Head Quarters who is a great favourite of the Marshals!

Lady Normanby was kind enough to send me a very pretty present from Florence by Captⁿ Lindsay – it is a small and well packed dressing case – She has done me the honour of asking me to pay her a visit on my return to England, but I doubt very much whether it will be feasible.

I hear from some Eton men of sense that you have chosen the best school master for youngsters in England. Let them be a year with him & then send them to Mr Coleridge Tutor to the lower school-boys –

Best remembrances to my Lady from

Y^{rs} very truly

W. G. Romaine

Cambridge University Library: Add. 7633: 5/48

[The letters and journal end here.]

Appendix 1

Raglan Papers at the National Army Museum

Correspondence of Mr Romaine, Deputy Judge-Advocate General

There are some fifteen letters and other documents but only those of particular personal reference to Romaine, or of significant interest are reproduced here. They include the proceedings of the Court of Inquiry into allegations of Russian ill-treatment of the wounded, Romaine's opinion on Dr Lawson's behaviour, and his legal opinion on the Army Works Corps' liability to the Mutiny Act, which he felt had cost him his CB.

66
Romaine to Lord Raglan

[Holograph. Pencil annotation 'Colonel Steele']   17th March 1854
Mr Romaine
4 Harcourt Buildings
Temple March 17. 1854.

My Lord

Having been informed that the appointment of Deputy Judge Advocate to the army now on its way to the East was with the Com[mander-in-]Chief I applied to him for it.

Having today heard that it rests with your Lordship I take the liberty of bringing my name under your notice.

The leaders of the Oxford Circuit M[r] W. J. Alexander M[r] Whately or M[r] Keating will readily answer any inquiries your Lordship might think proper to make.

I have the honour to be
Yr Lordship's
Obedt. Servt.
W. G. Romaine

NAM Accession 1968-07-293/2–3

67
Lord Raglan to Romaine

[Holograph]
<u>Written & sent</u>

Lord Raglan presents his compliments to Mr Romaine and begs to inform him in answer to his letter of the 17th Inst., that the appointment of Deputy Judge Advocate to the Army placed under Lord Raglan's orders, rests with the Judge Advocate General.
[Ordn]ance Office
[M]arch 18th 1854

NAM Accession 1968-07-293/4

68
S. C. Denison to Lord Raglan

[Holograph]   19 April 1854
                                                35 Gt George St

My dear Lord

Permit me to commend the bearer of this letter, M[r] William Govett Romaine, to your Lordship's notice, as the Deputy Judge Advocate to the Force under your Lordship's command. I believe him to be personally known to some members of your Lordship's Staff, and I dare say that they will bear me out in saying that he is a sensible handy man of business & entirely a gentleman in mind & manners.

As your Lordship is aware that the Government thought it expedient that the Office should be held by a Civilian, you will understand & excuse in a man fresh from Westminster Hall some want of familiarity with matters of Military practice: and I hope you will pardon the liberty I have taken in apprising M[r] Romaine that, should he happen to feel embarrassed by the novelty of the matters with which he has to deal, he may always count on your Lordship's kind assistance, & may safely act on your opinion.

With the most earnest wishes for your Lordship's welfare allow me to sign myself

Yours very truly

S. C. Denison

NAM Accession 1968-07-293/5–8

69
Romaine to Lord Raglan

[Holograph]   Camp Galata near Varna
                                                       July 31st 1854

My Lord,

It being currently reported that the army is about to embark for the Crimea, I venture to beg of your Lordship the very high honor of being allowed to act as an extra Aide de Camp to your Lordship at the landing and attack or siege of Sebastopol. If your Lordship should be unable to grant this request, I hope I may be permitted to accompany one of the regiments ordered on this service which may be willing to accept of me as a volunteer –

The army is behaving so admirably that I will undertake not to neglect my duties as Judge Advocate whilst I may be so engaged.

Allow me to suggest to your Lordship that there is a superabundance of Lawyers in England –

I have not mentioned the subject of this letter to anyone.

I have the honour to be
                    Your Lordship's obedient Servant
                              W. G. Romaine
                                 D.J.A.G.

NAM Accession 1968-07-293/9–11 (two copies)

70
Lord Raglan to Romaine

[Holograph]   Varna. August 1. 1854
Copy

My dear Mr Romaine,

I have received your letter of the 31st and am most flattered by the desire you express to be allowed to act as my Extra Aide de Camp, in the event of the British Army landing in the Crimea.

I cannot however consistently with my sense of what is due to a gentleman who is not a Military Man yield to your request, or permit you to serve with one of the Regiments as a Volunteer: but you will as a matter of course accompany the Head Quarters wherever they may go, & I hope will be able to see what may be worthy of observation without becoming a Combatant.

It is a satisfaction to know that in this uninteresting country where there is nothing to direct the mind or occupy the attention of the Soldiers, the Army is behaving so well. This good conduct has given you less employment than might have been anticipated, and has afforded me but few opportunities of communicating with you. They have however been sufficient to satisfy me that the selection of D.J.A.G. for this service was a very judicious one and that I can rely with confidence on your advice and opinion & equally so on your desire to render me every assistance in your power.

Signed/Raglan

NAM Accession 1968-07-293/12–13

71

Proceedings of a Court of Inquiry held at the Camp before Sevastopol the 9th day of November A.D. 1854, pursuant to an order of General Lord Raglan G.C.B. Commanding the Forces[87]

[Holograph]

Members

Brigadier General Sir John Campbell, Bart
Lieut Col The Honble Geo Cadogan Gren Gds
Lt Col Thomas Graham Egerton 77th Regt

Deputy Judge Advocate: W. G. Romaine

The order for the assembly of the Court was read.
Part of a Memorandum prepared for the Commander-in-Chief and which is as follows, was read.
Memorandum: The accusation has been made and is widely believed that the Russian soldiers in the battle of Inkerman have maltreated and killed the wounded and disabled soldiers of the British Army on the field of battle.

It is desirable that an accusation of conduct so opposed to the usages of civilized warfare should not be circulated to the world without other foundation than the rumours of a camp: And that the truth or falsehood of such a report should be satisfactorily ascertained. It is submitted that a Court of Enquiry be held –

To take the evidence of men on whose statements full reliance may be placed, on the general charge made against the Russian troops with which the British Army has been engaged in the Crimea.

The Board having assembled within the lines of the Light Division proceed to receive evidence.

1st Witness. The first witness called was Captain Sir Charles Russell Gren^r Gds. Captain The Honble Henry Neville of the Grenadier Guards told me in the Hospital tent "My dear fellow I am dying, raise me up, I am dying now." He then described to me in nearly these words the manner of his death wounds being received. "I was wounded and being carried to the rear by four drummers, the Russians pressed upon us and they had to lay me down to make their escape. A Russian came up and stabbed me in the body and then another bayonetted me in the arm and a third one stabbed me in the side of the head." Soon after – about two hours, he died –

2nd Witness John Lincoln. No 5508 P^c. John Lincoln of the 2^d. C^o. 3rd Batt^n. Gren Gds. States. I saw Sir Robert Newman an officer of my company about 30 yards from the redoubt we were sent to take, he was shot in the leg and fell to the ground. He said to me take hold of my hand and lift me up. I got hold of his hand and lifted him up, but he could not stand. At the same moment I was wounded myself in my right shoulder. I said "I am wounded myself Sir Robert I must either leave you or lose my life." He said "You must go." That was all he could say as the Russians were 20 yards off only. I came away and left Sir Robert, he had no other wound at that time than the one in the leg. He was in scarlet in full uniform lying on his cloak which had come unclasped from his neck.

3rd Witness. Ensign and Lt Robt. Hamilton. Ensign and Lieut Robert Hamilton Gren^r. Gds. I was sent to collect the wounded and to the left near the redoubt I found Sir Robt Newman lying on his back with his hands and arms stiffened, in the air without his coat, but with his shirt and trousers on. The firing of cannon by the Russians had not entirely ceased, when I went to bring in the wounded.

4th Witness. David Soper N° 4592. 2^d. C^o. 3^d Batt. Gr Gds. Sir Robert Newman was close by me when he was struck by a shot & fell he said "I am struck." I was ordered to advance and left him, this was our first advance, early in the day. About four o'clock or later, in the day I fell out with four others to bring him in, he was then stabbed with bayonets in the belly and on the forehead. I brought him in.

5th Witness. No 2666 P^e Charles Gavney 41st Reg^t. I saw an officer of the Guards, I believe, as a bearskin cap was lying within two yards of him. I saw five or six Russians come up, the first two stabbed him with their fixed bayonets and the remainder struck him with the butts of their muskets. I saw also one of my own comrades who had been wounded in the thigh and to whom I had spoken, when I went to pick him up, after the fight was over, his chest was broken in and his jaw broken with the butt of a musket.

6th Witness. Lieut & Captⁿ. Edwin Burnaby of the Gren^r. Gds. I was present when the body of Sir Robt. Newman was brought in, on examining it I found he had one bayonet wound in his left breast and another wound in his forehead.

7th Witness. Lieut & Captⁿ. Philip Crawley Cold. Gds I saw Captⁿ. Ramsden of the Coldstream Guards lying on the ground he said to me "The brutes have stabbed me repeatedly in the back after I was on the ground wounded." I sent for a stretcher and sent him to the rear as quickly as possible. He died I believe half an hour after he got to camp.

8th Witness. Assistant Surgeon John Wyatt 1st. Battⁿ. Coldstream Gds. I saw Captⁿ. Ramsden when he was brought in wounded. I told him I feared his wound was a mortal one, it was a musket shot through the chest passing out at the back. I saw his bayonet wounds. I thought it so barbarous that I made a memorandum of the fact. He said to me "When the Russians crossed over me after I was wounded I put up my hands & begged them to leave me as I knew I was badly wounded, but they stabbed me here" (pointing to his wounds).

I also saw the body of Lieut Greville of the Colds^m. Gds., he had been killed by a gunshot wound and had been bayonetted three times in the face and three times on the body also.

9th Witness. Drill and Colour Sergeant Shepherd Carter Colds^m Gds. I saw Thomas Hollingley N°. 5 C^o. Coldstream Guards. He was wounded in the leg I saw him on the ground tying up his wound. I saw him afterwards trying to escape, crawling along dragging himself from one bush to another. He had not gone far when we had to retire. The line halted & fronted and I saw three Russians slot him with the bayonet, the first bayonet went into his chest and he bounded up to them and fell dead. I saw Private John Pearson of N°. 8 Comp^y. He was wounded and lying on the ground by the side of the redoubt, while he was lying there I saw him wounded with a bayonet by one of the Russians, he gasped and died as the bayonet was drawn from him.

10th Witness. Robert Foulger 7th. C[o]. Colds[m]. Gds. 1st Batt. Reg[l]. N[o]. 2698. I saw Killingsley lying on the field of battle he had four bayonet wounds on his head, he had been shot in the leg and his leg was tied up in his handkerchief.

11th Witness. Charles Doggrel 5th. C[o]. Colds[m]. Guards I saw a private of the Fusilier Guards lying on the ground under a bush wounded. I saw a Russian with his bayonet fixed stabbing him once or twice as I was walking towards him. I shot the Russian through the head. I was about 40 yards from him. The Fusilier was dead when I came to him but quite warm. He had two or three wounds.

12th Witness. Lieut & Cap[tn] Gerald Goodlake of the Cold. Gds. While the battle of Inkerman was going on, about 12 noon, I met Capt[n]. M[c]Donald Adjutant of the 95 Reg[t] he told me he had been shot in the leg and fallen off his horse and after lying some time on the ground Murphy came to him and wanted to carry him to the rear, but that he ordered him to join his regiment as he was only shot in the leg and would do very well, that soon after he was surrounded by Russians who stabbed him five times and hit him three times, on the head with the butts of their muskets that he was then insensible, but that he thought they left him because they thought him dead. I looked myself and saw three bayonet wounds in his body, he was bleeding at the back of his head and had a fearful cut on his left temple.

13th Witness. Joseph Merritt No. 3787 – 8th C[o]. Cold[s]. G[ds]. I saw a Fusilier Guardsman wounded & sitting on the ground and while he was on the ground I saw a Russian at three yards distance take aim at him and discharge his piece at his head. I saw the Fusilier fall to the shot.

I helped to bring in Capt[n] Lionel D. Mackinnon, he was shot very high up in the thigh, he called to me by name to help him. He told me he had received a bayonet wound after he was shot and that the Russians would have killed him if we had not come up.

14th Witness. Assistant Surgeon John Wyatt of the 1st Batt[n] Colds[m]. Gds – Cap[n] Mackinnon was brought to me on a stretcher, he had been shot through the upper part of the thigh which was shattered. He said "Don't think that's the only place I am wounded, for I was stabbed in all directions", pointing to his face and a large wound in his head and also subsequently to two in his side. He said if the men had not come up when they did I should have been murdered. Amputation at the hip joint was performed about six hours afterwards. I had myself dressed the wounds on his head and body before the operation was performed. There were five bayonet wounds.

I attended a private who was badly wounded through the shoulder joint by a musket, upon whom an operation might have been performed with every probability of success, had he not been stabbed and jumped upon while lying on the ground wounded; from the effects of which injuries he died and not from the gunshot wound, this I am positive of.

15th Witness. No. 2934 P^te Thomas Boulter[?], 1st C°. 1st Batt. Cold^m. Gds. I went to help bring in Captn MacKinnon, he could not be moved because we had no stretcher. He said to me "The Russians have used me shamefully after I was knocked down and they ran the bayonet into me." Captn MacKinnon belonged to my Reg^t and I knew him when I saw him on the ground.

16th Witness. Serjeant W^m. Read of the 8th C°. Cold. Gds. I saw Abel Woodham of the 2^d. C°. He told me on the ground before he was removed that the Russians struck him four times with the butt of the musket after he was wounded and on the ground. He died that night. He had his great coat on. He said to me more of the Russians and one in particular who spoke good English asked him whether he was French or English and that when he said he was English they left him.

17th Witness. George Tibball 1st C°. Cold^m. Gds. I brought in Wm Whitehead of my company from the field he was shot and the leg broken and shattered. He told me that the Russians used him shamefully and knocked him about and stabbed him with the bayonet. He died that night –

18th Witness. Corporal James Smith 6th C°. Colds^m. Gds – Serjeant Thomas of the 8th C°. was wounded and lay on the ground. I saw him fall. We were obliged to leave him as we were hard pressed, though he asked us to take him with us. When we returned I saw him again he was stabbed in four or five places in his heart, and was dead. Serjeant Jakes lay near him and was also stabbed in several places. I saw him lie there.

19th Witness. Dr W^m A Anderson Surgeon of the 41st Regt. Col. Carpenter of the 41st. Regt. was brought to me on a stretcher between 11 and 12 on the day of the battle of Inkerman. He told me that he had had a gunshot wound through the thigh and another through his back, that he fell, that four men of his regt tried to carry him away, two of them were disabled and that the other two men were retiring, when a Russian came up & began to rifle his pocket when finding he was alone he clubbed his musket and struck him as he lay on the ground across the face. The cartilage of the nose was dislocated and turned on one side, three of the incisor teeth were nearly knocked out and he had a cut on the chin. He lived 15 hours and was conscious, but I had told him from the beginning that he was dying and he was aware that he was dying for he gave me his last wishes as to what should be done with his effects.

20th Witness. Corporal Patrick Hurley No 2698. I saw Col Carpenter lying under a bush and a Russian soldier rifling him. I shot the Russian soldier and then with three other men brought the Col. to the rear, his face was disfigured with blows, he told me he was wounded in the back besides. I had him put on a stretcher and carried away.

21st Witness. No. 1546.Corpl. Samuel Walsh B. Cº. 77th. Regt. When we charged on the left, the Russians retired in groups and it became a bush fight, at the corner of a stunted oak I saw a British soldier I think of the 88th. Regt. lying on his face apparently dead, motionless. I saw a Russian soldier as he came up to him run him through with his bayonet between the shoulder blades. I followed the Russian loading my piece as I was anxious to shoot him, keeping him in my eye for that purpose, but he was shot under the eye before I could get ready.

22nd Witness. No. 3477. Pte. Edward Cregh 1st Cº. Cold Gds. I saw George Washer of the 1st Cº. he died yesterday morning. He told me on the day of the battle that the Russians used him shamefully, that they stabbed him in several places and beat him about the head with the firelock after he was wounded and had his leg broken.

23rd Witness. Major Robert Jocelyn Straton 77th Regt. In action at the battle of Inkerman we were halted. I saw a serjeant of the 88th lying & groaning on the ground, he asked for assistance. I had none to give as we were hard pressed. I asked where he was hit, He said while I was on the ground, the rascals butchered me in the belly with their bayonets; I did not see him afterwards.

24th Witness. No. 3130. Pe. Oliver Kerry 8th. Cº. Cold Gds. I saw a man of the name of Timothy Sawyer of the Grenr. Gds. lying on the ground. I saw one of the Russians jab him three times three times [sic] through the back with his bayonet.

Near about the same time I saw a Guardsman shot through the leg or thigh he was sitting up, we were hard done and were firing and retiring, and passed this man sitting on the ground. When we got about 40 or 50 yards, I looked round to fire again and I saw a Russian soldier beating the Guardsmans brains out with the butt end of a musket.

Remarks by Court.

The proofs might have been almost indefinitely multiplied if we had considered it necessary but having already taken so many cases at length we merely append a list of men who were in waiting with a summary of the evidence they were prepared to give.

N$^{o.}$		
1998	Serj^t. Robt. Evans 41st. Regt	Saw four disabled men bayonetted
2404	Serjt Danl. Ford	Saw the same done in three or four cases
2182	P^e. Thomas Hodgkins	Saw one of the Rifle Brig^e. bayonetted when disabled
2411	P^e. Matthew Cassidy	D^o. one of the 47th. Regt.
2219	P^e. Chris. Moynishan	Saw disabled Serj^t. of 88th buttended
3164	P^e. John Kelly	Saw one of 41st. bayonetted by three Russ^{ns}. when crawling disabled on hands and knees
3113	P^e. Thomas White	Saw disabled man of 88th bayonetted
3387	P^e. W^m. Tipler	Saw three or four men bayonetted while on the ground
2370	P^e. James Jellico	Saw two disabled men of the Gren Guards and one of 38th. bayonetted and afterwards struck with butt end
3162	P^e. Patr^k. Donohue 41st	Saw one of our men bayonetted by three Russians when disabled
2463	P^e. Denish Knife	Saw one of 30th bayonetted by 2 Russians after he was shot in the leg & arm
3416	P^e. W^m. Watkins	Saw two of the Guards bayonetted in the same way
3020	P^e. Martin Kaine	Saw a disabled man of Scotch Fusiliers bayonetted by two Russians
2834	P^e. Thomas Richey	Saw one of the Guards wounded in the thigh bayonetted by four Russians
3065	James Bourke	Saw disabled man of the Guards ~~wounded in the thigh~~ bayonetted by four Russians, all of whom with the assistance of an Algerian soldier (or Zouave) witness afterwards killed

| 2175 | P^e John Marsh 77th. Regt. | Saw one of the 57th and one of 77th bayonetted by several Russians |
| 2626 | P^e Wm Jones 77th Regt. | Saw a man of the Guards who was disabled bayonetted two or three times |

The evidence of some witnesses taken on board the Evandale Transport N° 10 about to proceed to Scutari with wounded soldiers by the Deputy Judge Advocate was then read and appended to the Proceedings.

Serjeant Major Thompson of the 31st Regt. Stated. I was stabbed in the breast three times after I was shot in the leg which has been cut off. It was done by Russian soldiers whilst I was on the ground.

Corporal Isaac Osman 20th Reg^t stated. I was shot in the thigh which was broken and I was lying on the ground disabled when five or six of the Russians struck me with the butts of their muskets and one stuck me with a bayonet in the ribs.

Private Edwin Finnegan [?] of the 20th. Reg^t stated: I was wounded after we were ordered to support the Guards and I fell; when the Russians advanced one of them put his firelock to my breast and blew it open.

There were many other soldiers who had been treated in a similar way on board this ship, but were so severely injured that I refrained from taking their evidence. There were others who had seen the wounded stabbed with bayonets, but could not give the names of those so maltreated.

I was unable to see Captn Alexr. J. McDonald of the 95th Reg^t. as he was on board the Golden Fleece three miles off the harbour of Balaclava, but I have written to him by the Caradoc to send me his statement in writing.

Several vessels containing wounded soldiers whom I was anxious to examine had already sailed for Scutari.

W. G. Romaine
Deputy Judge Advocate

Opinion of the Court

We are of the opinion that the evidence of the witnesses given before us this day is that of men who may be implicitly believed.

That their testimony establishes beyond a doubt the charge of maltreating wounded and disabled British soldiers on the field of the battle of Inkerman

John Campbell Br Genl
Comg 1st. Brigade 3rd Division } President

G Cadogan
    Cap & Lt Coll. Act^g Major
    3rd B^n. Gren^r. Guards
Graham Egerton
    Lt. Colonel 77 Foot

W. G. Romaine
Dep. Judge Advocate
Novr. 10th. 1854

NAM Accession 1968-07-293/14–28

72
Romaine to Lord Raglan

[Holograph]
                         Camp before Sebastopol
                                 Novr. 12th. 1854

My Lord,

I have the honour to inform your Lordship that I have made a second attempt to see Mr Russell the Times Correspondent, but that he is still on board some ship at sea, the name of which I have not been able to ascertain.

I have left a letter for him with the Postmaster, conveying to him your Lordship's opinion of the letters dated Octr. 3^d. & Octr. 5th which appeared in the Times of the 23^d. of Octr. and requesting him to avoid carefully the insertion of anything which might be useful to the enemy and injurious to the public service.

I have no doubt that my representation will have the effect which your Lordship desires.

I have seen Mr Aber the Naval Correspondent of the Times who at once promised a compliance with your Lordship's wishes.

I have also spoken to M^r. Crowe of the Illustrated London News and M^r. Duncan of the Morning Chronicle who both expressed themselves most anxious to avoid giving any cause of complaint to your Lordship.

I have not been able to see either M^r. Wood of the Morning Herald, or M^r. Godkin of the Daily News as they live on board ships the names of which I could not learn.

    I have the honour to be
    My Lord
    Your Lordship's Obed^t. Servant
    W. G. Romaine
    Deputy Judge Advocate

NAM Accession 1968-07-293/29–31

73
Romaine to Lord Raglan

[Holograph]   Camp before Sebastopol
                                                                Novr. 25th. 1854

My Lord,

I have the honour to report to your Lordship that in reply to my application I have received a letter from Capt. Mc.Donald of the 95th with a statement of the manner in which he was treated by the Russians on the field of battle of Inkerman after he was disabled.

His name was mentd. in the evidence of Captn. Goodlake of the Coldstream Guards the 12th. Witness in the Court of Enquiry held here on the 9th. day of Novr. His statement is as follows:

"After the first repulse of the Russians from the small battery in front and to the right of the camp of the 2nd. Division before Sebastopol on the morning of the 5th. fresh bodies having come forward & gained the position I was retiring with a few stragglers of my own and other regiments and about forty guardsmen of what regiment I did not observe, the enemy were then advancing from three different points and were in our front rear and on one flank and pretty close; here I received my first wound, in the knee – (a gunshot) which unhorsed me and I fell under a bush About twelve or fifteen Russians as soon as they saw me commenced firing at me several bullets went through the bush under which I lay, but none struck me; I then struggled to my feet and pointed to my hand without a sword and my wounded knee (I had dropped my sword as I fell) they however took no notice of this but began to bayonet me, I warded off the thrusts as long as I could but soon fell, when they continued bayonetting me and beating me on the head with the butt ends of their muskets till they thought I was dead – I received in all 17 wounds and a contusion & lay where I fell, how long I cannot say till two privates of the 20th. Regt. came & carried me off."

(Signed) Alex^r. Macdonald

L^t. & Adj^t. 95th. Reg^t.

Witnesses to his Signature ⎰ H. Hume Major 95th. Reg^t.
                            ⎱ G. C. Viales Captn. 95th. Reg^t.

NAM Accession 1968-07-293/32–3

74
Romaine to Lord Raglan

Camp before Sebastopol
Novr. 25th. 1854

My Lord,

I have the honour to report to your Lordship that I have received the following written statements with regard to the Russian Major [blank space] now a prisoner at Balaclava and charged with ill treating disabled British soldiers at the Battle of Inkerman.

Copy

1st Witness

[Marginal note] This and the following statements were taken by Major Sillery 30th Regt. Commandant Scutari

Corporal John Head 3^d. Batt^n. Gren^r. Gds states that he heard men of his own regiment say that they saw a Russian officer stabbing English soldiers when laying on the ground wounded

(signed) John Head. Gren^r. Gds

{ Geo. Wells. Surg^n. 79th. Witness
{ Ch. Sillery Major & Commandant

Copy

Corporal Charles Pickett of the 3^d. Batt^n. Gr. Gds states:

That on the 5th. of Novr. after the Battle I was stabbed by a Russian officer, he was a man about 5 ft 7 inches in height, and a dark swarthy man. I saw several officers and soldiers stabbing our wounded.

(signed) Charles Piggott. Corpl. G.G.

Witness to signature & statement

Alexander Maclean }
A.S. 42^d. R^l. H^r.   }
Chas. Sillery   }
Major & Comt. }

Copy

Pay and Colour Serjt. Thos Austin of the 1st Batt^n. Coldm. Gds states that he saw a Russian officer near the Coldstream Hospital tent – several of the men around said that they saw him deliberately walking about the field stabbing our wounded he was about 5ft 7 inches in height and a dark swarthy man.

(signed) Thos Austin Serjt. Coldm. Gds

Witness

F. Holton MB }
A.S. 2^d Queens' Royals }
Chas Sillery }
Major & Comt. }

Copy

Serjeant Thomas Dawson of the 3^d. Battn. Gr. Gds states that he was laying in the Tent with a Russian officer he heard one of the men tell the Duke of Cambridge that the officer was the one that was stabbing our wounded. He was a dark swarthy man. He could recognise the officer if he saw him. He does not know anything about the officer giving any corporal money. This was on the morning of the 6th of Novr 1854.
signed Ths Dawson Serjt 3^d Batt Gr.Gds
Signed in presence of
W. Rutherford MD }
Staff Surgeon   }
Chas Sillery   }
Major & Comt   }

Copy

Corporal Robert Cowen 3^d Battⁿ. Gr. Gds says that he saw a Russian officer in charge of a Serjeant and the officer was recognized by men in the Hospital that did. I cannot to have stabbed our wounded on the field. I did not see him do so myself but there was [*sic*] men in the Hospital that did. I cannot name any of the men that did. The officer was about 5 foot 7 inches in height and of a dark complexion.
Signed R. C. [mark] [Marginal note: 'The initials are written in a shaky hand as if the witness was very weak. W. G. Romaine']
Witness
Charles Castle C^m. G^{ds}. }
Chas Sillery   }
Major & Comt.   }

Copy

Private Edward Lewis Cold^m. G^{ds} states While laying on board ship wounded Private Sawyer of the G^r. G^{ds}. told me that when he was in the General Hospital a Russian officer came to have his wound dressed & he recognized this officer to be one that stabbed our wounded, he told him of it – and the officer gave him a sovereign not to inform against him. I

seen him give the sovereign to a woman to change – Private Sawyer died
the day we arrived at Scutari
Signed E. Lewis Cm. Gds
(Witness)
Charles Castle C^m. G^ds ⎫
Chas Sillery ⎬
Major & Comt. ⎭
Scutari 20th. Novr. 1854

I have the honour to be
My Lord
Your Lordship's obedient Servant
      W. G. Romaine
      Dep. Judge Advocate

The following is the evidence of Pay and Colour Serjeant Thomas Austin
1st. Batt^n. Cold^m. Gds as to the death of Captn. Ramsden spoken to by
Witnesses N°. 7 and 8. Captn. & L^t. Crawley & Ass^t Surgeon J.Wyatt
Cold^m. Gds.
"I saw Captn Ramsden fall during the action and went to his assistance I
raised his head he says 'They have done for me' and desired me to take
his rings and watch – I took his rings, by this time the front was cleared
of our men. A Russian column was then in front. I told the Captain how
we were situated he said 'For God's sake don't leave me'. I took him in
my arms to carry him to the rear I had not gone more than five paces
when I was shot myself. I was then obliged to leave him I did not see him
again. When I first went to his assistance he told me he was shot through
the back."
(signed) Thos Austin Serj^t Cold G^ds
Witnesses
F. Holton MB
Asst Surgeon 2^d. Queens Royals
Chs. Sillery –
Major & Commandant.
[There follow twelve foolscap pages (pp. 40–55), written in copperplate
handwriting, repeating the proceedings of the Court of Enquiry noted
above.]

NAM Accession 1968-07-293/34–9

75
Lord Raglan to Romaine

[Holograph]   Decr. 5th. 1854
Copy

My dear Mr Romaine

I have read the proceedings of the Court of Enquiry and am much struck with the apathy, indifference and want of attention of Dr Lawson: and I will thank you to consider whether charges can be preferred against him –

It is absolutely necessary that I should do all in my power to arouse the Medical department to a sense of duty –

The system of throwing a heavy responsibility upon a very junior officer is vicious in the extreme and must be put a stop to – Dr Wilson Dr Hall says had been seven years in the Service – granted – He told Dr Lawson the day he went on board that he was unable to take charge of the sick, and yet he was not relieved. Dr Mills came on board the following day ill; the principal if not the whole labour fell on Dr. Read –

Dr Lawson applied no remedy even when his indifference allowed him to discover that a remedy was required –

The Commissariat are also to blame if even one sheep or one bullock was to be had at Balaklava –

I confess I pity the condition of our sick & wounded to be in such hands –

I return the proceedings and shall be glad to see you when you have considered the possibility of arraigning Dr Lawson before a General Court Martial.

    Yours
    (signed) Raglan

NAM Accession 1968-07-293/56–9

76
Romaine's draft for a General Order[88]

[Holograph]

It having been represented to the Commander of the Forces that the 297 sick and wounded on board the Steamship 'Avon' under orders to proceed to Scutari had not received that care and attention to which they were entitled, the Commander of the Forces directed a Court of Enquiry to meet on board that ship on Saturday the 2^d of Dec^r.

The Court of which Col. Cameron of the 42^d. Highlanders was president after making a personal inspection of the ship and receiving evidence has made its Report to the Commander of the Forces.

The Report takes notice of several deficiencies which in the opinion of the Court might with due care have been remedied.

The Report particularly draws the attention of the Commander of the Forces to the want of a sufficient number of Medical men and Hospital attendants for the service of the many sick & wounded on board –

The Report further states that this deficiency of medical men & attendants was known to Dr Lawson the Principal Medical Officer at Balaklava but that he took no steps to have it supplied.

[The following section deleted]

In this opinion after a careful perusal of the evidence the Commander of the Forces fully concurs.

[A section written in the margin, but then itself also deleted]

The Commander of the Forces has seen with pain and indignation the apathy and indifference of Dr Lawson to the suffering of the gallant but unfortunate men committed to his care. And the Commander of the Forces is compelled now to visit such conduct with his severest censure.

The Commander of the Forces is unable entirely to exonerate Dr Hall the Inspector General of Hospitals from all blame in this matter, as it was his duty either by personal inspection or by the Reports of his subordinates to have ascertained that the ship was furnished with everything necessary for the comfort of the many sick & wounded on board, which the public service could by any possibility afford.

In this opinion after a careful perusal of the evidence the Commander of the Forces fully concurs. Lord Raglan has seen with pain and sorrow the apathy and ~~apparent~~ want of interest* which Dr Lawson has exhibited as appears by the evidence ~~of the Ct xxx in the for~~ with respect both to the due care and the sufficient resupply [?] of which were requisite for the comfort and well doing [illegible, struck out] of the

---

* [Here the following words were struck out and the words above inserted] of Dr Lawson in which it was his unquestioned duty to provide for the due care and consideration of the sick.

suffering men who were† placed on board the Avon and he is compelled to visit such conduct with his severest censure.

NAM Accession 1968-07-293/60-4

77
Sir John Hall to Colonel Steele

[Holograph]   Camp before Sevastopol
6th December 1854

[Note added in a different hand: Col Steele Put with the papers connected with [illegible] of [illegible]]

Sir,

In reply to your communication of this date I have the honor to inform you that no leave of absence was granted to asst. Surgeon Wilson 7th Hussars – He was directed to take charge of the sick on board the 'Avon' down to Scutari and return, being one of the senior assistant Surgeons present, and there being no 2d Class Staff Surgeon disposable at the time.

Asst Surgeon Mills 63d Regiment not being able to do duty in the trenches on account of a Superficial ulcer on his shin, was recommended short leave to go on board ship in Balaklava Harbour, but Dr Lawson, not considering his disability sufficient to disqualify him for duty on board ship, and that the voyage down to Scutari and back would be beneficial to him named him, as he was already on board the vessel, one of the assistants – He is to return –

Staff Asst Surgeon Reade, having served the whole campaign with diligence and credit, was going down to remain on duty in the General Hospital at Scutari – He is the son of the late Chief Apothecary, whose death has been reported this day, and his mother and sisters are at Scutari.

---

† [Here the following words were struck out and the words above inserted] a duty which his inclination and xxx feeling as an officer should have brought him to consider xxx & all others.

[An earlier attempt at the words to follow here, struck out on a final page] Men whom it was his duty to see duly attended to the xxx and the Comdr of the Forces is compelled to visit his conduct with his severest censure.

Mr Wilson will now most likely remain at Scutari on account of his health; but I was not prepared for this contingency, as only a short time before the report of his sickness I had refused an application from him to rejoin his Division in camp, having no one of experience at the time with whom I could replace him on board the 'Avon'.

In conclusion I may mention that 2^d Class Staff Surgeon Ewing, who had just arrived in the country, was placed in charge of the sick on board the 'Avon', and a second Staff Asst Surgeon of the name of Smith was also put on board so that when the vessel sailed she had no less than five Medical Officers on board –

I have the honor to be

Sir

Your most obedient

Humble Servant

J Hall

D. Genl. of Hosps

NAM Accession 1968-07-293/65–6

78
Romaine to Colonel Steele[89]

[Holograph]   Jany. 18th. 1855.

My dear Steele,

After our conversation the other day I asked Mr Angela what his pay and that of Mr Smith the other Postmaster was.

He said Mr Smith received	350£ per annum
And 1.1.£ a day	383.5
⎰ Outfit	100
⎱ Cash for personal expenses	100
	933.5 the first year

Mr Angelo He receives (former Clerk in Post Office)

	150
A guinea a day	383.5
⎰ Outfit	90
⎱ Cash	100
	723.5

Besides this he had horses and saddles &c at Varna bought & paid for by the Department –

I do not remember any other civilian out here except our worthy friend Mr Russell of the Times who receives 800£ a year and a guinea a day expenses –

An officer who is appointed officiating Judge Advocate to conduct a Court Martial receives <u>besides his own pay</u>, two guineas a day as long as the Court sits, and is paid for any contingent expenses he may be put to. The Judge Advocate of the Army is employed every day –

Yrs. Truly

W. G. Romaine

NAM Accession 1968-07-293/76–8

79
Romaine to Lord Raglan[90]

[Holograph]   Head Quarters Camp
                                                June 21st 1855

My Lord,

I have carefully perused the despatch of Her Majesty's Principal Secretary of State for the War Department No. 156 dated 4th June 1855 and its enclosure from Sir J. Paxton dated 1st June 1855 referred to by your Lordship.

I am of opinion that the Army Works Corps on their arrival in this country will not be subject to the provisions of the Mutiny Act & Articles of War, neither the 2nd Section of the Act nor the 154th Article including such a Corps as the one now on its way to the Crimea.

They will be amenable to punishment for breaches of good order & discipline, under the 143 Article of War as all the followers of an Army in the field necessarily are – I have not seen a copy of the agreement signed by the members of the Corps, but I consider that their consent to be subject to the Mutiny Act and Articles of War, does not give power to the Commander of the Forces to apply those laws to them, any more than the want of such consent on their part would deprive him of the power ~~if he possessed~~ if he possessed it by force of law.

I believe that if one of these men should be sentenced to transportation under the supposed sanction of the Mutiny Act, that a judge of one of our superior Courts in England would refuse to make the order required by the 23^d. Section.

I think therefore that an act should be passed expressly subjecting them to the Mutiny Act & Articles of War, if that is thought desirable –

The punishment for offences against these laws are however, little adapted for the restraint of men earning high wages & hired for a limited period – Such for instance as stoppage of a penny a day of his pay for thirty days for drunkenness, or for a longer period for Habitual drunkenness

There is no place of imprisonment here in the field except a tent, where unruly men must be guarded & brought into collision with the soldiers –

The only punishment that can be conveniently applied is flogging, the policy of having recourse to which on all occasions to enforce order by discipline in a large body of civilians seems very questionable.

I would respectfully submit that if a large body of civilians, officers & men are permanently to be attached to the army, not only to perform ordinary labour but to go under fire in the trenches, a short code should be made for their governance and for regulating their trial for serious crimes by courts martial –* fines and forfeitures to be inflicted by their own officers for minor acts of misconduct, such fines to be proportional to their earnings† Led to the discontent now existing in the body of navvies at Balaclava & which last night ended in a strike & mutiny only arrested by the interference of the Provost Marshal and a body of soldiers sent by your Lordship's orders.

In the present spirit and temper of the navvies engaged on the Balaclava Railway it would perhaps be advisable that they should not be employed with a fresh body of labourers arriving from England –

The rules regarding gratuities and pensions for men wounded and disabled in action should be prepared before such casualties occur

I have the honour to be

My Lord

Your Lordship's obedient Servt.

W. G. Romaine

NAM Accession 1968-07-293/81–6

---

* [Marginal note] The Commander of the Forces to use the power to make rules and regulations and establish.

† [Inserted in margin] returns of all punishments to be made weekly to the Adjt. General for his approval.

    The right of the men to be put an end to their service with the army should be very carefully specified. The want of such knowledge of their obligation to serve as long as they may be required.

Appendix 2

Correspondence on Railway Matters

As noted, Romaine was asked to take on several extra tasks which were far from his legal duties and these included the correspondence between the Commander-in-Chief or his headquarters, and the railway engineers. Much of this was of trivial detail as revealed by the letters in the small sample which follows. They are drawn from the forty-one letters in the Edward Hall papers at Wigan.

80
Romaine to James Beatty

Headquarters
Camp before Sebastopol
January 26th 1855

Sir,

I am directed by the Commr of Forces to address the following questions and suggestions to you –

1. The Commr of the Forces was given to understand by you that stationary Engines could be used without difficulty on the Road from Kadikoi to the Turkish Flagstaff – But as it appears from the Minutes of the Board meeting yesterday that you intend to use Capstans and ropes in place of steam Engines, Lord Raglan wishes you to state in writing the reasons for such change of plan –

2. What portion of the road if any could be worked by Steam Engines – The saving of the labor of Men and horses being of the greatest importance.

3. How long a time it would take for a train of say ten carriages to go from Balaklava to the top of the hill –

4. Will the Capstan if used at the steep incline be worked to push up a train of say ten or more Carriages at once or only a single Carriage at a time –

5. Is there any intention of using locomotive Engines to move the Carriages when the top of the platform is reached or is the line when laid down to be worked by horses entirely.

Are the men required to take charge of these horses necessary for the work to be provided by the Army or by the men in your employ –

6. If the 500 men to be supplied according to your requisition remain constantly in your employ how long will it take to complete the line to Kadikoi? How long to complete the steep incline of about a third of a mile so as to have it in working order –

How long to complete the road to the Turkish Flagstaff on the top of the Hill –

How long to complete it to the Divisions encamped along the heights in front of Sebastopol –

I am also directed to request that you will take care that the landing of the materials for the Railway when they arrive may be so arranged as not to impede the traffic on the Wharf beyond your landing place, which is necessarily carried on there for the daily subsistence of the Army.

I have also to inform you that a steam[er] with an officer of the Commissariat and the necessary funds and an experienced non-commissioned officer of the Sappers to select Timber &c will be placed at your disposal to proceed to Sinope and bring such timber as can be obtained and the faggots you require they can be obtained according to such written instructions as you may give him –

M^r De Vere of the Royal Engineers who has been at Sinope will communicate with you as to what timber and materials are to be there obtained and will call on you for that purpose tomorrow.

The Commr of the Forces requests in order to save you the inconvenience of communicating with the different departments of the Army that you will address all your communications on the subject of the Railway to me –

I have &c
(signed) W. G. Romaine
D.J.A.G.

Edward Hall archive/21

81
James Beatty to Romaine

Balaklava January 27th 1855

Balaklava Railway

Sir

I beg to acknowledge the receipt of your letter of the 26th requesting for the information of the Commander of the Forces answers on certain subjects connected with the working and progress of the Railway –

Will you be kind enough to inform the Commander of the Forces that I purpose inspecting the whole line of route within the next two or three days and will give a reply to your enquiries at the very earliest moment –

I have seen M^r De Vere R.E. on the subject of Timber and Faggots from Sinope, from the information obtained from him it is very doubtful indeed if any Faggots could be obtained at all, in time to be of the slightest use towards the construction of the Railway and as regards Timber all that could be had when he was there was of the smallest size and only adapted for building huts – as we have a supply of these coming out along with the other materials I do not think I would be justified in employing a steamer on such a doubtful errand –

I feel very much obliged for the prompt manner in which my suggestion in respect to a vessel has been met but the report of M^r De Vere makes me doubt very much the information obtained at Constantinople; that a large supply of timber could be obtained at Sinope.

I have &c

(signed) James Beatty

Engineer in Chief

Edward Hall archive/29

82
James Beatty to Romaine

Balaklava Jany 30th 1855

Balaklava Railway

Sir,

I have been in daily expectation of being put in full possession of the yard & buildings occupied by some Turks in Balakava which was given for a Railway Wharf and which I was to have had possession of on the day after the Railway Board sat here.

This has not yet been done and the delay is very detrimental to the preparations for Railway operations. Will you be kind enough to give the necessary instructions for turning out these Turks & giving me possession of the premises.

I am &c

(Signed) James Beatty

Edward Hall archive/40

83
James Beatty to Romaine
Balaklava 6th Feby 1854 [*sic* – slip for 1855]

Balaklava Railway

Sir,

Will you be kind enough to direct the proper authority to deliver to my order 2 barrels of powder for Blasting –

Yours &c

(Signed) J. Beatty

Edward Hall archive/51

84
Romaine to James Beatty
Head Quarters Camp before Sevastopol
Feb 7th 1855

Sir,

I am directed by the Commander of the Forces to inform you that a Body of Croatian Labour has been engaged by the British Embassy at Constantinople for the service of the Railway on the following terms – Agreement

Article 1st 30 days pay in advance has been received for 100 labours –

Article 2nd Each labour will receive 3^d a day & rations on feast days or days they do not work they receive no pay only rations –

3. Nour Aga who contracted to supply these men will come with them to see that they do their* work properly –

---

*   [Marginal note] 'He receives 6^d a day and rations'.

<u>Art. 4</u>. An interpreter is come with them who speaks French and Turkish he is to receive 4s/6d a day & rations

<u>Art. 5</u>. They are to be sent home by the British Government

There are to be engaged by Nour Aga – 100

Engaged by Osman Aga – 207

Engaged by Osman Aga – 400

Tools to be provided by Government –

Ibrahim Kuks and an Interpreter are to come to see the men work properly until Osman Aga himself comes –

I have to recommend that care be taken to see that the Men are regularly paid & that <u>each individual</u> receives the money due to him –

That the Men are as well treated as circumstances will permit & their customs & prejudices respected and attended to.

I have &c

(Signed) W. G. Romaine

Edward Hall archive/51

85
Romaine to James Beatty

Head Quarters Camp before Sevastopol
Feb 7th 1855

Sir,

I am directed by the Commr ~~of the Forces~~ in Chief that the Commr^y. General has complained that his operations have been greatly impeded by the position taken up by the Ships unloading your materials.

He says that no wood can be landed for want of wharf room your ships lying alongside instead of end to the wharf –

Will you use your best endeavours to put this right – the wood is terribly wanted as fuel for the Army –

If it is an absolutely necessary obstruction I am sure you will be as anxious as anyone that it shall be removed as speedily as possible.

Yours &c

(Signed) W. G. Romaine

Edward Hall archive/53

86
Beatty to Romaine

Balaklava Railway Balaklava
Feby 8th 1855

Sir,

In reply to your two letters of the 26th & 30th January respectively asking for the information of the Commr of the Forces replies on certain subjects connected with the construction & working of the Railway.

Although I cannot give you definite answers to all the questions yet I will endeavour to do so as well as I possibly can –

As regards Engine Power

It is intended to erect a stationary Engine at the top of the 1. in 15. incline from Kadikoi to the French Camp as I do not doubt we shall get water to work it –

The other incline of 1. in 25. from the French Camp to the Flagstaff must for the present be worked by horses – there will be no difficulty in doing this –

The 1. in 15 incline is the only one we can at present work with Engine Power –

As regards the time required to go from Balaklava to the top of the Hill at the Flagstaff – two hours will be quite sufficient to calculate for taking a train of ten waggons –

Capstans will most probably not be required for the inclines. I hope to do everything with horses and Engine Power –

No locomotive Engines are provided, a further supply of horse power in addition to our own will have to be provided – but I think when the number of horses at present employed, which the completion of the Railway to the top of the incline will immediately relieve – that there will be no difficulty in giving us the assistance in horse power that we shall require, not amounting with the addition of our own to more than 100 horses –

I am quite of opinion that 100 horses with drivers in addition to our own presuming they arrive here all safe will be sufficient to work the Line – which will be done by the skilled men we have brought out.

I hope that the portion from here to Kadikoi will be available in 10 days from this date if the weather continues fine – The 200 men fatigue party being withdrawn and the Croatians being available for little more than carrying materials – I cannot undertake to say when the Line will be completed to the Flagstaff but I should hope in 3 or 4 weeks time.

It has retarded our progress very much taking away the <u>200</u> men of the 39th who were beginning to understand their work and did very well – As regards the extensions beyond the Flagstaff I hope the Comm[r]. of the Forces will excuse my asking a little further delay before giving any opinion about the compilation of that portion –

I am decidely of the opinion that all the force I can muster should be applied in the first place to completing the Line to the Flagstaff which will relieve the horses and men of the Army of the worst part of this work the extension beyond that being of secondary importance in comparison with the first 4 miles out of Balaklava –

The greatest care will be taken so as to interfere as little as possible with the traffic on the Quays –

In reference to your letter of the 30th –

<u>Weight of Waggons</u>

The weight of the waggons can be diminished but they will not be much under 1½ tons – I do not think it is at all advisable to attempt making the Artillery Wagons available for travelling on the Railway

<u>Harness</u>

I inspected a set of rope harness made by direction of Captn Heath which I conceive will answer very well for the Turkish horses –

I understand he was to order <u>100</u> sets of this harness to be made at Constantinople immediately*

In conclusion I hope that if all our men horses & materials arrive safely we shall be able to complete the Railway to the Flag Staff within one month and afterwards work it so as to set free the immense number of men and horses at present engaged in the transport of provisions &c between it and Balaklava. I also trust that difficulties which may now appear will gradually disappear as the Line progresses and that we shall within the time I have mentioned viz one month be able to render such assistance to the Army in the transport of every description of material that one is fairly entitled to calculate on by taking off 4 miles of the now worst & heaviest portion of the Carriage

I have &c

(Signed) J. Beatty

Edward Hall archive/54

---

* [Marginal note] 'Enquire of Mr Pritchard if Captn Heath undertook this – & where the pattern set is'.

Glossary of Military Terms

24 lb, 68 pr, 13 inch, etc. (as applied to guns). Once systems of artillery had been standardised, guns were referred to by the weight of roundshot they fired, e.g. a 9-pounder gun fired a 9-lb roundshot. When shells (q.v.) were introduced this was inapplicable and the calibre of shell guns was quoted in inches. Both types also fired various other projectiles including case shot and carcass (q.v.) but shell guns did not fire roundshot. There were many exceptions to the general rule, and the lighter field howitzers fired shells but were referred to by weight.

Abattis. Trees cut down and trimmed with the branches intertwined to present a dense obstacle to attacking infantry.

Ambuscade. Place of concealment for a surprise attack.

Araba. Native two-wheeled cart.

Blindage. A cover for troops made of heavy timber frames or other materials.

Boyau. Zig-zag branch of a trench.

Cacolet. French ambulance litter fitted to horse or mule, carrying two sick men, slung on each side of the animal.

Caisson. Ammunition wagon for small arms and artillery.

Canister or case shot. Multiple small iron or lead shot similar in size to musket balls contained in a light cylindrical casing so that the shot dispersed at the muzzle. The artilleryman's short-range weapon against infantry or cavalry, devastating in effect.

Carcass. A hollow iron shell pierced with three or four large holes and filled with an inflammable composition which could not be extinguished by water, thus making an incendiary shell.

Case shot *see* Canister.

Casemate. Room in wall of fortress, providing safe shelter for troops.

Cohorn, Coehorn. Small mortar (q.v.) used in the trenches.

Communication trench. A trench connecting two parallels (q.v.).

Embrasure. Opening in a parapet for a gun.

Enfiladed. Vulnerable to fire from open flank.

Entonnoir. Crater of a mine.

Fascine. A tied bundle of sticks used to fill enemy ditches so that they could be crossed.

Firelock. Common term for a musket or rifle.

Fougasse. An early form of anti-personnel mine consisting of a buried box of gunpowder. When trodden on, a glass tube of acid would break and set it off.

Gabion. A cylindrical construction normally of wickerwork which could be placed in position and rapidly filled with earth or stones to form a protective wall, or the filled 'basket'.

Gorge. An opening in a fort wall.

Grape. Projectile consisting of iron shot of sizes between golf and tennis balls, usually nine or twelve, arranged in layers and held to an iron frame by canvas which disintegrated in flight leaving the individual balls to continue flying forward. A term frequently misused when *canister* (q.v.) is intended.

Howitzer. A short-barrelled gun which lobbed shells at high elevation and short range.

Lancaster. An experimental rifled gun invented by a London gunsmith and first used in the Crimea where rebored 68-pounders and 8-inch guns were sent with great expectations of success which were not realised. The bore was oval and twisted, and the shells were elongated and of oval cross-section. The shells carried more powder and had a greater range than the spherical shells used in conventional guns, but were expensive to make. The Lancaster guns were soon used to fire conventional ammunition, frustrating the purpose of the special bore.

Mamelon. Any rounded isolated hill, but especially the fortified hill in the Sevastopol defences forward of the Malakhov (*see* Map 6).

Masking. Covering of an embrasure to keep out enemy fire.

Minié. The popular term for the Pattern 1851 Rifle Musket, standard issue for most of the British troops at the start of the campaign. It had a longer range and greater accuracy than the smooth-bore musket it replaced.

Mortar. Short large-bore weapon for throwing bombs short distances at very high angle.

Palisaded ditch. Ditch with walls reinforced by wooden fence.

Parallel. A long trench first dug some distance from the objective out of range of the defending artillery, and then further trenches dug successively nearer to the objective, parallel to the first (hence the name) and connected with the earlier parallels by communication trenches (q.v.).

Pit, rifle pit. A hole dug in front of the defences to provide shelter for sharpshooters to fire at the enemy.

Redoubt. Fort.

Revetted. Strengthened, as in the wall of an earthwork.

Rifle pit *see* Pit.

Rocket. Projectile driven by combustion of the propellant within it.

Round shot. Solid cast-iron sphere, colloquially called 'cannon ball'.

Sap. A pit dug beneath the enemy works and filled with explosive to be fired.

Shell. A hollow sphere containing explosive, which detonated after a time set by its fuse.

Shot *see* Round shot.

Sutler. Civilian following the army to sell food, etc., to the soldiers.

Tête de point [*sic*]. Actually *tête de pont*, field work on enemy side of river, defending bridge, i.e. bridgehead.

Tirailleurs. French light infantry used individually, especially for skirmishing [cf. Voltigeurs].

Traverse. A trench connecting parallels (q.v.).

Trou de loup. Loophole: a narrow vertical slit in the wall of a fort, etc.

Tumbril. Open two-wheeled cart.

Voltigeurs. French light infantry used in formed groups (cf. Tirailleurs).

Zouaves. Originally native troops from North Africa, with French officers, but later composed mainly of European soldiers.

Biographical Notes

Ranks shown are contemporary and many officers reached higher ranks, and received decorations later. At that time the staff were divided into two categories. The Adjutant General, and his juniors such as the Assistant Adjutant General (AAG), or Deputy Adjutant General (DAAG), dealt with personnel matters such as discipline, promotions, courts-martial etc. The Quartermaster General, and staff officers such as the AQMG, or DAQMG, dealt with what are now called 'logistic' matters: supply of weapons and equipment, ammunition, stores, clothing and rations. At that time there was no branch of the staff dealing with operational and training matters (in later times known as 'G' matters, in contrast to the 'A' and 'Q' matters described above) and these were also the province of the QMG. Thus, until a Chief-of-Staff to the Commander-in Chief (C-in-C) of the Army of the East was appointed when General Sir James Simpson joined Raglan's HQ, the QMG was effectively the Chief-of-Staff. It was therefore, for example, the QMG who wrote out Raglan's fourth order at Balaklava. Commanders of brigades and above also had Aides-de-camp (ADCs). Many of the staff officers are shown as 'unattached' as this was necessary to take them off their original regimental establishment. The personal numbers in Kane's List are shown for Royal Artillery officers.

Abdul Medjid, Sultan, ruler of the Ottoman Empire.

Airey, Richard. Brigade Commander in Varna, QMG in Crimea; Major-General 12 December 1854.

Alexander II, Tsar, born 1818, succeeded his father as ruler of Russia 2 March 1855, assassinated March 1881.

Ali, Mehmet, Grand Vizier to the Sultan Abdul Medjid.

Alison, presumably a local agent.

Anderson, Mrs, wife of Staff Surgeon Anderson, q.v.

Anderson, Arthur, Staff Surgeon 1st Class, Principal Medical Officer 4th Division at Balaklava and Inkerman.

Astley, probably John Dugdale Astley, Brevet Major 12 December 1854, wounded at Alma.

Aylmer, Fenton John, 97th Regiment. Lieutenant 8 December 1854.

Bainbrigge, Philip John, Royal Engineers. Captain 1 April 46.

Banbury, Romaine's friend at home.

Barnard, Henry, Brigade Commander, later Chief-of-Staff, then Commander 2nd Division; Major-General 20 June 1854.

Bate, Lord, an example of an aristocrat, presumably in disgrace, enlisting as a soldier.

Beatty, James, Chief Engineer of the railway. Injured in an accident, returned to England and died 11 March 56, aged thirty-five.

Bentinck, Lieutenant-General Sir Henry, Brigade Commander Guards Brigade, later Commander 4th Division; Major-General 20 June 1854.

Biddulph, Michael A. S., Royal Artillery, Kane 2010. Brevet Major 12 December 1854, in charge of submarine telegraph.

Bizot, General, French Chief Engineer. Killed visiting English trenches 1 April 1855.

Blane, Robert, unattached. Lieutenant-Colonel 12 December 1854, Assistant Adjutant General at HQ, then Military Secretary.

Bosquet, Maréchal Pierre, French commander of 2nd Division, later of Corps of Observation.

Bostock, John Ashton, MD, Scots Fusilier Guards. Surgeon 17 February 1854.

Boutinieff, Russian naval captain.

Brackenbury, Mr, agent for the Crimean Army Fund, organised to provide comforts to the troops.

Bright, John, MP, radical member for Birmingham and opponent of the war.

Brodin, aide to Lord Stratford.

Brown, General Sir George, Division Commander, Light Division. A stickler for discipline. A Peninsular veteran and Raglan's confidante; Lieutenant-General 11 November 1851.

Browne, The Hon. Cavendish, 7th Fusiliers. Captain 4 August 1854, killed 22 March 1855.

Brownrigg, Studholme, Grenadier Guards. Assistant Adjutant General 1st Division, Colonel 2 November 1855.

Bruat Admiral, French navy. Second-in-command French Black Sea squadron, then Commander. Died en route to France, 25 November 1854.

Brunet, General, French divisional commander. Killed 18 June 1855 leading attack on Little Redan.

Buchanan, George, a constituency official in Chatham, Romaine's chosen parliamentary target.

Buller, General Sir George, Commander 2nd Brigade of the Light Division at Alma; Major-General 12 December 1854.

Burghersh, Lord Francis William Henry, unattached. ADC to Raglan, Lieutenant-Colonel 20 September 1854.

Burgoyne, Lieutenant-General Sir John, GCB, Royal Engineers. Adviser at HQ, and main advocate of a formal siege; General 5 September 1855.

Cadogan, The Hon. George, Grenadier Guards. Colonel 28 November 1854. Later Commissioner at Sardinian HQ.

Calthorpe, The Hon. Somerset John Gough, 8th Hussars. ADC to Lord Raglan. Brevet Major 2 November 1855. Defendant in a celebrated libel case brought by Lord Cardigan after the war for suggesting in his book, *Letters from*

Headquarters, that Cardigan had abandoned his men after reaching the Russian guns in the Charge of the Light Brigade.

Calvert. The references may be to Frank Calvert, British Consul at Gallipoli, or to Charles Cattley, Raglan's intelligence chief at HQ who had been Vice Consul at Kertch until expelled, and who now used the name Calvert as 'cover'. Kinglake records that Cattley warned about the Crimean winter while the army was in Bulgaria – but Calvert also knew the region well and could equally have done so. Romaine may have referred to the two different persons at different times: we can only guess from the context. Thus 'Calvert' attached to HQ must be Cattley, and it was Cattley who died in 1855 from cholera.

Cambridge, George, Duke of, cousin of Queen Victoria – hence the nickname 'The Royal George'. Commanded 1st Division at Alma and Inkerman; Lieutenant-General 19 June 1854. Went home sick shortly afterwards but rose to be C-in-C of the army.

Cameron, Duncan, 42nd Black Watch. Commanded battalion, later Highland Brigade; Colonel 20 June 1854.

Camidge, Charles, Chief Cashier of the railway. Became ill and was sent home in June 1855.

Campbell, Sir Colin. Commanded Highland Brigade at Alma, later C-in-C of British troops in the Indian Mutiny and created Lord Clyde; Major-General 20 June 1854.

Campbell, Sir John, Bt. Commanded a brigade in 3rd Division, later temporarily commanded 4th Division, and then a brigade in 4th Division. Died leading assault on Redan, 18 June 1855; Major-General 12 December 1854.

Canning, The Misses. The Hon. Louisa (b. 1828) and The Hon. Katharine (b. 1835), daughters of Lord Stratford de Redcliffe who had recently arrived in the *Caradoc*.

Cannon, Colonel Robert. A British officer with considerable experience in various armies and continents. He joined the Madras army in India and fought in the Coorg war. While in Britain on sick leave he joined the 'legion' raised by Sir de Lacy Evans to fight the Carlists in the Spanish Civil War, rising to command the 9th Irish regiment. He returned to India as a commissioner in Mysore but resigned on marrying and was in England when the Crimean War broke out. He was asked to join the Turkish army and was known to them as Behram (or Beiram) Pasha. He rose to be a Lieutenant-General, or *ferik* after service on the Danube. He was said by Omar Pasha to have saved Silistria, and led his men with great skill and gallantry at the Battle of Giurgevo, July 1854. He commanded the 1st Turkish Division at Eupatoria, and later joined the relief column for Kars.

Canrobert, Maréchal François. Commanded French 1st Division, succeeded St Arnaud as C-in-C but resigned in May 1855 and reverted to command a division. Indecisive and known to the British as 'Bob Can't'.

Cardigan, Earl of. Commanded the Light Brigade of Cavalry in the Charge. Major-General 20 June 1854.

Cathcart, Lieutenant-General Sir George. Success in Kaffir War led to his commanding 4th Division, with dormant commission to succeed Raglan, but he was killed at Inkerman; Local Lieutenant-General 30 January 1852.

Cator, William, Royal Artillery, Kane 1134. Brigadier-General. Commander Royal Artillery in Bulgaria but went home sick from there in August 1854.

Cattley, *see* Calvert.

Caulfield, Francis William, 44th Foot. Captain 29 December 1854, killed at the Redan 18 June 1855.

Chapman, Frederick E., Royal Engineers. Captain 1 April 46, Brevet Colonel; surveyed the defensive lines at Boulair; with 1st Division at Alma. Director of Left Attack, to which he gave his name.

Chetwode, George, 8th Hussars. Captain 24 February 1854.

Claremont, Edward Stopford, unattached. Commissioner to French at Paris. Lieutenant-Colonel 14 September 1855.

Cobbe, Henry, 4th Foot. Brevet Colonel 20 June 1854. Wounded at Alma and on 18 June 1855.

Cockerill, R.W., medical officer with Royal Artillery. Assistant Surgeon 24 May 1854. Wounded in an advanced battery in the April bombardment. Tried by general court martial on 15 June 1855 with neglect of duty to a patient, and found guilty. Sentenced to be severely reprimanded and placed at the bottom of the seniority list of Assistant Surgeons of the Ordnance Department (General Orders, 17 June 1855). Resigned 1 August 1855.

Cocks, Octavius Yorke, 4th Foot. Captain 4 August 1854.

Codrington, General Sir William. Rose from Guards Company Commander in Varna to command brigade at Alma, later Light Division and finally in October 1855 the whole Army of the East; Major-General 20 June 1854.

Cole, Arthur Lowry, 17th Foot. Lieutenant-Colonel 9 March 1855.

Coleridge, Mr. Tutor at Eton College with a high reputation.

Comyn, a friend of Romaine's at home.

Cork, a friend of Romaine's at home.

Cunynghame, Arthur Augustus Thurlow, late 51st Foot. Colonel 20 June 1854, AQMG 1st Division and then Major-General Turkish Contingent.

Curzon, The Hon. Leicester, Rifle Brigade. Brevet Lieutenant-Colonel 8 September 1855, ADC to Raglan and later Assistant Military Secretary.

Dacres, Richard, Royal Artillery, Kane 1668. Lieutenant-Colonel commanding artillery of 1st Division, succeeded Fox-Strangways, who was killed at Inkerman, as overall Commander of the Royal Artillery at Raglan's HQ.

D'Aguilar, C.L., Royal Artillery, Kane 1911. Commanded one 18-pounder at Inkerman and distinguished himself on several occasions during the siege.

D'Autemarre, General. French general commanding brigade in Bosquet's Corps of Observation.

de Bathe, Henry Percival, Scots Fusilier Guards. Captain and Lieutenant-Colonel 17 February 1854.

De Morel, Charles, Carew, 67th Foot. ADC to General Estcourt (Adjutant General); Brevet Major 12 December 1854.

De Revel, Comte, French officer. Lieutenant Joachim du Perrin, Comte de Revel, served under Admiral de Grasse in the American War of Independence and the officer named here may have been his grandson, perhaps also in the navy.

Delane, John Thaddeus,. Editor of *The Times* throughout the war. Initially a strong supporter of Aberdeen's government, he visited the army in autumn 1854 and witnessed their disembarkation in the Crimea. He saw with his own eyes the defects of the military organisation and instructed William Howard Russell (q.v.) and his other correspondents to tell the truth without fear or favour. The fall of the government in early 1855 was in large part due to the fierce criticism it received from Delane's correspondents and leader writers.

Della Marmora, General. Commanded the Sardinian Contingent.

Denison, Stephen Charles. The Judge-Advocate General (proper) was a political appointment held by a junior member of the government. The day-to-day administration of his organisation was overseen by a deputy, namely Denison. He was born in 1811, educated at Eton and Oxford, called to the Bar 1839 and appointed Deputy Judge-Advocate General in 1851.

Derby, Earl of. Prominent politician and government critic but would not form a ministry himself.

Derriman. Romaine's servant?

Dickson, Collingwood, Royal Artillery, Kane 1824. Initially with Raglan at HQ as Turkish interpreter and later as commander of Right Attack, and instrumental in getting up 18-pounder guns at Inkerman. Awarded VC for his gallantry in the batteries. Brevet Colonel 29 June 1855.

Dixon, Matthew Charles, Royal Artillery, Kane 1929. Brevet Major 17 July 1855. Awarded VC for bravery in the batteries.

Drummond, Hugh F., Scots Fusilier Guards. Lieutenant and Captain 8 November 1850, Adjutant 14 July 1854, killed 13 August 1855.

Dugatty, Dugald. Officer of the Land Transport Corps.

Dundas, Sir James Whitley, Vice Admiral, Royal Navy. Naval C-in-C in the Black Sea. Over-cautious and ready to leave matters to his deputy, Sir Edmund Lyons, who replaced him on 21 December 1854. Cruelly dubbed 'Damned Ass' by many. Not to be confused with Rear Admiral Richard Saunders Dundas who commanded the Baltic Fleet in 1855 and was no relation.

Dunkellin, Lord Ullick Canning, Coldstream Guards. Captain and Lieutenant-Colonel 3 November 1854, short-sighted and taken prisoner by the Russians on 22 October 1854.

Edward, Prince of Saxe Weimar, Grenadier Guards. Captain and Lieutenant-Colonel 18 May 1855 – a regimental officer, albeit with good connections.

Edwards, Clement Alexander, 18th Foot. Lieutenant-Colonel 9 March 1855.

Edwards, Richard Lloyd, 68th Foot. Captain.

Egerton, The Hon. Algernon. Honorary agent in Crimea to administer the Crimean Army Fund.

Egerton, Thomas, 77th Foot. Commanded his regiment, Brevet Colonel 28 November 1854, killed 20 April 1855.

Ellenborough, Earl of. Opposition politician who had been First Lord of the Admiralty and was to return to government with Lord Derby in February 1858.

England, Sir Richard, Lieutenant-General. Commanded 3rd Division; Major-General 11 November 1851.

Espinasse, General, French Brigade. Commander in Bosquet's Corps of Observation.

Estcourt, James, Major-General, Adjutant General at HQ until death on 24 June 1855.

Evans, Lieutenant-General Sir de Lacy. Commanded 2nd Division; Lieutenant-General 20 June 1854.

Eyres, Major-General Sir William, KCB. Commanded brigade then 3rd Division; Major-General 12 December 1854.

Fellowes, Edward, 11th Hussars. Brevet Major 12 December 1854; DAQMG Cavalry Division.

Fenton, Roger, photographer. Present in Crimea from March 1855 to July 1856.

Filder, William, Commissary-General. Reviled chief of the commissariat, hidebound by regulations and replaced July 1855.

Fitzherbert, a friend of Romaine's at home.

Foley, The Hon. St George, unattached. Lieutenant-Colonel 12 December 1854; Assistant Commissioner at French HQ.

Follett, a friend of Romaine's at home.

Forey, General Elie, French army. Commanded siege corps before Sevastopol.

Fremantle, Charles. H., Rear Admiral, Royal Navy. Sent to sort out the confusion over transport ships and port facilities. He favoured use of Kazatch Bay, but was over-ruled.

Gabriel, Sacry. Romaine's servant.

Gambier, Gloucester, Royal Artillery, Kane 1783. Lieutenant-Colonel 6 July 1854. Not, it seems, highly regarded by his colleagues, nor by the men.

Gavin, Dr Hector. One of three Sanitary Commmissioners (Dr Sutherland and Mr Rawlinson were the others) sent out by the government in February 1855. Accidentally killed in April 1855 when a pistol was discharged by his brother William (q.v.). Dr Gavin was a leading sanitary reformer.

Gavin, William, veterinary surgeon with the 17th Lancers, attached to the Land Transport Corps. Accidentally killed his brother, but a Court of Enquiry exonerated him from all blame. Died in the Crimea himself on 9 June 1855 from disease.

Glyn, St Leger. Reconnoitred for the Crimean Army Fund with Jervoise Smith (q.v.).

Goodall, not traced.

Gordon, George Grant, Scots Fusilier Guards. Lieutenant and Captain 26 December 1854. Later ADC to General Simpson. Referred to by Romaine as 'Gerry'.

Gordon, John W., Royal Engineers. Brevet Colonel 29 June 1855. Set out the trenches and batteries of the Right Attack on Frenchman's Hill, which became known as Gordon's Battery; severely wounded on the night of 22–23 March 1855.

Gordon, Samuel Enderby, Royal Artillery, Kane 2052. Brevet Major 12 December 1854; ADC to Fox-Strangways and then Dacres.

Gortchakoff, General Prince. Russian commander in Danubian Principalities and succeeded Menshikov as Crimean commander in 1855.

Govett, Charles Albert. Brother of Romaine but retained the surname Govett when Romaine's father, and Romaine, changed theirs. An attorney (an early form of solicitor). Practised from various addresses including Mitre Court, 10 Lincoln's Inn Fields and 10 King's Bench Walk.

Graham, Gerald, Royal Engineers. Lieutenant 17 February 1854. Awarded the VC for his gallantry leading the ladder party in the assault of 18 June 1855.

Grant, Miss, a friend at home.

Greville, a friend of Romaine's at home.

Grey, Sir G. Made Secretary for Colonies when the dual role of Secretary for War and for the Colonies was split in June 1854.

Hall, Sir John, MD, Principal Medical Officer in Crimea; Inspector General of Hospitals 28 March 1854.

Hardinge, The Hon. Arthur Edward, Coldstream Guards. Brevet Major 12 December 1854; DAQMG 3 Div, later AQMG at HQ. Son of Lord Hardinge (q.v.).

Hardinge, Viscount, C-in-C at Horse Guards; General 20 June 1854, Field Marshal 2 October 1855.

Harvey, John, a friend of Romaine's, living at Ickwell Bury, Biggleswade, Bedfordshire.

Hay, Lord John, Royal Navy. Commander 20 August 1852. Ashore with the Naval Brigade from command of HMS *Wasp*, screw corvette, 14 guns.

Hayter. Perhaps a constituency official in Chatham?

Hepburn, Henry Poole, Scots Fusilier Guards. Captain and Lieutenant-Colonel 20 June 1854.

Herbert, The Hon. Percy Egerton, unattached. Colonel 29 June 1855, QMG after Airey returned to England.

Hill, Arundel Edmund, 89th Foot. Captain 3 October 1848; taken prisoner 27 March 1855 and died of wounds.

Hughes, Mr. Not identified.

Jervoise, Henry Clarke, 42nd Foot later Coldstream Guards. Lieutenant and Captain 6 April 1855; ADC to QMG.

Jones, Major-General Sir Harry KCB, Royal Engineers. British commander in siege operations at Bomarsund; Commander, Royal Engineers, Crimea, February 1855.

Jordan, William Walker, 34th Foot. Lieutenant 6 June 1854, killed 22 March 1855.

Kains. Chairman of the constituency party at Chatham where Romaine was seeking selection as candidate.

Keith, The Hon. Charles. James, 4th Light Dragoons. Lieutenant 31 October 1851; ADC to Lieutenant-General England, GOC 3rd Division. Keith had served three years as a midshipman.

Kelly, Richard D, 34th Foot. Lieutenant-Colonel 9 March 1855, wounded 22 March 1855.

Keppel, The Hon. Henry, Royal Navy. Captain 21 May 1853, Ashore from command of HMS *St Jean d'Acre*, to command the Naval Brigade in succession to Captain Lushington.

Kinglake, Alexander William, 1809–91. Educated at Trinity College, Cambridge, called to the bar, MP 1857, author of *Eothen*. Went as a civilian to Crimea with Raglan. Later, at Lady Raglan's invitation, wrote the standard contemporary history in eight volumes, *The Invasion of the Crimea (to the death of Lord Raglan)*.

Kirkland, John Agmondisham Vesey, 21st Foot then unattached, Brevet Major 12 December 1854, DAAG at HQ.

Korniloff, Vice Admiral Vladimir. Inspirational Russian commander of the Sevastopol defences until killed by gunfire 20 October 1854 in the first Allied bombardment.

Layard, Austen H., MP. Visited the Crimea and was critical of the conduct of the war. Kinglake (q.v.) says that it was to Layard that the French General Bosquet made his famous comment on the Charge of the Light Brigade: 'C'est magnifique mais ce n'est pas la guerre. C'est folie.'

Lempriere, Audley, 77th Foot. Lieutenant 11 August 1854, Captain?, killed 19 April 1855.

Lewis, Miss. A lady at home, perhaps a member of Lord Mulgrave's household.

Lindsay, Robert James, Scots Fusilier Guards. Lieutenant and Captain 6 November 1854.

Liprandi, General Pavel. Russian commander.

Lucan, Earl of, GCB. Commanded the British cavalry and was blamed for the disaster of the Charge of the Light Brigade – many consider unfairly.

Luders, General Count Alexander. Russian commander of Crimean army from 1855.

Lyons, Sir Edmund, Royal Navy. Rear Admiral, 14 January 1850; As second-in-command to Dundas (q.v.) supervised the landing at Kalamita Bay. Gave invaluable support to the army in the siege of Sevastopol while Dundas cruised well off-shore, and replaced him as C-in-C in December 1854.

Lysons, Daniel, 23rd Royal Welch Fusiliers. Landed with the battalion, was immediately taken onto the staff, returned to command after Alma, later temporarily, and then permanently. Later Brigade Commander. Colonel 17 July 1855.

McDonald, The Hon. James William Bosville (Jim), unattached. Lieutenant-Colonel 12 December 1854, equerry and ADC to Duke of Cambridge, commanding 1st Division.

Maclean, Sir George. A Peninsular veteran who replaced Filder (q.v.) as Commissary-General in August 1855.

McMurdo, Colonel William, Director-General of Land Transport Corps, local Colonel 28 November 1854.

McNeill, Sir John. A distinguished Scottish surgeon appointed with Colonel Tulloch to inquire into the management of the Commissariat Department.

Markham, Frederick. Major-General 28 November 1854, Commander 2nd Division from July to September 1855. Left Crimea, sick, and died the same year.

Marsh. Not identified.

Martimprey, General Edmond Charles de. French Chief-of-Staff.

Maule, The Hon. Lauderdale, 39th Foot. Half pay Lieutenant-Colonel on HQ staff; died during 1854.

Maxse, Henry F. B., 21st Foot. Captain 29 December 1854, ADC to Cardigan and wounded in the Charge.

Mayran, General. French; commanded 3rd Division of 2 Corps, mortally wounded on 18 June 1855.

Mazza, Consultore. Presumably an official in Naples.

Menshikoff, Prince. Russian General, Negotiated at the 'Porte' before the war. Commanded in the Crimea.

Messiter, Sussex Lennox Aubrey Beauclerk, 28th Foot. Captain 29 December 1854.

Molesworth, Sir William. First Commissioner of Works in both Aberdeen's and Palmerston's cabinets. Became Secretary for the Colonies in July 1855. Died October 1855.

Montagu, Horace W., Royal Engineers. Brevet Major 2 November 1855; wounded and made prisoner 22 March 1855.

Mulgrave, Lady. Laura, wife of Lord Mulgrave (q.v.).

Mulgrave, Lord. George, son and heir of Marquess of Normanby. MP (Lib.) for Scarborough. A friend of Romaine's from Trinity College, Cambridge.

Munchausen, Karl Friedrich Hieronymus, Baron de. An eighteenth-century German aristocrat, known for his boastful tall tales.

Napier, Sir Charles, Royal Navy. Vice Admiral of the Blue 28 May 1853. C-in-C Baltic Fleet in 1854.

Napier, William Craig Emilius. Colonel 28 November 1854, Assistant Director General, Land Transport Corps.

Napoleon III, Emperor, ruler of France.

Napoleon, Prince. Napoleon Joseph Charles Paul Buonaparte, son of Jerome (1784–1860), youngest brother of Napoleon I, by Catherine of Wurttemburg. Commanded 3rd French Division at Alma and Inkerman. Later married Clothilde, daughter of King Victor Emmanuel II of Sardinia. When Napoleon

III's son, the Prince Imperial, was killed in Zululand in 1879 Prince Napoleon became pretender to the throne. Exiled in 1886, died in 1891.

Neville, Edward, Scots Fusilier Guards. Brevet Major 12 December 1854, ADC to Sir Richard England, commanded 3 Div; left in November 1854.

Newcastle, Henry Pelham Clinton, 5th Duke of, Secretary for War June 1854 to February 1855.

Newlands, Mr. Sanitary inspector who went to the Crimea with the Sanitary Commission (*see* entry for Dr Sutherland). Newlands had worked on the new Liverpool sewers and was an outstanding engineer in this new specialisation.

Nicholson. A friend of Romaine's.

Niel, Adolphe. French General. Served in Baltic and at capture of Bomarsund. Chief Engineer in the Crimea after the death of Bizot, April 1855.

Nolan, Lewis Edward, 15th Hussars. A great horseman and theorist on the use of cavalry. To the horror of his fellow British cavalry officers he had written a book! Initially employed to purchase remounts, later ADC to General Airey (QMG) and carrier of the fateful order to Lucan which led to the Charge of the Light Brigade in which he was the first man killed.

Normanby, Lord and Lady. The Marquess, Constantine Henry, and Marchioness, Maria Liddell, parents of George, Lord Mulgrave (q.v.). Marquessate created 1838. Lord Normanby was ambassador to the Court of Tuscany, 1854–8. Seat: Mulgrave Castle, Whitby, Yorks.

Norton, Edward, 88th Foot. Major 28 Jul 1854. Died of cholera 20 May 1855.

Oglon. A local mule dealer.

Omar Pasha. Turkish commander in Bulgaria, and later at Eupatoria. A Croat convert to Islam. The Turk most respected by the Allies.

Osten Sacken, General Count Dmitri. Russian commander at Odessa and briefly in Sevastopol.

Pacha, Ruschie. Principal adviser to the Ottoman Sultan, Abdul Medjid.

Paget, Lady Agnes. Young and beautiful wife of Lord George Paget (q.v.) who joined him in the Crimea.

Paget, Lord Clarence, Royal Navy. Captain 29 October 1853, commanding HMS *Princess Royal*, 91-gun screw line of battle ship. Third son of the 1st Marquess of Anglesey.

Paget, Lord George, 4th Light Dragoons. Commanded his regiment at Alma and in the Charge of the Light Brigade at Balaklava. Took leave for 'urgent private affairs' (he had just married) and was ostracised in London. Returned to Crimea to command Light Brigade and later the Cavalry Division.

Pakenham, The Hon. William Lygon, unattached. Colonel 17 July 1855. Originally AAG at HQ but succeeded Estcourt as Adjutant General after Estcourt's death in June 1855.

Panmure, Baron, Secretary for War from 1855. Earl Dalhousie from 1860.

Parker, John. A railway official, originally employed as Horsemaster.

Parlby, William, 10th Hussars. Colonel 20 June 1854.

Pasha, Selim. Turkish general killed at Eupatoria on 17 February 1855.

Paulet, Lord William. Originally commanded the lines of communication at the Bosphorus, and after the fall of Sevastopol commanded the Light Division; Colonel 20 June 1854.

Pearson, Richard L. Otway. Probably a reference to an officer of the 7th Fusiliers, Lieutenant 4 April 1851, ADC to Sir George Brown, Commander of the Light Division.

Peel, William, Royal Navy. Captain 10 January 1849. Ashore from HMS *Diamond* with the Naval Brigade, he led the scaling ladder parties on 18 June 1855 and was severely wounded.

Pélissier, Maréchal Amiable. French. Commanded 1 Corps from February 1855 and succeeded Canrobert in May 1855. Considered by the British as a great improvement on his predecessor.

Pennefather, General Sir John. Commanded 1st Brigade of 2nd Division and later the division.

Polignac. Probably Alphonse Armand Charles George Marie, French Artillery officer, Captain 10 May 1855, sometime ADC to the Commander 4th Division, Forey.

Raglan, Field Marshal Lord. Had been Wellington's ADC and Military Secretary, and rose steadily on the staff until Master General of the Ordnance in 1852. Selected to command the Army of the East; died in office 28 June 1855, supposedly broken-hearted at the failure of the assault on 18 June.

Rokeby, General Lord. Commanded the Guards Brigade in 1st Division from 1855, and then the division.

Rolt, Chancellor. A law officer in England.

Ross, Robert Lockhart, 93rd Foot. Brevet Major 12 December 1854, DAQMG at Balaklava.

Rosser, Charles Potts, 10th Hussars. Captain 26 June 1855, ADC to Lieutenant-General commanding Cavalry Division.

Roupell, Charles Morris, barrister at Lincoln's Inn; called 1842. A friend of Romaine's.

Russell, Lord John. Foreign Secretary 1852–5. An advocate for Reform.

Russell, William Howard. Correspondent of *The Times* – the first war correspondent.

St Arnaud, Maréchal. French C-in-C until his death shortly after Alma and the Flank March to Sevastopol.

St-Pol. French General of Brigade, commanding the 1st Brigade of Duloc's 4th Division. Killed 8 September 1855 in the assault on the Little Redan.

Samary. Apparently a local mule dealer.

Sankey, William, 47th Foot. Brevet Major 12 December 1854, Brevet Lieutenant-Colonel 2 November 1855. DAQMG at HQ.

Selwyn, Charles Jasper. Born 13 October 1813, the youngest son of William (1775–1855) and Laetitia Frances, daughter of Thomas Kynaston Esq. Brother of George Augustus Selwyn who became Bishop of Lichfield. Educated at

Ealing and Eton. Admitted pensioner at Trinity College, Cambridge, in 1832 and successively scholar and fellow; BA 1836, MA 1839, LL D 1862. Admitted at Lincoln's Inn 1836 and called to the Bar in January 1840. A close friend of Romaine's from Trinity College, Cambridge days (Romaine was admitted in March 1833 and both were on the 'side' of George Peacock, generally regarded as the best of the three tutors at the time). Selwyn specialised as an equity draftsman, drawing up pleadings for use in Chancery Court proceedings, and also as a conveyancer. He is said to have amassed a vast fortune. His chambers were at 7 Old Square, Lincoln's Inn. He was 'commissary' of Cambridge University from 1855–8. Went on to have a distinguished political and judiciary career, as MP for the University 1859–68 and again in 1876, Queen's Counsel 1856 and Bencher of Lincoln's Inn the same year, Knighted 1867, Solicitor-General in Lord Derby's administration 1867, appointed Lord Justice of Appeal and Privy Councillor by Disraeli 1868. He died on 11 August 1869.

Shadforth, Thomas, 57th Foot. Lieutenant-Colonel 7 November 1854. Killed in action.

Shadwell, Lawrence, unattached. Major 12 December 1854, formerly Sir Colin Campbell's ADC and later AQMG of the Highland Division. Lieutenant-Colonel 2 November 1855.

Shewell, Frederick George, 8th Hussars. Colonel 28 November 1854, led the 8th in the Charge of the Light Brigade.

Shute, Charles Cameron, 6th Dragoons. Brevet Lieutenant-Colonel 12 December 1854, AAG Cavalry Division.

Siggs. Lord Mulgrave's keeper.

Simmons, John Linton Arabin, Royal Engineers. Brevet Major 14 July 1854, Brevet Lieutenant-Colonel 12 December 1854. After distinguished service in Canada was in Turkey in 1853 and was employed by Lord Stratford de Redcliffe on special missions with Omar Pasha, laid out the defences of Slobodzie and Georgevo on the Danube, and then of Eupatoria. HM Commissioner with the Ottoman army throughout the war.

Simpson, General Sir James. Sent out to sack incompetent staff at Raglan's HQ, he supported them and stayed as Chief-of-Staff. On Raglan's death he reluctantly accepted the position of C-in-C but was out of his depth and knew it. After the fall of Sevastopol he gratefully handed over to Codrington.

Smith, Abel. A London banker.

Smith, Sir Fred. A political figure in the Chatham constituency which Romaine coveted.

Smith, Jervoise. Reconnoitred on behalf of the Crimean Army Fund with Glyn (q.v.).

Somerset, Edward Arthur, Rifle Brigade. Lieutenant-Colonel 23 March 1855.

Somerset, Poulett George Henry, Coldstream Guards. Lieutenant-Colonel 3 March 1854, ADC to Lord Raglan. Horse killed by explosion of shell within it at Inkerman. Retired after Raglan's death.

Soyer, Alexis, The chef of the London Reform Club who travelled out to the Crimea at his own expense after reading of the soldiers' problems in cooking food. He invented a stove which bore his name (it continued in use for civil defence and disaster relief until recently), he planned the layouts and equipment of hospital kitchens and he devised 'receipts' (recipes) which transformed the nutritional value of the men's meals.

Spratt, Thomas Abel Bremage, Royal Navy. Commander 5 March 1849, Commanding HMS *Spitfire*, steam surveying vessel. A brilliant surveyor.

Steele, Thomas Montagu, Coldstream Guards. Colonel 29 June 1855, Military Secretary at Raglan's HQ.

Sterling, Anthony Coningham, unattached. Lieutenant-Colonel 20 June 1854. Initially Brigade Major to the Highland Brigade, then AAG to the Highland Division.

Stewart, Houston, Royal Navy. Rear Admiral of the White 16 June 1851, Second-in-command Mediterranean to Admiral Lyons.

Stoppard. Not identified.

Stratford de Redcliffe, Lord. Ambassador in Constantinople 1842–58, wielded huge influence on the Ottoman ruler and committed Britain to support them.

Straubenzee, Charles T. van, 3rd Foot. Colonel 20 June 1854, commanded a brigade from June 1855.

Sutherland Dr John. Head of the three Sanitary Commissioners sent out in February 1855 with three inspectors by the new government. The others were Dr Hector Gavin (q.v.) and Mr Robert Rawlinson, a civil engineer. The inspectors were Mr Newlands, Mr Wilson and another. Dr Sutherland had been a GP in Liverpool and had worked with Dr William Duncan, the first Medical Officer of Health in the UK.

Synodent, Lord. Presumably an official at Cambridge, perhaps the Vice Chancellor.

Talbot, Charles, Royal Navy. Captain 25 November 1830. Commanded HMS *Algiers*, a 91-gun screw ship which was employed carrying troops to the Baltic and to Sevastopol.

Tennant, Henry, of Cadoxton Lodge, Glamorganshire. Father-in-law of John Harvey (q.v.), and to be Romaine's own father-in-law when he married Frances Tennant in 1861.

Tonsky. A Polish officer who was head of the French intelligence service.

Tower, Thomas. Honorary agent in Crimea to administer the Crimean Army Fund.

Trollope, General Charles. Commanded 1st Brigade of 2nd Division and later 2 Brigade of 3rd Division.

Tryon, Henry, Rifle Brigade. Lieutenant 12 October 1852. Killed in action 20 November 1854.

Twyford, Samuel, Royal Navy. Lieutenant 12 July 1849, Killed in action 9 April 1855.

Tylden, Richard, Royal Engineers. Major 28 May 1853.

Tylden, William Burton, Royal Engineers. Colonel 21 September 1850; Commander Royal Engineers until after Alma.

Upton, Mr E. N., son of Colonel Upton, the Englishman who had designed and built the superb docks in Sevastopol, and other civil engineering works. Upton junior was employed by the Russian government in a similar capacity. On the arrival of the Allies he went to Lord Raglan but refused to give information about the docks and buildings in the town which his father and he had built, on the grounds that he could not honourably do so. He was detained, with his wife and daughters, at Balaklava and seems to have been the subject of legal proceedings, presumably for treason, though Romaine does not say. He was eventually repatriated to England with his family.

Vernon. A Conservative MP for the Chatham constituency.

Vicars, Hedley Shafto Johnstone, 97th Foot. Captain 3 November 1854. A religious young officer respected by all his men, killed in action 22 March 1855. *Memorials of Captain Hedley Vicars* was published in 1858.

Vico, Commandant. French commissioner at Raglan's HQ; died from cholera a few days after Raglan.

Vynoi, General Joseph. French commander of brigade and later division.

Walker, Mark, 30th Foot. Lieutenant 3 February 1854. The adjutant, an ex-ranker with over nine years' service.

Warde, Edward Charles, Royal Artillery, Kane 1751, Brevet Colonel 28 November 1854, Commanded Siege Train January to August 1855.

Warre, Henry, 57th Foot. Commanded after death of Shadforth (q.v.).

West, Lord Charles R. Sackville, 21st Fusiliers. Brevet Colonel 17 Jul 1855. As 2nd Lieutenant-Colonel took 1st Brigade of 4th Division out of action on 18 June 1855 though wounded. Commanded 1st Brigade in Kinburn Expedition.

Wetherall, Edward Robert, Scots Fusilier Guards. Brevet Major 12 December 1854, DAQMG at HQ.

Wilshere, Charles Willes. A visitor to the Crimea, a 'travelling gentleman', who had been a contemporary of Romaine, Selwyn and Harvey at Trinity College, Cambridge.

Windham, Charles Ash, unattached. AQMG 4th Division, later Brigade Commander in 2nd Division, then Division commander and finally Chief-of-Staff. Famed for his leadership in the final assault 8 September 1855.

Wood, John Stewart, 13th Foot. Brevet Lieutenant-Colonel 12 December 1854, AAG 3rd Division and later at HQ.

Wredo, General. Russian commander, better known as 'Read'. Killed at Chernaya, August 1855.

Wright, The Revd Henry Press. Army Chaplain since 5 May 1853.

Yan. Romaine's Polish servant.

Yea, Lacy Walter, 7th Fusiliers. Colonel 28 November 1854, much loved commanding officer, killed in assault on the Redan, 18 June 1855.

Zamoiski. Presumably Count Wladyslaw Zamoyski (1803–68), a Polish patriot who lived in London where he was involved in the emigré organistion set up by his uncle Prince Adam Czartoryski, to work for a free Poland. The reference to Zamoiski's Polish legion is no doubt to that organisation. It was not one of the three British legions of foreign mercenaries which were raised: they were German, Swiss and Italian. None of their officers were named Zamoiski, nor were any apparently Polish.

Notes

1 The word 'Deputy' in the title indicates the level in the hierarchy of the appointment, not a position as second-in-command. The Deputy Judge-Advocate was the only lawyer at Raglan's HQ.

2 See the correspondence in Appendix 1.

3 Much of this information is from the *Dictionary of National Biography*.

4 For a full discussion of this see, for example, J. M. Roberts, *A History of Europe*, Oxford 1996.

5 See Map 2.

6 The leading British troops were the light cavalry but when Russian artillery was seen on the heights on the other side of the valley they were ordered by Raglan to withdraw, receiving as they did so derisive comments from the infantry – normal inter-regimental rivalry, but also starting the myth that Lord Lucan was reluctant to engage the enemy.

7 This was another incident which damaged Lucan's reputation for when the cavalry at last came up, Raglan rebuked him. In fact the responsibility was with Wetherall on the HQ staff as he had been sent as pathfinder to lead the cavalry and it was he who had got lost.

8 This decision has been widely criticised by modern writers, but they cannot have visited Sevastopol as no one who has, and who has seen the width of the estuary, could prefer the north route. It would have involved capturing the Star, or Severnaya, Fort but, more importantly, it led to a dead end for a fearsome water crossing from the northern shore of the estuary would have been necessary towards the heavily fortified southern side. The flank march was sound in every way; the mistake was not to attack at once from the western and southern sides of the town.

9 Romaine reveals that the token shots fired by the Greek colonel in command of the Genoese Fort very nearly killed Raglan!

10 That part of Constantinople north of the Golden Horn, and the 'modern European' part of the capital.

11 This and the next two rumours were a reference to the Royal Navy campaign of summer 1854 in the Baltic Sea.

12 There was general satisfaction in the Army of the East with the reports printed in *The Times* and it was then sufficient to refer in letters home to the reports, and not to bother giving full accounts of actions, etc.

13 This was the 'sore-back' reconnaissance referred to in the Introduction.

14 Huge diplomatic pressure from Austria and fear of the results of ignoring them led to the Russian withdrawal from the Principalities they had illegally entered.

15 In accordance with the Mutiny Act a judge-advocate attended all general courts martial to advise on the law and to record the proceedings, but district and garrison courts martial would be conducted by regimental officers without a lawyer present, with the officer appointed as president of the court standing in his place. Nevertheless a judge-advocate could advise on the framing of charges, and to ensure that all was in order could scrutinise the records of proceedings afterwards before they were sent to the Judge-Advocate General at Horse Guards.

16 Russia and Greece were still using the Julian calendar beloved of the Orthodox church in which a leap year came every four years, one day too many every thousand years. Western Europe had changed to the more accurate Gregorian calendar (Britain changed in 1752). From 1700 to 1800 the date in the Gregorian was twelve days more, thus Julian 1 September was Gregorian 13 September.

17 See Romaine's letter (no. 69) in Appendix 1.

18 The Duke of Cambridge, q.v.

19 The Russian artillery had prepared in a very professional way and had placed markers at known ranges along the approaches to their position so that when the Allies were seen near the markers the precise range to them was known.

20 It was widely believed by the English that the French had inflated their own casualties to give the impression that they had fought harder in the battle than they had. They were thought to have done this by including casualties from disease during the invasion and march. Kinglake writes that Lord Raglan believed that their total loss was sixty killed and 500 wounded.

21 This was Sankey, referred to a line or two later.

22 The aqueduct was part of the works connected with the large complex of docks at Sevastopol, built by Englishman Colonel Upton. It included a dry dock, and the aqueduct brought the water to refill it.

23 'riff-raff'.

24 A reference to William Howard Russell of *The Times*.

25 20 degrees of frost on the Réaumur scale is equivalent to $-25°C$.

26 Henry Fuseli (1741–1825) was a Swiss-born painter who settled in London and became famous for his drawings and paintings of figures caught in strained and violent poses suggestive of intense emotion. He also painted macabre fantasies which influenced William Blake.

27 While the British army struggled to find reinforcements, the French seemed to have an inexhaustible supply of fresh troops. Their population was then approximately 36 million, considerably more than that of the United Kingdom (21 million).

28 This place has defied all attempts to identify it, and has probably been transcribed wrongly, but repeated examination of the original cannot improve

on the transcription shown. He was presumably referring to the landing at Old Fort.

29 Mulgrave's parents.

30 Kamiesch Bay, the French harbour.

31 General Orders of the 13 December savagely (and publicly) criticised Dr Lawson, Principal Medical Officer at Balaklava, for neglect of sick and wounded placed on board ship there and ordered that he be relieved from his position. It went on to record that Dr Hall, Inspector General of Hospitals, could not be exonerated from all blame in the matter. These were astonishing public rebukes.

32 Equivalent to 5°F or −15°C.

33 In the North Pacific!

34 The battle of Miani, 17 February 1843, in the conquest of Sind, Baluchistan. In the battle General Napier with 2,800, men attacked and defeated 30,000 Baluchis in savage hand-to-hand combat. The sixty-one-year-old General, musket in hand, personally led his troops. It was his capture of the town which led to the story – possibly apocryphal – that to announce his success he sent the single word 'Peccavi', Latin for 'I have sinned'.

35 The report of the Court of Inquiry is in Appendix 1 (no. 71).

36 No one identified. Possibly a literary reference to the name used by Ford when he visited Falstaff in Shakespeare's *Merry Wives of Windsor*.

37 A reference to the standard legal work, *Abridgement of the Law of Nisi Prius*, written by Selwyn's father, William Selwyn (1775–1855), and published in three separate parts in London, 1806–8. *The Dictionary of National Biography* notes that it was a work of great merit; it went to thirteen editions. It was referred to colloquially as 'Selwyn's N.P.'.

38 'Cost what it may.'

39 Mother Shipton (circa 1486–1561) was a legendary English witch and soothsayer, known as the Yorkshire Sibyl. She is supposed to have been born at Dropping Well, Knaresborough, Yorkshire, in about the year 1486.

40 *The Hundred Wonders of the World, and of the Three Kingdoms of Nature, described according to the best and latest authorities, and illustrated by engravings* was written by Sir Richard Phillips under the pseudonym Rev. C. C. Clarke and published in London, 1818.

41 'Lady John', and 'Johnny' on the next line: Lord John and Lady Russell.

42 This entry should be dated 18 *February*. One deduces that when Romaine consolidated his diaries and notebooks, the first volume ended with 17 January 1855 and, intending to start the second volume at 18 January, he inadvertently turned to 18 February in his diary. The first volume of his journal is lost.

43 *Samson* was not in fact involved. One British ship, probably *Viper*, and the French *Veloce* and Turkish *Schefer* were (Clowes, *The Royal Navy*, vol. 6, p. 450).

44 This entry should be dated Monday 19 *February* 1855. See note 42 above.

45 The last part of this letter is cross-written over the previous page.
46 The Volkynia and Selinghinsk Redoubts.
47 'I have expressed my feelings.'
48 Properly an Albanian, especially one in the Turkish army, but often applied to Greeks as well because of the similarity in their traditional costume.
49 Romaine must have misread, or misremembered, the number on the button. The shoulder strap indicates the soldier was in 12 Division, and the button must have been 24, not 44. He was in either the Dnieper Infantry Regiment, or the Odessa Jäger Regiment. Each division had two infantry regiments and two jäger. They wore the same buttons and they were distinguished by white leather equipment (infantry) or black (jäger).
50 Cox and Co. were founded by Richard Cox in 1758 when he was appointed agent to the 1st Foot Guards. Later the firm became agents to most regiments including the entire Household Brigade, the Royal Artillery and Royal Engineers. As the duties of regimental agent were taken over by the Army the company's business as personal bankers was expanded and eventually they were taken over by a major British clearing bank. They continued their special relationship with the army under the name Cox and King's and exist to this day.
51 This happened the night before. Three trains were run to take 300 troops down to Balaklava, and the last ran out of control as the brakes skidded on wet rails. Several wagons left the track and one soldier was killed and another had his right leg severed. Beatty himself was aboard and badly shaken.
52 Twyford intended. See Reilly, *Siege of Sevastopol*, p. 75.
53 A favourite viewpoint, especially to see the French operations. It was due south of the Dockyard Creek, and roughly in line with Traktir Bridge and Cathcart's Hill, the British viewpoint.
54 *A Proposed New System of Fortification*, by James Fergusson, was published in 1849.
55 One rumour which circulated amongst the British was that he had been discovered spying for the Russians!
56 Royal Navy steam frigates of sixteen and twenty-eight guns respectively.
57 See note 54 above.
58 The Troad is the north-west corner of Asia Minor where the site of ancient Troy was presumed to be. The Calverts were an expatriate English family consisting at this time of three brothers, Frederick, James and Frank, each of whom held a consular appointment. They owned a farm which included part of Mount Hisarlik. Frank believed this to be the site of ancient Troy and told Heinrich Schliemann, subsequently credited with the discovery. (The Calverts should not be confused with Charles Cattley, Lord Raglan's head of intelligence and former vice-consul at Kertch, who used the alias 'Calvert'.)
59 For Upton, see Biographical Notes.
60 Romaine has clearly written 88th, and it seems that Raglan and he were

convinced that the Regiment had behaved badly at Alma. However, it is likely that Raglan and staff were actually watching the 95th withdraw. As both regiments had yellow facings and buttons in pairs, and as they would not have expected the 95th to be with the Light Division, they assumed – wrongly – that they were watching the 88th.

61 The telegraph entered the sea at St George's Monastery, west of Balaklava.

62 Wellington, of course.

63 A reference to his reputation in Algeria – see note 69.

64 'There are masses of fine fellows wholly focused on frustrating the ambition of one man.'

65 In Vienna. The major powers were seeking to persuade Russia to accept their terms.

66 A comparison with Field Marshal Sir Hugh Gough (1779–1869), a fine fighting general in the Peninsula, China and India, especially in the Sikh Wars.

67 Brevet Colonel Duncan Cameron, 42nd Highlanders, commanded the brigade of British troops.

68 Peto, Brassey & Co. were the engineering contractors who constructed the Balaklava Railway.

69 An incident in the French campaign in Algeria on 18 June 1845. It brought Pélissier some notoriety at the time. The Kabyles were properly the people who were smoked in the caves, not the location of the caves.

70 There was no such officer, and this appears to be a slip of the pen for Lawrence *Shadwell*.

71 Read 'tête du pont' – bridgehead.

72 'It is a pity that they have not communicated their ideas.'

73 Beatty's report to his employers, Messrs Peto, Brassey and Betts, was published in the *Illustrated London News* of 12 May 1855. It made clear that Filder was not making full use of the railway.

74 This is a well-known photograph by Roger Fenton, showing Raglan wearing a straw hat with a scarf tied round it, Omar Pasha complete with fez, and Pélissier resplendent in full dress. All are sitting at a table outside an open door. See Helmut and Alison Gernsheim, *Roger Fenton: Photographer of the Crimean War*, Secker and Warburg, 1954, Plate 76.

75 Ickwell Bury, John Harvey's house.

76 John Arthur Roebuck, a barrister, was Member of Parliament for Sheffield. In January 1855 he had moved for the appointment of a Select Committee to investigate the conduct of the war which was a public scandal. This led to the fall of Lord Aberdeen's government. The committee reported to Parliament in June 1855 and Roebuck threatened a Vote of Censure against the former government, including those who had continued to serve in the new one. As Romaine rightly judged, it came to nothing.

77 A species of wild sheep with large curved horns, ancestor of the domestic sheep. It has many subspecies, including *Ovis ammon ammon*, the largest

known sheep, but *Ovis ammon hodgsoni* is the one whose habitat is the Himalayas.

78 The new Commissary General who had replaced Filder.

79 Rokeby was clearly trying to get home and Romaine describes his moves as if they were siege operations.

80 The croaking noise made by the chorus in *The Frogs* by Aristophanes.

81 In the summers of 1854 and 1855 there were important campaigns by the Royal Navy and the French in the Baltic Sea. The grand finale in 1855 was the bombardment on 9 and 10 August of Sveaborg, the naval base outside Helsinki (then known as Helsingfors) from which hundreds of Finns watched as if it was a fireworks display. Over fifty British warships, many of them mortar-vessels, and some French ships took part. The base was destroyed.

82 In the few days before 18 June 1855, when Sevastopol was assaulted by British and French forces, both navies fired by night on the sea and town defences. Some nine British steam frigates or sloops were involved, including HMS *Terrible* which had returned from Kertch. It was intended to repeat this on 8 September but a north-west gale and heavy sea made it impossible.

83 The French assault was made at about noon as they had observed that the Russians withdrew their men from the fortification then, and that the replacements marched in afterwards, leaving a gap in which no defenders were present.

84 'Travelling gent' – an irreverent term applied to the civilians who went to the Crimea during the war as sightseers.

85 A slang reference to the King of Naples.

86 The line which had run to the Crimea, landing at a point near St George's Monastery, had been damaged and had failed.

87 These papers are folded in four and on the spine is the following note: 'W. G. Romaine Proceedings of a Court of Enquiry 9th Nov 1854. On the treatment of the wounded by the Russians during the battle of Inkerman.'

88 This appears to be a draft by Romaine, with sections crossed out and replaced. The papers are folded in four and marked on the spine: 'Dr Lawson, Court of Inquiry. Ld. Raglan's G.O. on the subject 6 Dec 54.'

89 The pages are folded in four, and on the spine is written: 'From Mr Romaine 18th Jan.55 representation on the difference in pay between him and other Civil Appoint. Post master &c.
    'See private letter to D of Newcastle 19th Jan 55 recommending £800 a year and a field allowance.'

90 The sheets are folded in four and labelled on the spine: 'From Mr Romaine 21 June 55 Opinion regarding the position of the Army Works Corps with reference to Crime.'

Select Bibliography

Allen's Navy List 1855, facsimile reprint, Savannah Publications, 2002

Arnaud, René, *The Second Republic and Napoleon III*, Heinemann, 1930

Bazancourt, Baron de, *The Crimean Expedition*, trans. R. H. Gould, Sampson Low, 1856

Bonner-Smith, D., *Russian War 1855, Baltic*, Navy Records Society, 1944

—— and Dewar, A. C., *Russian War 1854, Baltic and Black Sea*, Navy Records Society, 1943

Burke's Peerage, Baronetage and Knightage, various years, Burke's Peerage Ltd.

Calthorpe, S. J. G., *Letters from Headquarters*, John Murray, 1858

Clowes, William Laird, *The Royal Navy: A History from the Earliest Times to 1900*, Sampson, Low, Marston and Company, 1901.

Cook, Frank and Andrea, *Casualty Roll for the Crimea*, Hayward, 1976

Cooke, Brian, *The Grand Crimean Central Railway*, 2nd edition, Cavalier House, 1997

Dewar, A. C., *Russian War 1855, Black Sea*, Navy Records Society, 1945

Dictionary of National Biography

Douglas, Sir George and Ramsay, Sir George Dalhousie, *The Panmure Papers*, Hodder and Stoughton, 1908

Elphinstone, H. C. and Jones, H. D., *Journal of the Operations of the Royal Engineers in the Crimean War*, 1859, by order of the Secretary of State for War, printed by Eyre and Spottiswoode.

Hargreave Mawson, Michael, *Eyewitness in the Crimea*, Greenhill, 2001

Hart's Army Lists, 1854, 1855, 1856, 1857, 1860, 1870

Jocelyn, J. R. J., *History of the RA: Crimean Period*, John Murray, 1911

Kane, J., *List of Officers of the Royal Regiment of Artillery*, 4th edition, Royal Artillery Institution, 1900

Kelly's Handbook to the Titled, etc. Classes, various years, Kelly and Co.

Kinglake, A. W., *The Invasion of the Crimea*, Blackwood, 1863–7

Lambert, Andrew, *The Crimean War*, Manchester University Press, 1990

—— and Badsey, Stephen, *The War Correspondents: The Crimean War*, Sutton 1994

McGuigan, R., *Into Battle! British Orders of Battle in the Crimean War*, Withycut House, 2001

Marsh, Philip, *Beatty's Railway*, New Cherwell Press, 2000

Nolan, E. H., *The History of the War against Russia*, Virtue, 1857

Parliamentary Papers, *Returns relating to Officers in the Crimea*, House of Commons, 1857 ('Wetherall')

Porter, Major-General W., *History of the Corps of Royal Engineers to 1885*, Longman, 1889

Reilly, Major-General W. E. M., *Siege of Sevastopol: Operations by the Royal Artillery and Royal Naval Brigade*, Clowes, 1859.

Robins, Major C. D., *The Murder of a Regiment*, Withycut House, 1994

—— *Captain Dunscombe's Diary*, Withycut House, 2003

Royle, Trevor, *Crimea*, Little Brown and Co, 1999

Russell, W. H., *The War*, Routledge, 1855

—— *The British Expedition to the Crimea*, Routledge, 1858

Sayer, Frederick, *Despatches and Papers*, Harrison, 1857

Shepherd, John, *The Crimean Doctors*, Liverpool University Press, 1991

Simmons, T. F., *Courts Martial*, 4th edition 1852

Stanmore, Lord, *Sidney Herbert: A Memoir*, John Murray, 1906

Tyrrell, H., *The History of the Present War with Russia*, London Publishing and Printing Co., 1855–8

Venn's *Alumni Cantabrigiensis*

Index

INDEX

Edwards, Capt R.L. 285
Egerton, Hon A. 83, 140, 286
Egerton, Lt Col T. 68, 106, 124, 127, 252, 260, 286
Egyptian Treasury xxv
Eisk 155
electric telegraph (*see* telegraph, electric)
Ellenborough, Earl 120, 286
Elvas 130
embrasures 99, 109, 114, 115, 116, 117, 119, 155, 158, 175, 205
Emperor of France (Napoleon III) 1
Emperor of Russia (*see* Tsar)
England, General Sir Richard 59, 96, 180, 185, 286
Enikale (*see* Yenikale)
Espinasse, Général (French) 119
Estcourt, Maj Gen J. 24, 95, 110, 118, 122, 124, 177, 286
Eton 248
Eupatoria 32, 50, 76, 77, 80, 82, 94, 98, 107, 108, 123, 127, 132, 140, 183, 189, 192, 202, 204, 223, 225, 230, 232, 283
Evans, Lt Gen Sir De Lacey 11, 15, 75, 286
Eyre, Maj Gen Sir W. 136, 139, 140, 159, 171, 175, 176, 182, 191, 199, 200, 201, 286

fascines 17, 44, 56, 144, 153, 159, 219
Fellowes, Bt Maj E. 113, 286
Fenton, Roger 107, 151, 286
Ferguson's plan 117, 125
Filder, W. 48, 55, 60, 64, 77, 82, 88, 103, 107, 108, 115, 120, 147, 148, 173, 211, 246, 286
Fitzherbert, Mr 16
Flagstaff Battery 112, 116, 119, 120, 122, 125, 126, 132, 152
Florence 47, 49, 53, 54, 81, 248
Foley, Lt Col Hon St G. 77, 79, 248, 286
Follett, Mr 38, 286
Foreigners Enlistment Bill 65
Forey, Général (French) 121, 286
Fort Alexander 220, 234
Fort Catherine 216, 227
Fort Constantine 35, 149, 175, 223, 227
Fort Michael 167

Fort Nicholas 167, 201, 220, 234
Fort Paul 158, 217
Fortnum & Mason 37, 83
France 1, 183, 231, 240
Fremantle, Rear Adm C.H. 181, 286
French
 Events:
  Louis Napoleon declared himself Emperor 1
  army sets out for East 2
  told by Emperor to 'do what we do' 3
  confusion over plan at Alma 4
  troops sent from Algeria 7
  works at Gallipoli 8
  embark at Baltchik Bay 17
  Battle of Alma 19
  full share of sickness 27
  seek assistance at Alma 28
  attempt to steal captured cannon 27
  account of Alma exaggerates their part 28
  numbers of troops a mystery 34
  cut roads and establish redoubts 40
  Canrobert and Raglan get on well 48
  fail to turn out for night march 78–80
  fail to take earthwork, marines run away 85
  Romaine visits advanced trench 86
  clash with British by mistake 97
  Romaine considers British soldier best 102
  reclaim ground lost on 25 October 1854 107
  prepare to capture Mamelon 119
  Général Forey recalled to France 121
  review of troops 131
  prepare for Kerch expedition 134
  recalled by Emperor after sailing 137
  Pelissier replaces Canrobert 142
  capture trenches and pits 144
  cross Chernaya at Traktir 145
  attack on June 7th, 1855 153–5
  attack on June 18th 166, 170–2, 174, 176
  Battle of Chernaya 195–8
  final assault on Sevastopol 206–8
  destruction of forts and docks 226, 234, 240
  move of cavalry to Eupatoria 225

308